Belief and imagination

Ronald Britton's writing on belief is based on the premise that in addition to the instincts of love and destruction there is an independent instinct for knowledge. Just as there is potential conflict between love and hatred, so there is conflict between the wish to love blindly and the need to know the truth.

The author suggests that belief is a function of the instinct for knowledge that operates from the outset of life. He argues that we are influenced in our feelings and actions by unconscious beliefs, and can only modify them by making them conscious. The relinquishment of redundant belief is only accomplished through a process of mourning, and those who have difficulty mourning have difficulty giving up their beliefs.

A further area of exploration is the concept and internal phantasy of the imagination as a mental location. Britton explains that this begins as the unknowable place – 'the other room' in which the principal figures of our lives spend their lives when not with us. The nature and use of the imagination is explored both from the point of view of clinical practice and by using literature as a field for inquiry. Britton finds in the works of Wordsworth, Rilke, Milton and Blake a source of understanding of the concepts of belief and imagination which are central to psychoanalysis.

Bringing together Britton's influential work on these concepts over many years, *Belief and Imagination* is an important addition to psychoanalytic literature and presents valuable sources of inquiry relevant to philosophy and literary criticism.

Ronald Britton is a psychoanalyst in private practice in London, and training and supervising analyst of the British Psycho-Analytical Society.

THE NEW LIBRARY OF PSYCHOANALYSIS

The New Library of Psychoanalysis was launched in 1987 in association with the Institute of Psycho-Analysis, London. Its purpose is to facilitate a greater and more widespread appreciation of what psychoanalysis is really about and to provide a forum for increasing mutual understanding between psychoanalysts and those working in other disciplines such as history, linguistics, literature, medicine, philosophy, psychology and the social sciences. It is intended that the titles selected for publication in the series should deepen and develop psychoanalytic thinking and technique, contribute to psychoanalysis from outside or contribute to other disciplines from a psychoanalytic perspective.

The Institute, together with the British Psycho-Analytic Society, runs a low-fee psychoanalytic clinic, organises lectures and scientific events concerned with psychoanalysis, publishes the *International Journal of Psycho-Analysis* (which now incorporates the *International Review of Psycho-Analysis*) and runs the only training course in the UK in psychoanalysis leading to membership of the International Psychoanalytical Association – the body which preserves internationally agreed standards of training, of professional entry, and of professional ethics and practice for psychoanalysis as initiated and developed by Sigmund Freud. Distinguished members of the Institute have included Michael Balint, Wilfred Bion, Ronald Fairbairn, Anna Freud, Ernest Jones, Melanie Klein, John Rickman and Donald Winnicott.

Volumes 1–11 in the series have been prepared under the general editorship of David Tuckett, with Ronald Britton and Eglé Laufer as associate editors. Subsequent volumes are under the general editorship of Elizabeth Bott Spillius, with, from Volume 17, Donald Campbell, Michael Parsons, Rosine Jozef Perelberg and David Taylor as associate editors.

ALSO IN THIS SERIES

NEW LIBRARY OF PSYCHOANALYSIS

——— 31 ———

General editor: Elizabeth Bott Spillius

Belief and Imagination

EXPLORATIONS IN PSYCHOANALYSIS

RONALD BRITTON

Routledge
Taylor & Francis Group
LONDON AND NEW YORK

First published 1998
by Routledge
27 Church Road, Hove, East Sussex BN3 2FA
Simultaneously published in the USA and Canada
by Routledge
711 Third Avenue, New York, NY 10017
Routledge is an imprint of the Taylor & Francis Group, an informa business

Typeset in Bembo by Routledge

British Library Cataloguing in Publication Data
A catalogue record for this book is available from the British Library.

Library of Congress Cataloguing in Publication Data
Ronald Britton. Belief and imagination: explorations in psychoanalysis.
Includes bibliographical references and index.
1. Belief and doubt. 2. Imagination. 3. Psychoanalysis. 4. Psychoanalysis
and literature. 5. Klein, Melanie. I. Title.
BF173.B824 1998
98–19593
153.3–dc21
CIP

ISBN 0–415–19437–7 (hbk)
ISBN 0–415–19438–5 (pbk)
ISBN 978–0–4151–9438–9 (pbk)

For Ritaclare, and to our children, and their children

Contents

Contents

Acknowledgements

I want to express my gratitude to my wife for both her participation and her support in the making of this book. I am deeply indebted to my psychoanalytic teachers, particularly Betty Joseph, Hanna Segal, Ruth Malcolm and the late Herbert Rosenfeld; also to my colleagues in the Betty Joseph Workshop for hours of clinical discussion, notably Michael Feldman and John Steiner, with whom I share the West Lodge Conferences. I am grateful to overseas colleagues, particularly the members of my postgraduate seminar in Frankfurt, Germany, for enthusiastic shared explorations. I owe a double debt to Elizabeth Spillius as a colleague and ever supportive editor. A number of literary scholars have informed and inspired me, particularly at the Grasmere Conferences, especially my friends Robert and Pamela Woof, Jonathan Wordsworth, Thomas McFarland and Duncan Wu.

I want to thank the Melanie Klein Trust for permission to use material from *The Writings of Melanie Klein*, *The Oedipus Complex Today* and a footnote from the *Envy & Gratitude* typescript; the Wordsworth Trust for permitting me to quote from the *I.F. Manuscript*; Karnac Books for permission to use *The Missing Link: Parental Sexuality in the Oedipus Complex* from *The Oedipus Complex Today* (ed. J. Steiner); *the International Journal of Psycho-Analysis* for material from R. Britton and J. Steiner, 'Interpretation: selected fact or overvalued idea?', and R. Britton, 'Psychic reality and unconscious belief', 'Psychic reality and unconscious belief: a reply to Harold B. Gerard' and 'Publication anxiety: conflict between communication and affiliation'. *Psychoanalytic Inquiry* gave me permission to use 'The blindness of the seeing eye: inverse symmetry as a defence against reality' (vol. 4, 1994) and Yale University Press gave me permission to use 'Reality and unreality in phantasy and fiction' from *On Freud's 'Creative Writers and Day-dreaming'* (ed. E. S. Person *et al.*, 1995). W. W. Norton & Co. gave permission for the use of material from W. Wordsworth (1979) *The Prelude 1799, 1805, 1850*

William Wordsworth (ed. J. Wordsworth, M. H. Abrams and S. Gill, New York); *John Milton: Paradise Lost* (Scott Elledge, 2nd edn, 1975); *Letters of Rainer Maria Rilke 1910–1926* (trans. J. B. Greene and Herter Norton MD). I am grateful to Oxford University Press for material from *Blake: Complete Writings* (ed. Geoffrey Keynes), and to Cambridge University Press for *William Wordsworth: The Pedlar, Tintern Abbey, The Two Part Prelude* (ed. J. Wordsworth and E. P. Thompson) and *Witness against the Beast.* I was given permission by Random House, Inc., New York, to use R. M. Rilke, *The Notebooks of Malte Laurids Brigge* (trans. Stephen Mitchell, 1983), and by Anvil Press Poetry to use R. M. Rilke (1981) *An Unofficial Rilke* (ed. and trans. Michael Hamburger, Hogarth Press). Random House, London, gave permission to quote from the *Complete Psychological Works of Sigmund Freud, The Writings of Melanie Klein, Selected Papers of Karl Abraham*, H. Segal, *Introduction to the Work of Melanie Klein*, and D. W. Winnicott, *Through Paediatrics to Psycho-Analysis*.

Introduction

We are so constituted that we believe the most incredible things.
(Goethe 1774: 51)

This book is based on papers written over a period of fifteen years on a variety of subjects but with the same preoccupations and theme. One preoccupation has been about the status of phantasies in the mind of the individual and not simply their content. When are they regarded as facts, probabilities, possibilities or mere fancies? This line of thought culminated in the ideas put forward in Chapter 1, on 'Belief and psychic reality'. A second line of thinking that converges with the first has been on the internal relationship of subjectivity with objectivity and its origins in the primitive Oedipal triangle. This line of exploration led to the theory developed in Chapter 4, on 'Subjectivity, objectivity and triangular space'. A third line followed from the recognition that when a phantasy is not taken to be real or given the status of a belief it might be consigned to the *Imagination*. But what is and where is the *Imagination* in any modern model of the Mind? Ever since the demise of *faculty psychology* over a hundred years ago it has been homeless, not even having a proper place in modern philosophy according to Mary Warnock (1976). Nevertheless, as both a mental function and location the *Imagination* has continued to have a robust existence in literary scholarship and common speech. How can we conceive of it in psychoanalytic terms? This is the third strand which runs through these explorations and it is the explicit focus of attention in Chapter 9, on 'Daydream, phantasy and fiction', and Chapter 10, on 'The other room and poetic space'.

The ideas I put forward about belief and phantasy in relation to reality and imagination pervade all the chapters – sometimes explicitly, sometimes implicitly. The first seven chapters describe various aspects of belief, its vicissitudes and its consequences as I have encountered them in analytic

1

practice. Chapters 7 and 8 continue this concern but also bring into play the analyst's beliefs and their impact on the analysis.

In Chapter 9 I explore the relationship between psychic reality and fictional writing; I suggest that some fiction is truth-seeking and some truth-evading, just as some phantasies form the basis of psychic reality and some are created to escape it. Chapter 10 is an attempt to account for the development of the *Imagination*, conceived as an imaginary mental space in which imagined events can take place. In Chapters 11 to 14 the themes of phantasy, belief and reality continue in the work of specific poets: Wordsworth, Rilke, Milton and Blake. All four were in different ways exploring the issues of belief and reality in themselves. The final chapter, on 'Publication anxiety', discusses the problems that arise when it comes to making private professional convictions public.

At times the explorations in this book enter territory usually occupied by philosophy, literary scholarship and theology. I am neither a philosopher nor a theologian, and the study of poetry has long been a passion of mine but not a profession. These incursions have not occurred simply because of personal interest; they have happened, I think, because psychoanalysis necessarily finds itself exploring the areas of mental life that have been the concern of philosophers, theologians and poets. As Bion wrote, 'The psycho-analyst's experience of philosophical issues is so real that he often has a clearer grasp of the necessity for a philosophical background than the professional philosopher' (Bion 1967: 152). Before the eighteenth-century period of Enlightenment the imperative, subjective issues of psychic life were formulated in theological terms. The issues remain the same. We encounter them in psychoanalytic practice and think of them in our own terms. Poetry has, for me, long been more than a pleasure; it is a source of understanding and a departure point for psychological exploration. However, the real source of the thinking in this book is my own clinical experience. The psychoanalytic theories learnt from books, teachers and colleagues come to life only when the phenomena they describe are met in practice. When I find a conjunction between understanding gained in one sphere and that gained in another it stimulates in me, not only a sense of excitement, but also an urge to tell others about it. I suspect that there is a basic desire for the corroboration of belief and an innate wish to share beliefs with others that bind us all in groupings of one sort or another. The snag is that we can substitute concurrence for reality testing, and so shared phantasy can gain the same or even greater status than knowledge.

The background of psychoanalytic theory against which I write is mainly that of Freud, Klein, Bion and the group of London analysts now generally known as post-Kleinians.

Several concepts are used throughout this book. Belief is, of course, central but others are *Wissentrieb*, as used by Freud and Klein; Klein's concepts of the paranoid-schizoid and the depressive positions; the Oedipus complex and its integral relationship to the depressive position; Bion's concept of the container; the concept of defensive organisations; phantasy and imagination; projective identification and anxiety. Some of these concepts are the subjects of particular chapters; others are used throughout. I will take this opportunity to discuss them briefly.

Wissentrieb, meaning literally the urge for knowledge, was translated as *the epistemophilic impulse* by James Strachey, and this academic-sounding term has stuck. Both Freud and Klein thought of it as a component of one or other of the two instincts, the life instinct or the death instinct. Whatever the translation, I think it is simpler to treat *Wissentrieb* as on a par with love and hate, and to regard epistemophilic development as complicated by and merged with love and hate but not derived from them. Taking Melanie Klein's formulation that 'there is no instinctual urge, no anxiety situation, no mental process which does not involve objects, external or internal' (Klein 1952a: 53), I think it is better to say that we love things, hate things and want to know things than to speak of abstract drives. In view of the fact that we have an internal world of object relations in addition to a world of external objects, I envisage that love, hate and knowledge are also deployed in our relationship with ourselves. In both external and internal situations we have desires for and from our objects. We want to love, to hate and to know our objects, and we also need to be loved, fear being hated and want to be understood. Internally we are inclined to love ourselves, loathe ourselves and want to understand ourselves.

The two psychic complexes, *the depressive position* and *the Oedipus situation*, are an essential background to the ideas developed in this book; their essential interrelatedness is discussed in Chapter 3. The concept of the *infantile depressive position* was introduced by Melanie Klein in her paper 'A contribution to the psychogenesis of manic-depressive states' (1935) and further developed by her in 'Mourning and its relation to manic-depressive states' (1940). Donald Winnicott thought it was her most important contribution and that it ranked in importance with Freud's concept of the Oedipus complex (Winnicott 1962). Klein saw that some of the defences against the depressive position themselves led to pathology. She focused particularly on the manic defence, with its reliance on denial, contempt, triumph, omnipotent restitution, and on the obsessive-compulsive attempts to undo phantasised destruction when manic assertion failed magically to remove or to restore the damaged object.

Joan Riviere (1936), armed with the Klein's new concept of the *depressive position*, enlarged on Freud's suggestion that unconscious guilt caused the *negative therapeutic reaction*. She linked *narcissistic character* with the *manic defence*, and emphasised that patients prone to negative therapeutic reactions – which included those suffering from incipient melancholia – anticipated that catastrophe would follow from the development of insight. She wrote of a general system of defence organised and perpetuated against this danger. This notion of *defensive organisations* has been central in post-Kleinian thinking as a means of producing what Betty Joseph (1989) has called *psychic equilibrium*. We have met descriptions of such systems as *narcissistic organisations* (Rosenfeld 1971), *defensive organisations* (O'Shaughnessy 1981) and *pathological organisations* (Steiner 1987). John Steiner has emphasised that what he now calls *psychic retreats* are seductive because they offer not only security of tenure but also secret perverse pleasure and a place in which to confine sadism.

John Steiner's part in this book is not limited to indirect influence, as Chapter 8 is based on a paper we wrote together in 1992–3 on the problem of distinguishing between the analyst's intuitive choice of an organising *selected fact* and the imposition on unorganised psychic material of an *overvalued idea* (Britton and Steiner 1994). We emphasised in the paper that, while the analyst is dependent on his intuitive selection of a central element in the patient's communication to orient his understanding of the material, he is always subject to error due to the interference of his own belief systems and preoccupations. For this and other reasons, constant monitoring of the effects of the analyst's interventions has become an essential aspect of analytic technique.

Throughout the book the term *phantasy* is used with the larger meaning that Melanie Klein attached to it, and not the more restrictive use made of it by Anna Freud and her followers. Susan Isaacs's definition is that 'Phantasy is (in the first instance) the mental corollary, the psychic representative, of instinct. There is no impulse, no instinctual urge or response which is not experienced as an unconscious phantasy' (Isaacs 1952: 83). The word '*phantasy*' came into English from the translation of the German *Phantasie*, which one would usually translate as '*imagination*'. Differences of usage of the English word 'imagination' bedevilled the literary scene in a way similar to that in which different uses of the word 'phantasy' have the psychoanalytic world. The use Coleridge and Wordsworth made of the term 'imagination' is very similar to Klein's use of 'phantasy' as a fundamental process underlying all mental activity, whereas others used it only to describe intentionally unrealistic representations. Coleridge suggested that the word '*fancy*', an older English alternative to imagination, should be kept for deliberately fanciful or plainly wish-fulfilling mental productions. The history of the term and the controversy surrounding it are discussed in some detail in Chapter 12, as part of an exploration of the relation between *truth-seeking* and *truth-evading* fiction.

4

Projective identification

Another concept used throughout the book is that of *projective identification*. Since when I use it I do so without specifically describing what I mean by it, I will briefly do so now. First I will mention the varying ways the term is used and then give my own classification. Klein wrote:

> By projecting oneself or part of one's impulses and feelings into another person, an identification with that person is achieved. . . . On the other hand, putting part of oneself into the other person (projecting), the identification is based on attributing to the other person some of one's own qualities. Projection has many repercussions. We are inclined to attribute to other people – in a sense, to put into them – some of our own emotions and thoughts; and it is obvious that it will depend on how balanced or persecuted we are whether this projection is of a friendly or a hostile nature. By attributing part of our feelings to the other person, we understand their feelings, needs, and satisfactions; in other words, we are putting ourselves into the other person's shoes. There are people who go so far in this direction that they lose themselves entirely in others and become incapable of objective judgement. At the same time excessive introjection endangers the strength of the ego because it becomes completely dominated by the introjected object.
>
> (Klein 1959: 252–3)

These last two sentences describe precisely a problem articulated by the poet Rilke in his *Duino Elegies* and his novel *The Notebooks of Malte Laurids Brigge*: whenever he was prompted to love or felt loved, he felt he risked losing his identity. I discuss this in Chapter 12 as part of a study of Rilke's poetic self-analysis; it also forms part of the discussion of existential anxiety in Chapter 4. Klein, however, also makes it clear that projective identification is the basis of empathic understanding and she makes the observation that, 'If projection is predominantly hostile, real empathy and understanding of others is impaired' (*ibid.*: 253).

In the passage quoted above Klein describes projective identification as an attributive process; elsewhere, as in 'On identification', she has described it as a means of entering into and assuming another's identity (Klein 1955: 141–75). The analysis of this form of projective identification has been used by Herbert Rosenfeld (1965) and Leslie Sohn (1985), particularly in their understanding of psychotic patients. For the purposes of classification I call this form *acquisitive projective identification*. In its crudest form it could be illustrated by a schizophrenic patient I met years ago in the North of England who believed that he had become overnight the Roman Emperor

5

Hadrian. In a less omnipotent patient this might have been recounted as a dream.

Bion added to the theory of projective identification of the *attributive* kind the notion that 'The patient, even at the outset of life, has contact with reality sufficient to enable him to act in a way that engenders in the mother feelings that he does not want, or which he wants the mother to have' (Bion 1962b: 31). This idea formed the kernel of his theory of containment. It meant a distinction could be made between attributive projective identification which was simply an omnipotent phantasy, with no resonant effect on the object of the projection, and that in which subtle acts by the subject would evoke in the object the state of mind projected by the subject. Elizabeth Spillius has coined the term '*evocatory*' to describe this form of attributive projective identification which produces effects on its host (Spillius 1988: 83). Some analysts have taken to using the term '*projective identification*' only for the evocatory attributive form where the individual's activity produces an effect on the other person. Joseph Sandler has introduced the term '*actualised*' to indicate situations where the projection has been realised in a relationship (Sandler 1976a, 1976b). Other analysts however, including myself, continue to use the term for the whole class of phenomena described above and to indicate which is signified at any particular point.

To summarise my own classification:

- *Acquisitive projective identification*: 'I AM YOU' – that is, another person's identity or attributes are claimed for the self. The more omnipotently this is done the more delusional the result.
- *Attributive projective identification*: 'YOU ARE ME' – that is, an aspect of the self is attributed to another person. This may be *evocatory*, inducing change in the other, or *non-evocatory*, when no action is taken to give effect to it.

Anxiety

Another area of psychic phenomenology that forms part of the background of my thinking in the book is that of *anxiety*. Freud, in his great papers of his late period, completely reorganised psychoanalysis by placing anxiety at its centre. Anxiety was no longer to be seen as a transformation of undischarged affect, nor simply as an undesirable consequence of conflicting wishes, but as the core of neurosis and psychosis, and one of the mainsprings of human endeavour.

Melanie Klein's eventual theory organised what she earlier described as persecutory and depressive anxiety into the paranoid-schizoid position and the depressive position. She distinguished fear of the destruction of the self from fear of the destruction of the world. From Freud's account of the innate death instinct she drew the conclusion that we are born with a fear of annihilation. As I see it, this is not simply fear of death in adult terms, but a more inchoate anxiety: a terror of non-existence, a fear that something will annihilate the past, present and future, whereas the adult fear only relates to the death of the individual's future. Clinically, I think we meet individuals tempted to seek actual death in order to escape from the anxiety of annihilation.

Bion's *nameless dread* is, I think, a manifestation of this terror when, in infancy, maternal containment fails completely. Later, when whole object relations are established and part no longer equals whole, it expresses itself in this more partial form of existential anxiety, the fear of loss of identity. In Chapter 4 ('Subjectivity, objectivity and triangular space') I discuss the relationship of nameless dread, failures of containment and fear of chaos, and in Chapter 12 I follow Rilke in his poetic exploration of existential anxiety. In Chapter 6 ('Before and after the depressive position') I attempt to describe the inevitable, alternating anxieties of integration and disintegration inherent in development by proposing a model of psychic development and regression, expanding Bion's formula $Ps{\leftarrow}{\rightarrow}D$ to $Ps(n){\rightarrow}D(n){\rightarrow}Ps(n+1)$ and incorporating John Steiner's pathological organisations. That chapter also draws attention to the way in which defensive organisations erected against anxiety can themselves become the source of further anxiety. A simple example of this is the use of acquisitive projective identification to evade separation anxiety, giving rise itself to a fear of entrapment.

Those familiar with Thomas Kuhn's writing on 'The structure of scientific revolutions' (1962) will recognise that what I call $Ps(n+1)$ in Chapter 6, the de-integration of a previously coherent belief system, has a good deal in common with Kuhn's notion of post-paradigm states of scientific belief. He suggests that a science moves from the establishment of a new *paradigm*, through a period of its development and application, to its eventual destabilisation by the accumulation of anomalies. There is then a phase of some confusion and scientific insecurity before a new paradigm emerges. This phase creates acute anxiety in those postulating new theories, as in Darwin's case. I discuss this in the final chapter on 'Publication anxiety', which contains a brief description of Kuhn's theory.

The situation, whether in personal life or in science, is not a simple one of moving on and changing beliefs; we are attached to our beliefs and have difficulty relinquishing them. This is the subject of Chapter 1.

1

Belief and psychic reality

we call a belief an illusion when a wish-fulfilment is a prominent factor
in its motivation.

(Freud 1927a: 31)

Since I wrote the papers on which this chapter is based (Britton 1995b,
1997b) several people have pointed out to me that surprisingly little exists
in the psychoanalytic literature on the subject of belief. It is surprising
because the daily work of psychoanalysts includes the exploration of their
patients' conscious and unconscious beliefs. It is also a continuous task for
practising analysts to examine, as best they can, their own. It seems to be
the case that not only the exploration of beliefs in daily psychoanalytic
practice is taken for granted, but also the role of belief in everyday life. Our
moment-to-moment sense of security depends on our belief in the well-
being of ourselves, our loved ones and our valued objects. Belief rests on
probability, not certainty, and yet it produces the emotional state that goes
with certainty. The state of mind consequent on losing the security of belief
is one in which anyone might find themselves; some unfortunate individuals live constantly in doubt of everyday beliefs. They are often the same
people who are afflicted with beliefs of which they cannot rid themselves
with the aid of reality. One so afflicted I will describe later in this chapter,
who believed she would go blind if she did not see her mother, who in fact
was dead.

A belief in a specific impending calamity may be unconscious, so that we
are anxious without knowing why. If we have an unconscious belief that
someone has betrayed us we hate them without apparent cause; if we
believe unconsciously that we have done them an injury we feel guilt
towards them for no obvious reason. Psychopathology can, in this way, be a
result of the nature of unconscious beliefs and we might describe this as

8

neurosis. There can also be, I think, disorders of the belief function itself. It is the latter that I will concentrate on mainly in this chapter, but first I need to make clear my ideas on the role and place of belief in mental life, and to explain what I mean by *psychic reality*.

I will itemise the description of the steps in the development and testing of beliefs that I proposed in the two papers mentioned above for the reader to use as a guide to the rest of this chapter:

1 Phantasies are generated and persist unconsciously from infancy onwards.

2 The status of belief is conferred on some pre-existing phantasies, which then have emotional and behavioural consequences which otherwise they do not. Beliefs may be unconscious and yet exert effects.

3 When belief is attached to a phantasy or idea, initially it is treated as a fact. The realisation that it is a belief is a secondary process which depends on viewing the belief from outside the system of the belief itself. This depends on internal objectivity, which in turn depends on the individual finding a third position from which to view his or her subjective belief about the object concerned. This, I think, as I explain in later chapters, depends on the internalisation and tolerance of the early Oedipus situation.

4 Once it is conscious and recognised to be a belief it can be tested against perception, memory, known facts and other existing beliefs.

5 When a belief fails the test of reality it has to be relinquished, in the same sense that an object has to be relinquished when it ceases to exist. As a lost object has to be mourned by the repeated discovery of its disappearance, so a lost belief has to be mourned by the repeated discovery of its invalidity. This, in analysis, constitutes part of *working through*.

6 The repression of a belief renders the particular belief unconscious but does not abolish some of its effects. Other measures that are taken to deal with threatening beliefs are directed at the belief function itself. Counter-beliefs may usurp the place of disturbing beliefs, creating an alternative to psychic reality, as in mania. The function of belief may be suspended, producing a pervading sense of evenly distributed psychic unreality, as in the '*as-if*' syndrome; or the apparatus of belief may be destroyed or dismantled, as may be found in some psychotic states.

7 What is perceived requires belief to become knowledge. Disbelief can therefore be used as a defence against either phantasies or perceptions.

Psychic reality

In 1897 Freud wrote: 'Belief (and doubt) is a phenomenon that belongs wholly to the system of the ego (the Cs. [the conscious]) and has no counterpart in the Ucs. [the unconscious]' (Freud 1897a: 255–6). He equated belief with 'a judgement of reality' (Freud 1895: 333). 'If after the conclusion of the act of thought the indication of reality reaches the perception, then a *judgement of reality, belief, has been achieved*' (*ibid.*: 313). In addition to the physical senses, 'indications of reality' could be achieved through speech, but this would apply only to '*thought reality*', which was different from '*external reality*' (*ibid.*: 373). This difference between thought reality and external reality is his first formulation of this crucial distinction: 'Psychical reality is a particular form of existence not to be confused with material reality' (Freud 1900b; 620). He did not subsequently describe belief as a process in his writing, leaving it in place in his theoretical account of psychic function as something accomplished by conferring the status of reality on perceptions and thoughts. He was convinced that this function was located in the 'system of the ego' (Freud 1897a: 255); he never changed that opinion and was adamant that the *system Ucs*, later called the *id*, knew nothing of belief, reality, contradiction, space or time (Freud 1933a: 74). Unlike the id, he thought the 'Ego has the character of Pcpt.-Cs. [perception]', which places all its material in space and time (*ibid.*: 75). Freud returned repeatedly to Kant's philosophical assertion that space and time are necessary forms of the human mind, claiming that the system unconscious did not conform to the philosopher's theorem, but that the Ego, because of its roots in the conscious perceptual apparatus, necessarily disposed itself in conformity with that system's construction of space and time. I suggest that our beliefs necessarily conform to this construction of space/time, as does what we describe as our 'imagination', in which we locate some phantasies. I discuss this further in Chapters 9 and 10 ('Daydream, phantasy and fiction' and 'The other room and poetic space').

When he wrote about belief in 1897, Freud equated the ego with consciousness. By the time he wrote 'The ego and the id' he was quite clear that 'A part of the ego . . . undoubtedly is *Ucs*.' (Freud 1923a: 18) and he regarded mental processes as themselves unconscious (Freud 1915b: 171). I take believing to be such a process, and therefore unconscious, and I think that the resulting beliefs may become conscious, remain unconscious or become unconscious.

Freud, having established the term *psychic reality*, somewhat confuses the issue by the way he uses it in two senses. He does the same with 'internal reality' as he does with 'external reality'. Following Kant, he regards the *thing in itself* as unknowable, the noumenon, and the reality experienced, that is, created by perception (Freud 1915b: 171). Sometimes when he refers to reality he means the thing in itself and sometimes he means perceptual reality. In the same way, sometimes he equates psychic reality with an unknowable unconscious system: 'The unconscious', he wrote, 'is the true psychical reality; in its innermost nature it is as much unknown to us as the reality of the external world' (Freud 1900b; 613). At other times he means psychic reality to be something created by the '*judgement of reality, belief*' (Freud 1897a: 333). It is in this latter sense that I am using psychic reality – that is, as that which is created by belief – and I regard belief as the function that confers the status of reality on to phantasies and ideas. I suggest that belief is to psychic reality what perception is to material reality. Belief gives the force of reality to that which is psychic, just as perception does to that which is physical. Like perception, belief is an active process, and, like perception, it is influenced by desire, fear and expectation – and, just as perceptions can be denied, so beliefs can be disavowed. Freud thought that in neurosis belief was 'refused to repressed material' and displaced 'on to the defending material' (*ibid.*: 255–6). I am modifying this by making use of his later notion of an unconscious ego to suggest that there are repressed beliefs which may produce neurotic symptoms.

Beliefs have consequences: they arouse feelings, influence perceptions and promote actions. Phantasies, conscious or unconscious, which are *not* the object of belief do not have consequences: disavowal therefore can be used to evade these consequences. Unconscious beliefs have consequences, so we feel and act quite often for no apparent reason, and may find a spurious reason to explain our feelings and actions. Rationalisation is the artefact of a constructed logical justification for a strongly held conviction that is really based on an unconscious belief.

The role and place of belief

I regard the epistemophilic instinct (*Wissentrieb*) to be on a par with and independent of the other instincts; in other words, I think that the desire for knowledge exists alongside love and hate. Human beings have an urge to love, to hate, to know, and a desire to be loved, a fear of being hated and a wish to be understood. Unlike Freud and Klein, I do not think of *Wissentrieb* as a component instinct, but as an instinct with components. Exploration, recognition and belief are among such components. They can be thought of as mental counterparts of basic biological functions such as molecular recognition and binding.

We need to believe in order to act and react, and a good deal of the time we have to do so without knowledge. I think that we believe in ideas in a similar way to that in which we 'cathect' objects. A belief is a phantasy invested with the qualities of a psychic object and believing is a form of

11

object relating. I think belief, as an act, is in the realm of knowledge what attachment is in the realm of love. The language of belief is clearly cast in the language of a relationship. We embrace beliefs or surrender to them; we hold beliefs and we abandon them; sometimes we feel that we betray them. There are times when we are in the grip of a belief, held captive by it, feel persecuted by it or are possessed by it. We relinquish our most deeply held beliefs, as we relinquish our deepest personal relationships, only through a process of mourning. It is my observation that those people who have difficulty relinquishing objects have difficulty relinquishing beliefs.

Belief and knowledge

To believe something is not the same as to know it. The following philosophical distinction is helpful and relevant, not only in theory, but also in analytic practice. Belief is defined as:

> The epistemic attitude of holding a proposition p to be true where there is some degree of evidence, though not conclusive evidence, for the truth of p . . . while *knowing p* would generally be considered to entail . . . that p is true, *believing p* is consistent with the actual falsity of p.
>
> (Flew 1979: 38)

My purpose in offering a philosophical dictionary definition of the term '*belief*' is not to enter into a philosophical discussion of the concepts of belief and knowledge, but to provide an acceptable description of the word 'belief'. In ordinary usage we happily describe someone as believing something even if we are aware that what they believe is not the case. We would not describe them as knowing something if we were aware that what they believed was untrue; in both philosophy and common speech the use of the two words differs. My reason for emphasising this point is that claiming *to know* something means that one asserts that it is incontrovertibly true, whereas stating that one believes something is saying that one takes it to be true but accepts the possibility that it may not be true. However, our emotional reactions and often also our actions do not wait for knowledge but are based on belief. In other words, we are apt initially to treat believing as knowing and beliefs as facts. We are captives of our beliefs while we regard them as knowledge, never more so than when they are unconscious; the realisation that they are only beliefs is an act of emancipation. I think that such psychic emancipation is a function of psychoanalysis. Only through psychic development do we recognise that we actively believe something and that we are not simply in the presence of facts. This recogni-

12

tion is a first stage in the relinquishment of a redundant belief as it admits the possibility of doubt. Cognitive, scientific and cultural development is not simply the acquisition of new ideas but an act of emancipation from pre-existing beliefs. I suggest that this involves the bringing together of subjective experience with objective self-awareness so that one sees oneself in the act of believing something. This depends on internal triangulation, and that in turn requires the toleration of an internal version of the Oedipal situation. I suggest that the recognition that one has a *belief* rather than that one is in possession of a *fact* requires what I describe as *triangular psychic space* – a *third* position in mental space is needed from which the *subjective self* can be observed having a relationship with an idea. The basis of triangular space and the origin of the third position in the primitive Oedipus situation – and the relation of that to subjectivity and objectivity – are the subject of Chapter 4 ('Subjectivity, objectivity and triangular space').

In the model I am proposing subjective belief comes first before objective evaluation or reality testing. *Objective evaluation* may use external perception, in reality testing, or it may simply involve correlation internally with known facts or related beliefs. The *internal objective evaluation* of a subjective belief is particularly crucial in situations where direct perceptual confirmation is not possible. It depends on two processes, both of which provoke resistance. One is the correlation of subjective and objective points of view, and the other is the relinquishment of an existing belief. The former involves the *Oedipal triangle* and the latter *mourning*.

Just as beliefs require sensory confirmation (reality testing) in order to become knowledge, so what is perceived requires belief to be regarded as knowledge. Seeing is not necessarily believing. *Disbelief* can be used, therefore, as a defence against both phantasies and perceptions, and it plays a familiar role in neurosis and everyday life, where it is usually called *denial*. It can also be a manifestation of aversion towards otherness. If any cognitive tie outside the existing belief system of the self is treated as a dangerous link to something alien, then all such mental links may be destroyed, as Bion described in his paper 'Attacks on linking' (1959). This may eliminate the capacity for belief in anything.

A state in which belief is treated as knowledge is usually described as omniscience, and the resultant beliefs as delusions. However, initially in my scheme of mental events beliefs are taken to be facts, and I would not describe this as delusional, but as naive, just as I would not call infantile mentation psychotic just because adults who use it are psychotic. It would be more useful to describe delusion belief which is treated axiomatically as knowledge even though it runs counter to perceived reality. My starting point in this business of considering belief was, like Descartes's, the realisation that I had held in the course of my life, without question, fallacious beliefs. Descartes wrote in his *First Meditation*: 'Some years ago I was struck by the large number of falsehoods that I had accepted as true in my childhood, and by the doubtful nature of the whole edifice that I had subsequently based on them' (quoted in Ayer and O'Grady 1992: 111).

For me, the doubtful edifice I accepted without question as a young child included the existence of God. As a child I did not realise until I first encountered the word 'atheist' that I *believed* in God; until that moment I thought God was a fact. There was an unnerving precedent for this discovery, which was that at a much earlier age I met a child sceptic, and it was only then I realised that Father Christmas was not a fact but a belief of mine. This transition from assumed knowledge to belief was to be followed eventually by disbelief. I can remember thinking when my friend shocked me by telling me what an atheist was, 'I hope this doesn't turn out to be like Father Christmas.' It needed the discovery that it was possible not to believe to discover that I had a belief and did not know a fact. It is the shift from thinking one knows a fact to realising that one has a belief which is linked to self-awareness.

Before discussing the psychopathology of belief I will summarise the sequence I have been describing. The *unconscious* that is there all along, as Freud thought of it, is unknowable, and contains phantasies which are unreconciled with each other and uncontaminated by beliefs about the outside world. From this source arise ideas that may become the objects of belief. Once ideas become beliefs they have consequences. Beliefs may be conscious or unconscious, but they cannot be tested or relinquished without becoming conscious. Beliefs require reality testing to become knowledge. Reality testing occurs through perception of the external world or through internal correlation with already known facts and other beliefs. If subsequent experience and knowledge discredit a belief it needs to be relinquished; this requires a process of mourning if it is an important or precious belief.

Disorders of the belief function

In addition to disorders arising from the content or denial of particular beliefs, there are disorders of the belief function itself that give rise to psychic impairments.

The annihilation of the function of belief

This is a drastic measure. It can be found in severe psychoses, in which ordinary belief systems are lost and normal thinking unavailable. Belief,

14

conscious and unconscious, is necessary for a sense of psychic reality. If this function is annihilated the ordinary unthought sense of certainty of self-continuity and the everydayness of the perceived world is lost. The individual is then detached, not simply from external reality, but also from psychic reality. Everything is possible and nothing is probable. Delusional certainty may be substituted to fill the void in some cases, as Freud suggested in the Schreber case (Freud 1911a). In such cases belief is asserted to be knowledge and it may also be imposed on perception, resulting in hallucination. In other psychotic states an arbitrary – sometimes capricious – kaleidoscope of ideas floats freely, untethered by belief, giving a facile, often foolish quality to thinking.

Presumably the belief function may be undeveloped or impaired because its basis in brain function is not intact; in other words, the 'hardware' may be defective. In other instances the 'software' may have been deleted; that is, the mental apparatus of belief may have been dismantled or destroyed to abolish any attachment to ideas. I think this dismantling is analogous to abolishing emotional ties to all objects, thereby producing a loss of a sense of reality; similarly, abolition of the capacity to believe produces a loss of a sense of psychic reality.

The suspension of belief

In a footnote to *Studies in Hysteria* Freud drew attention to a state of mind which he described as the 'blindness of the seeing eye', in which 'one knows and does not know a thing at the same time' (Freud 1893–5: 117). Later he was to use the noun '*Verleugnung*' to describe this non-psychotic form of denial, which Strachey translated as 'disavowal' (Freud 1924b, 1927b, 1938). I am suggesting that the *suspension of belief* is a non-psychotic form of disavowal in which one believes and does not believe a thing at the same time. Coleridge suggested that in order to be enthralled by drama we *willingly suspend disbelief*, thus conferring a sense of reality on what we know to be unreal (Shawcross 1968, vol. II: 6). I suggest that in certain psychic states of everyday life and analysis the reverse takes place. Belief is willingly suspended to avoid the emotional consequences, and the resultant state is one of *psychic unreality*. This may be an intermittent phenomenon temporarily arising in analysis to deal with emerging beliefs, or it may be persistent and pervasive.

If disavowal is all-pervasive it manifests itself in the state of *inconsequentiality* that is found clinically in the *as-if personality*. In this state all beliefs are treated as is recommended for religious beliefs in the *as-if philosophy*. Vaihinger suggested that although religious beliefs were now untenable in a scientific age they could be maintained on an *as-if basis* – that is, 'they perish only as theoretical truths; as practical fictions we leave them all intact' (Vaihinger 1912; quoted in Freud 1927a: 29, fn). Therefore, in the analysis of a patient in such a state interpretation (the analyst's belief) or insight (the patient's belief) can be treated as only practical fictions, useful but not truthful. Belief as a function is thereby suspended along with disbelief, and phantasies are treated as neither true nor untrue – or, more accurately, *true and untrue*. It is the *either/and* state of mind evading either/or. Not only is belief suspended, but so are its emotional consequences, and calmness is purchased at the price of a prevailing sense of unreality. Ambiguity is used as a defence against ambivalence. The place in the mind sought or created by this suspension of belief is, I think, related to Winnicott's notion of *transitional space*, which he described as 'an intermediate area of experience which is not challenged (arts, religion, etc.)' (Winnicott 1951: 240). It is not challenged with a question as to whether its contents were conceived or found. This, I think, is a space where the question 'Do you believe it?' is not to be asked. An individual who spends his life in such an area could be described as an *as-if personality*; a clinical discussion of this is the subject of Chapter 5 ('The suspension of belief and the "as-if" syndrome').

Counter-belief

Counter-beliefs may be produced as a defence against the unconscious beliefs that constitute the individual's psychic reality. As Winnicott said in his paper on the 'Manic defence', 'Omnipotent fantasies are not so much the inner reality itself as a defence against the acceptance of it' (Winnicott 1935: 130). If wish-fulfilling beliefs are used to serve the defensive purpose of denying psychic reality, anxiety increases the tenacity with which they are held. Considerable violence may be used to enforce such beliefs and to prevent their being challenged and discredited. Many political and religious beliefs fall into this category. Such counter-beliefs are at the heart of pathological organisations. I find very convincing Freud's definition from 'The future of an illusion', quoted at the head of this chapter:'Thus we call a belief an illusion when a wish-fulfilment is a prominent factor in its motivation, and in doing so we disregard its relations to reality, just as the illusion itself sets no store by verification' (Freud 1927a:31). To this I would add that an illusional belief sets no store by psychic reality and thus creates psychic unreality.

The conclusion I come to differs in one regard from that of Freud on the subject of religion. Some religious beliefs are illusional in the sense that they are the products of wish-fulfilling beliefs running counter to psychic reality, but others, even though based on psychic and not external reality,

16

seek the truth. As I discuss at greater length in Chapter 9, this is also the case with fiction; some fiction is true and some is false.

Some counter-beliefs form the basis of transference illusions, which defend the patient from the psychic reality of transference fears, conflicts or pain. For example, the following typical counter-belief was found in the analysis of a young woman patient. The patient believed that she (as daughter) shared a special analytic understanding (secret relationship) with her analyst (as father) which his wife (as mother) and other patients (as her siblings) did not possess. This wish-fulfilling *counter-belief* defended the patient from *believing* her existing phantasies associated with exclusion from the parental relationship. It produced complacency and stasis; her relinquishment of this counter-belief was followed by the emotional flux one hopes to meet in analysis. This sort of transference situation is described in Chapter 7 ('Complacency in analysis and everyday life').

The failure to relinquish belief

Relinquishing beliefs involves mourning; I have found that those who are unable to relinquish their discredited beliefs are the same people who cannot relinquish their lost objects.[1] The relinquishment of the lost object is linked with realising *and* tolerating the distinction between what is mental and what is material. The maintenance of the differentiation between belief and knowledge is also linked with realising *and* tolerating this distinction. Thus, the person who cannot make a distinction between belief and knowledge is unable to give up beliefs. To conclude, therefore, I will briefly describe a patient who could have been said to suffer from a surfeit of beliefs that were immune to the experience of reality.

The patient, Miss A, could not hold to the distinction between belief and knowledge. She could not derive any security from belief unless she regarded it as knowledge; *probability* did not exist for her, only *possibility* or *certainty*. Unless, therefore, she believed she *knew* her object's exact whereabouts she was in a panic. For this reason she developed elaborate strategies to avoid any occasion that would prompt her to doubt for a moment that she knew the whereabouts of her primary object. This meant manipulating not only her environment but also her mind. Her ultimate weapon against uncertainty was a system of counter-beliefs which she treated as knowledge. These counter-beliefs, in turn, plagued her as they had dire consequences. One such counter-belief was that she would go blind. From childhood her greatest fear was the fate of her mother if she was 'out of sight'. Her mother's continuing existence 'out of sight' meant she was 'in the other room'. The 'other room' was her parent's room, the setting of the primal scene, which for this patient was a murderous scenario. The counter-

17

belief she mounted as protection from her own phantasy was that her mother was not out of sight but that she herself was blind. This then became the belief that unless she saw her mother she would go blind. Finally it took the form 'if my mother dies I will go blind'. This was the form in which it emerged in the transference, when she believed that my disappearance would cause her blindness. The only means of ridding herself of this belief was to take a number of physical actions representing evacuation of her mind symbolically, such as flushing the toilet repeatedly.

There was compelling evidence that this inability to relinquish a belief was parallel with an inability to relinquish her object. Following the death of her mother, while she accepted the external reality of this event, she could not accept it psychically. She perceived her mother's absence, she knew of her death, but she did not believe it. Her fearful delusion soon returned; once more she believed that *if* she did not see her mother she would go blind. This counter-belief was now a means of denying the reality of her mother's death.

My patient's pathological mourning resembled a situation described by Hanna Segal (1994: 397); her idea of her mother was like a dead concrete object inside her, not a symbolic presence, and therefore could only be revived in the flesh and not in spirit. Freud wrote: 'the distinction between imagination and reality is effaced . . . when the symbol takes over the full functions of the thing it symbolises' (Freud 1919: 244). He went on to link this with 'the over-accentuation of psychical reality in comparison with material reality – a feature closely allied to the belief in the omnipotence of thoughts' (*ibid.*). Hanna Segal's (1957) work on the failure of symbolisation clarified this phenomenon when she linked it to a failure to work through the depressive position, and hence an inability to achieve normal mourning.

I think there are complex reasons why particular individuals have problems distinguishing material from psychic reality, symbol from object and belief from knowledge. By relinquishing objects I do not mean simply accepting the fact of their loss but, rather, accepting all the necessary changes in beliefs about the world that follow from that loss. One such belief which has to be relinquished is that the lost object is indispensable to life. In that sense, some people have the same difficulty with beliefs as they do with objects: they cannot accept that their beliefs are not indispensable to them.

Note

1 I prefer 'relinquish' to Strachey's 'renounce' for Freud's '*nicht aufgeben will*' (Freud 1916a).

2

Naming and containing

Life reposed with my daughter Order,
the one within me, the other without me.
I rose over them, but their arms were around me.
(Rundle Clark 1959: 45)

This chapter is about Wilfred Bion's concept of *the container* and *the contained*. He derived this notion initially from his clinical work, particularly with borderline and psychotic patients, and applied it in a very general way to individual and group behaviour. I want to approach my discussion of his concept through its clinical manifestations in analysis, and I will begin with a description of a patient who resembles those who provoked the idea in Bion's mind.

Miss A, as I shall call my patient, was compelled by threats from within herself to empty her mind of the thoughts she was having. She did this by repeatedly flushing them down the lavatory. There were days when she did this so often that she broke the mechanism. By the time she would tell me about this in her session she no longer knew what these thoughts were. The process, however, of emptying out was so severe that she felt empty of any ideas and any mental life; she complained of feeling 'unreal'. The quality the outside world acquired in this process was a sense of menace. As a consequence of this mental evacuation of 'something bad', she found it impossible to travel outside an imaginary boundary, which roughly coincided with the outskirts of London, where she lived. Thus she was menaced from within by an inner presence or from without by unspecified dangers. If she took things in and held them in her mind she was in danger; if she expelled them from her mind she produced a menacing outside world. She could neither introject nor project without producing a fearful situation.

Her dilemma was epitomised in a memory she often repeated to me of an episode that occurred during the Second World War, which served as a paradigm. It was what Freud called a screen memory; that is, a condensation of experience which functioned as an expression of earlier unconscious memories and a prototype for later experiences. In this memory of adolescence she was in a public air-raid shelter during a bomb attack. She felt suffocated in the shelter, where she was with her mother, whose anxiety had always oppressed her. She felt very urgently that she must escape. At the threshold she was terrified when she saw the bombs falling and the street on fire. An air-raid warden confronted her in the entrance and ordered her to stay. Her conflict was intense and apparently unresolvable. She collapsed in the doorway, retaining consciousness but becoming paralysed, mute and entirely without bodily sensations, so that she could not feel the pins which the examining doctors stuck into her. It was this state of anaesthesia that has been used by her internal voice as a threat ever after, compelling her to perform compulsively her irrational activities – 'If you don't do this you will get the feelings'. The 'feelings' which she so dreaded were actually the experience of having *no* sensation.

The threshold remained a crucial place materially and symbolically for her. When she embarked for her sessions with me she would repeatedly go in and out of her flat, which she shared with her mother, before she could leave to come and see me. The to-and-fro movement was to ensure that she did not bring the 'wrong ideas' with her from her flat.

What she sought from me was basically two things: one was to find sanctuary and the other was to find meaning. She found sanctuary the moment she was under my roof. Once she was in the waiting room – and she was always early – she felt free of what she called the noise in her mind. Once in the session, she would immediately seek meaning from me, reiterating 'What does it mean? What does it mean?'

Sanctuary seemed to be a sense of being in a safe place, which expressed an idea of being inside something good. Winnicott called this a sense *of being held* (Winnicott 1960a). Esther Bick equated it with a sense of envelopment like a skin around oneself which protects and enfolds (Bick 1968). Bion himself, in an early description of containment, referred to a mental skin. My patient found sanctuary when she felt that she was in my mind. Having rung the bell and gained admission to the waiting room she was confident I had her in mind. If she could leave with a conviction that I would keep her in mind she felt safe. The other thing that she sought from me was meaning and knowledge. This, she believed, would provide internal coherence to her thoughts, the disconnectedness of which persecuted her. When the thinking broke down further she had to ask people for the name of everything and everyone in a desperate effort to arrest an otherwise uncontained flooding sense of 'not knowing'.

When sanctuary, a sense of being inside something safe, is lost the individual feels that he or she is falling forever. When meaning is lost a sense of tormenting perplexity is felt. My patient, Miss A, found this intolerably distressing. That which I described as giving sanctuary to my patient, a sense of being in safely bounded space, is one function of containment; the other is providing meaning. This comes from the relationship between the two components 'the container' and 'the contained'. If a name enshrines a psychic quality – like love, for example – the word provides a container for the emotional experience, putting a semantic boundary around it. It also places it in a ready-made context of significance provided by the place in human affairs of love and the place of the word in an existing language. At the same time, the experience of the emotion gives meaning to the word for that individual. Thus the experience as container gives meaning to the word 'container' (Bion 1962b, 1970). The analytic situation could be described as endeavouring to provide both a bounded world and a place where meaning can be found.

'The container' and 'the contained' were terms Bion used in 1962 in his book *Learning from experience* (Bion 1962b), but the concept was developed earlier in a series of three papers: 'On arrogance' (1957), 'Attacks on linking' (1959) and 'A theory of thinking' (1962a). In the last of these papers he expounded his theories on the nature of thought and the capacity for thinking. This, I believe, is a piece of major metapsychology and a notable contribution to psychoanalysis. It has not only shed new light on psychopathology but also furnished a new rationale for the efficacy of psychoanalysis, namely his notion of the transformation of experience through the process of containment.

Bion defines his terms in *Learning from Experience* as follows:

> Melanie Klein has described an aspect of projective identification concerned with the modification of infantile fears; the infant projects a part of its psyche, namely its bad feelings, into the good breast. Thence in due course they are removed and re-introjected. During their sojourn in the good breast they are felt to have been modified in such a way that the object that is re-introjected has become tolerable to the infant's psyche.
>
> From the above theory I shall abstract for use as a model the idea of a container into which an object is projected and the object that can be projected into the container; the latter I shall designate by the contained. The unsatisfactory nature of both terms points to the need for further abstraction.
>
> (Bion 1962b: 90)

What Bion added to Melanie Klein's account of projective identification was, first, the observation that projective identification was often not simply an omnipotent phantasy as she described, but that the patient took steps to give effect to his phantasy, for example that it is not the patient who is afraid, angry, helpless, despairing, impotent or whatever, but that it is the analyst who experiences such feelings as a consequence of the patient's verbal and non-verbal behaviour. The second additional point that Bion made was that this is a repetition of a normal stage of development between mother and infant, which provides a primitive method of communication and is the forerunner of thinking. The mother, if she is receptive to the infant's state of mind and capable of allowing it to be evoked in herself, can process it in such a way that in an identifiable form she can attend to it in the infant. In this way something which in the infant is near-sensory and somatic is transformed by the mother into something more mental which can be used for thought or stored as memory. The nearly sensory-somatic qualities Bion called β elements, and those which become more mental in character he called a elements. The process by which β is transformed into a he called a function because its nature is unknown, and he did not want to give the impression by giving it a name that the process was identified and not simply inferred.

In the original infant–mother relationship it is the mother's a process that functions or malfunctions for the infant. In due course the mother's capacity is introjected by the infant. If this process badly misfires something like the state of mind of Miss A can result. I would like to return to that in order to illustrate what I have been describing in theory. If the elements of potential experience are unprocessed – that is, if they remain as β elements – they cannot be treated as ordinary thoughts or emotions, or as ordinary perceptions of the material world; they are on the boundary of somatic and psychic. Miss A was consciously aware of them, and she tried to describe something which she regarded as mental and yet could experience only as physical, something which had mental status but could only be physically removed. She would say to me, 'I know it sounds mad, but I do feel that these terrible things in my mind should be cut out. If only someone would X-ray my mind and do an operation.'

Of the various forms of removal to which she had already resorted, I have already referred to one, flushing the lavatory; others were repeated hair washing, compulsive bathing and repetitious disposal of rubbish. In a long history of psychological troubles she had used different routes and locations for the disposal of these elements. Since she could not make them mental she could not keep them in her mind in the sense that one might keep thoughts as conscious, preconscious or unconscious.

Basically, there are three spheres where these precursors of thought, β elements, might go out of the mind: first, into the body; second, into the perceptual sphere; and, third, into the realm of action – in other words, into psychosomatic dysfunction, perceptual hallucinations or symptomatic action. Miss A had at different times used all three. She had suffered a good deal of psychosomatic ill health; it seems likely that these unprocessed elements had been discharged through physical channels into her body. At other times these elements were projected into the perceptual sphere so that she 'heard' or 'saw' things that she knew were not real. These episodes frightened her and she described them as 'like having nightmares' while still awake. Her life was dominated by symptomatic acts.

Miss A functioned as though she lacked a process for producing things in a form that could be kept in mind, and also appeared to lack a mind that could keep things in it. Bion formulated the notion that *thinking* is dependent on the successful outcome of two main mental developments: the development of thoughts and the apparatus necessary to deal with the thoughts. Sometimes he called this the 'mental apparatus', sometimes simply 'thinking'. Therefore, he argued, thinking comes about in order to deal with thoughts. Either of these two developments may go wrong. These capacities have their origins in the link between infant and mother in which knowledge develops. He designated this knowledge the K link, to distinguish it from the two other links between objects that he referred to, namely love, which he called the L link, and hate, which he called the H link. The origin of the K link was the process between mother and child based on the infant's use of projective identification and the mother's capacity to receive and modify it. The subsequent introjection by the child of a maternal object with this capacity provided the child with an internal object capable of knowing and informing. In other words, people who internalise such an object are capable of self-knowledge and communication between different aspects of themselves.

If a mother fails to absorb the infant's projective identification and resists any attempt by the child to know her mind she gives the child a picture of a world that does not want to know it and does not want to be known. How this internal situation manifests itself in analysis was first described in Bion's paper 'On arrogance', where he described the presence of *a triad of arrogance, stupidity and curiosity* which indicated the presence of psychotic thinking, a consequence of what he called a 'primitive mental catastrophe' (Bion 1957: 89). The 'stupidity' was the manifestation of something obstructing the process of 'taking things in' which underlies communication. Familiarity with its operation has made it clear that this problem is something that crops up in many analyses, not only as a major feature in severely disabled patients. This obstruction is sometimes felt to be in the analyst, sometimes in the patient and sometimes in some other location altogether, from which it intervenes to thwart understanding. If it is felt by the patient to be in the analyst, the analyst is thought to be impermeable to the reality of the patient. If it is active in the patient, the patient cannot 'take in' what the analyst is saying and appears to be stupid. If it is in a third position it manifests itself by intrusive thoughts, destructive comments or sometimes threats.

A patient considerably less disturbed than Miss A said to me: 'The reason why I go on and on at you is that I must let you know how I feel. I don't feel I get it across to you just by saying it. I have to make you feel it. I don't think that you take it in.'

How this obstructing force moves around within a session I can illustrate from another patient. This patient started a session by saying, 'I'm deaf in one ear'; he then remained silent for some time, before he commented, 'I feel thick-headed'. He went on despondently, 'It's not going to be any good today, I won't be able to think. I feel muddle-headed'. As the session proceeded I sensed a quiet despair in my patient, and I thought to myself that he believed I did not want to know what he was thinking and feeling. So I said this to him. He said 'yes' very promptly, and went on: 'You must be feeling impatient, waiting for me to get on with this analysis. But I feel muddled, unclear about anything – stuck.' In contrast to himself, he believed that I already knew what he should do, already knew what was in his mind and knew what it all meant. All I knew in reality, however, was that my patient felt he could not enlighten me about himself. When eventually he did begin to talk he did so in an unusual way. Its effect on me was that I could not remember what he said and was unable to make anything of it. I felt muddle-headed and stupid and impatient with myself; I blamed myself. I tried to think about the sense of impatience I had with myself, then I realised that I was imagining privately that other colleagues, whose abilities I admired, would know with crystal clarity the meaning of what was being said. It was only then that it occurred to me that this was the internal situation that my patient had brought with him. He had arrived to talk to an analyst who he imagined did not know what it felt like to be ignorant and in comparison with whom he felt ignorant. In other words, once the preliminary work of the session had been done he had begun to communicate his state of mind to me, not in words but by projective iden-tification. Therefore I said that his words today gave me a sense of what it was like to feel muddled and unsure of what was happening, in contrast to an imaginary superior person who he thought always knew what was happening. He reiterated that he felt there was something that he ought to know and did not know which I would expect him to know. It was only then that I remembered that shortly before this session I had told him, unexpectedly, that I would not be working on a particular day a few weeks thence. It occurred to me that he felt ignorant about my activities outside the sessions. This for my patient always reactivated a lurking sense of inferi-ority which he felt about any activities of mine which, like his parents' sexual life together when he was a small child, was beyond his comprehen-sion. He appeared to experience it as a form of exclusion which condemned him to a shameful exposure of inferiority.

The belief that they are dealing with an impermeable object coated with an impregnable sense of superiority drives some personalities to violence. It underlies a good many of the situations of spiralling violence that occur in professional situations, whether in psychiatry or social work, in teaching or in psychoanalysis. If the patient, client, child or whoever feels that he or she cannot 'get through', is making no impact or impression on the person that he or she is addressing, then an intensification may occur in his or her efforts to project and enforce feelings within the professional recipient. This often produces a vicious circle, since we are all apt to respond to such pressure from patients by 'hardening' inside. We may communicate this hardening in our choice of words, in our expression or in our tone of voice; this, in turn, provokes more efforts to intrude forcibly. In other people at other times the sense of being faced with an impervious object induces an acquiescent despair. This was so in the patient I have just been referring to.

Fear of the containing object does not only take the form of a fear of being denied access, ingress or acceptance. Other fears result from a phantasy of the projected self being taken in and then destroyed, of one's nature being taken in by another's devouring curiosity and consumed in the process, of oneself being comprehended and nullified during the process. It is a not uncommon fear that analysis will strip the individual of his or her individuality, or that particular gifts will be lost, but in severe forms this idea can lead to profound fears of a psychotic kind, as in my patient Miss A. She feared entombment while still alive. One version of this was her fear that she would be buried alive, incarcerated in a coffin unable to speak or move. It was one of several versions of a configuration that haunted her, in all of which she would be enclosed, confined and denuded of life. When she was a small child one form this had taken was a phantasy she had of being trapped in a 'tube' inside her mother. Her mother did, in fact, have a 'tubal' (ectopic) pregnancy. She had heard a lot of conversation about this, and it was for this reason that her mother was hospitalised. This image gave shape to pre-existing phantasies which derived from early infancy with her mother. As a little girl she grasped that this 'tubal' pregnancy meant death for one or the other party, mother or baby. She repeated this fear symbolically in her treatment with me. There were times when she became afraid that I would listen to what she said, take it in and then I would tell her that it meant nothing – literally nothing or that it added up to nothing, that it made no sense. This would have meant she was mad. A related fear was that I would take in what she said and forget it. This was a cause of great panic because she could not remember things once she had told them to me and thus feared that they were lost completely.

The analysis of the other patient was very different. One important difference was that Miss A's father was psychotic and hostile to her relationship with her mother. Mr B's father was a more normal and helpful person. I have noticed that where the problem has its roots mainly in maternal difficulties of containment the patient is often very responsive to the kind of analytic approach that I have been describing. However, I find that such patients are markedly dependent on the analytic process itself, and are very vulnerable to interruptions such as those caused by breaks and particularly prone, I find, to lose their functional capacities during breaks.

In Miss A's case her father's mad destructiveness provided an external location for her own conspicuous envious and nihilistic trends, as a result of which there was, by projective identification, a fusion between that hostile aspect of herself and her perception of her father's hostility. This introduced into her personality what I have called an 'Alien Object' (Britton 1986), which she experienced as both part of herself and not part of herself. In fact she used to say, 'It must be me but it doesn't feel like me'. This enabled her to exonerate her mother from any attribution of malignancy as she split this off from her mother, attached it to her idea of her father and cemented it there with her own projected hostility. Her mother was consequently internally represented as inadequate and restricted, a lifeless object in which she felt entombed. Her father was perceived as unrestrained, totally free and dangerous – a picture of uncontained violence, a man who destroyed any relationship he entered, just as my patient envisaged him destroying the peace of mind of her childhood home. The air-raid shelter memory, functioning as a condensation in the way that a dream image might do, could be seen as a representation of the alternative of a sheltering, confining mother, and outside that relationship was an attacking air-raid father, with his bombshell curses and angry words, which she could not keep out of her mind.

Bion, as I said earlier in this chapter, applied this basic relationship of the container to the contained in a very general way to individual and group relationships. He saw it as a predetermined form, a *pre-conception*, which would seek its first expression in the mother–infant relationship. Whatever phantasies it engendered in that early encounter would fundamentally shape for the individual his or her expectations of all subsequent situations and also the relationship inside himself, as we picture ourselves containing ourselves. In this picture of our own self-composition we sometimes see ourselves as containing vital things such as vital organs or other vital components, or at other times we see ourselves as inhabitants of our bodies. In older language we might have said that sometimes we see ourselves as our bodies containing a soul and at other times as our souls confined within a body.

A degree of mutual recrimination between container and contained seems inevitable. Some amount of friction is, after all, part of life. I think this was eloquently expressed by the seventeenth-century metaphysical poet Andrew Marvell, that most sensuous of Puritan poets. His poetic account of the relationship I have been describing followed the fashion in the late seventeenth century for literary debates between body and soul: 'Marvell is somewhat unusual in the way he avoids favouring one side or the other in the dispute, or resolving the problem of the mutual incompatibility of the participants' (Wilcher 1986: 219). In his even-handed dialogue between the Soul and the Body we see a mild mutual persecution, a sort of exasperation at the human condition. Soul begins by complaining of imprisonment within his mortal frame:

> Oh, who shall from this dungeon raise
> A soul enslaved so many ways?
> With bolts of bones that fettered stands
> In feet, and manacled hands.
> Here blinded with an eye, and there
> Deaf with the drumming of an ear.
>
> (Marvell; cited in Wilcher 1986: 17)

Body replies, complaining of the tyranny he suffers from his Soul, who by breathing life into him 'Has made me live to let me die' (*ibid.*: 19). Soul's riposte is to grumble at the affliction from Body of sensations of grief and pain. He says, 'I feel, that cannot feel, the pain' (*ibid.*: 18). Body, however, has the last word, and perhaps speaks for all of us, describing what it is to be afflicted with the qualities of psychic life, giving us a catalogue familiar to those who have suffered the pangs of the depressive position. Body complains that thanks to containing a Soul he suffers from hope, fear, love, hate, joy, sorrow, knowledge and memory:

> . . . first the cramp of hope does tear,
> And then the palsy shakes of fear;
> The pestilence or love does heat,
> Or hatred's hidden ulcer eat;
> Joy's cheerful madness does perplex,
> Or sorrow's other madness vex;
> Which knowledge forces us to know,
> And memory will not forgo.
>
> (Marvell; cited in Wilcher 1986: 18)

In a description of the 'container' in an unpublished paper entitled 'Catastrophic change', Bion said that 'Some aspect of the personality is stable and constant, and that this is maintained as the only force likely contain emergent ideas which express new awareness of reality of the self the world' (Bion 1966). If the relationship between this continuous self and the changing emergent self is mutually enhancing, development takes place. He described this relationship as *symbiotic*. If, however, that continuous identity which he called the container would be disrupted by new self-development or new self-discoveries, psychic change would be experienced as catastrophic since the changes would disintegrate the sense of self-continuity. When this happens the subjective experience is one of fragmentation. In these circumstances in order to preserve a sense of continuity of existence *all* change may be resisted and no new experience allowed to emerge. This mutually destructive relationship of container and contained Bion called *parasitic*; I prefer to call it *malignant containment*. As I have described, faced with these two catastrophic alternatives – incarceration or fragmentation – some people, like my patient Miss A, remain paralysed at the frontier, on the threshold. If she left the shelter and confines of her already-existing ideas about herself and her mother, which could not accommodate any growth, she thought that her world would be shattered and her continuous self annihilated. However, if she remained confined to her cramped, rigid view of her mother and herself it meant the stifling of thought. I was to see this pattern repeating itself again and again as we tried to enlarge her view of things by the inclusion of new ideas within the context of her relationship with me, which took years to change. This describes what we might call a persecutory view of containment. There is, of course, a corresponding belief in its opposite, namely ideal containment, in which an absolute fit between container and contained would exist. In this, perfect understanding would be the order of the day, failing which a feeling of persecution would follow. In some personalities small discrepancies in understanding, or between words and meaning, or between intention and execution, or between interpretation and experience, or between ideal and real cannot be tolerated. In Chapter 4 ('Subjectivity, objectivity and triangular space') this phenomenon is discussed at length.

3

Oedipus in the depressive position

Here is the instance, here is Oedipus, here is the reason
Why I will call no mortal creature happy
(Sophocles, *Oedipus Rex*; in Watling 1947: 59)

The earliest version of this chapter was a paper I read in Vienna (Britton 1985), which was modified and published as 'The Oedipus situation and the depressive position' (Britton 1991). In that I said that we resolve the Oedipus complex by working through the depressive position, and the depressive position by working through the Oedipus complex; that neither are ever finished and both have to be reworked in each new life situation.

The Oedipus complex has occupied a central place in psychoanalytic theory from the beginning, and though much has changed it remains so. What substantial additions have been made to our knowledge about it since Freud? I consider that the most significant new additions to our perspective on this were made by Melanie Klein, partly in her clinical observations of Oedipal manifestations in very small children, partly in her papers on the Oedipus complex (Klein 1928, 1945), and indirectly by her concept of the depressive position (Klein 1935, 1940). Donald Winnicott considered that her most important contribution to psychoanalysis was the concept of the depressive position, which, he wrote, 'ranks with Freud's concept of the Oedipus complex' (Winnicott 1962: 176).

In this chapter I will describe some of what she added to the understanding of the Oedipus situation, what is meant by the depressive position and how in my view the introduction of this concept necessarily changes our understanding of the Oedipus complex. As I see it, these two situations are inextricably intertwined in such a way that one cannot be resolved without the other; we resolve the Oedipus complex by working through the depressive position and the depressive position by working through the Oedipus complex.

29

A century has passed since Freud first put pen to paper to describe the complex. In May 1897, in a letter to his friend Wilhelm Fliess, he wrote that he now thought an 'integral constituent of neuroses' (Freud 1897a:255) was hostile impulses against parents: 'This death wish is directed in sons against their father and in daughters against their mother' (*ibid.*). He wrote a succinct further note: 'A maidservant makes a transference from this by wishing her mistress to die so he can marry her (cf. Lisl's dream about Martha and me)' (*ibid.*). Lisl was the Freuds' nursery maid, and she had reported a dream of her mistress having died and the professor marrying her.

Five months later Freud described in a further letter his discovery of a similar configuration in himself in the course of his own self-analysis. This persuaded him that such wishes might be ubiquitous. And he conjured up for the Greek drama of *Oedipus Rex* a universal audience in which 'Each member was once, in germ and in phantasy, just such an Oedipus' (Freud 1897b: 265). Freud refers to the horror generated in the audience by the 'dream fulfilment here transplanted into reality' (*ibid.*) – the horror, that is, of Oedipus killing his father and marrying his mother, leading Jocasta, his mother, to suicide and Oedipus to blinding himself. However, whether it is the royal court of Thebes or Lisl in the nursery, we notice in the two different sexes the same elements: a parental couple (symbolic in Lisl's case); a death wish towards the parent of the same sex; and a wish-fulfilling dream or myth of taking the place of one parent and marrying the other.

Though Freud referred to *Oedipus Rex* in his letter of 1897 and expanded on the myth in *The Interpretation of Dreams* (Freud 1900a: 261–4), he did not use the term *Oedipus complex* in a paper until 'A special type of choice of object made by men' was written in 1910. In this paper he puts it that the boy who begins to desire his mother anew and hate his father as a rival 'comes, as we say, under the dominance of the Oedipus complex. He does not forgive his mother for having granted the favour of sexual intercourse not to himself but to his father, and he regards it as an act of unfaithfulness' (Freud 1910b: 171). The parents' sexual relationship is centre stage in this account and is at war with the child's exclusive relationship with his mother, as it is in Freud's other accounts of the Oedipus complex during this period, culminating in his account of the 'primal scene' as the centrepiece of the case study usually known as the 'Wolf Man' (Freud 1918). During that analysis (1910–14) Freud began to speculate on 'primal phantasies', an archaic inheritance of innate ideas, one variety of which would be some sort of primitive precursor to the primal scene (editor's footnote to *Moses and Monotheism*, Freud 1939: 102). Such innate ideas, were they universal, would predispose us all to construct some version of parental intercourse fleshed out by experience and imagination. In the *Introductory Lectures on Psycho-Analysis* he said: 'I believe these *primal phan-*

tasies . . . are a phylogenetic endowment' (Freud 1916b: 370–1). But Freud never incorporated the primal scene and its associated phantasies into the Oedipus complex itself. Melanie Klein not only did so but made it central in her account of what she called the Oedipus situation (Klein 1928, 1945).

Klein was to find ample confirmation of Freud's primal phantasies in the analyses of young children. She also found that such phantasies occurred very early, and that in very young children they were at times idyllic, and at times violent, terrifying and bizarre. She also found that, in conjunction with the aggressive phantasies of children against parental intercourse and mother's body containing unborn babies, there was guilt and despair at the damage done in phantasy and there was a wish to repair the damage. Where this reparative wish failed the damage was denied and magically restored by omnipotent manic reparation. When this belief faded obsessional methods were resorted to, with compulsive acts of symbolic significance carried out in desperate efforts to undo what had been done in imagination.

In Klein's view, the Oedipal situation began in infancy and underwent a complex development lasting years, before reaching its zenith at the age of 4. This was the age of what has come to be called the classical Oedipus *complex*, as described by Freud. Klein also emphasised that the development of the epistemophilic impulse, the urge to know, is considerably influenced by these early experiences of the Oedipus situation. She described the enormous hatred that could be stimulated by the child's feeling of ignorance in the face of the irreducible mysteries of parental sexuality, and how in some children an inhibition of all desire for learning could follow. In one of her earliest papers, in 1926, she wrote:

> At a very early age children become acquainted with reality through the deprivations which it imposes on them. They defend themselves against reality by repudiating it. The fundamental thing, however, and the criterion of all later capacity for adaptation to reality, is the degree in which they are able to tolerate the deprivations that result from the Oedipus situation.
>
> (Klein 1926: 128–9)

What are these deprivations? Why are they so crucial that they influence our hold on reality and therefore our sanity? We are better equipped to consider these questions in the light of the notion of the depressive position, a concept Klein first formulated a decade later (Klein 1935, 1940). In Klein's view, the phenomena of the depressive position, which begin to develop between the ages of 3 months and 6 months and continue thereafter, involve major steps forward in psychic integration. Part-objects such as the anatomical and functional components of the primary object are recognised to be parts of one single, whole object and not entire objects in their own right. It is realised that love and hate, previously attached to what seemed to be separate objects, are directed towards the same object. The infant begins to feel guilt over his or her attacks on the good object, and becomes afraid of the damage done to it and afraid of losing it; the infant has a strong wish to repair the object believed to be damaged.

Klein pointed to the close connection between the phase in which the depressive position develops and the early Oedipus complex: 'The early stages of the Oedipus complex and the depressive position are clearly linked and develop simultaneously' (Klein 1952c: 110). In her paper 'Envy and gratitude' she reiterated her belief that:

> Jealousy is based on the suspicion of and rivalry with the father, who is accused of having taken away the mother's breast and the mother. This rivalry marks the early stages of the direct and inverted Oedipus complex, which normally arises concurrently with the depressive position in the second quarter of the first year.
>
> (Klein 1957: 196)

If the integration of the depressive position fails the individual cannot progress fully towards developing a capacity for symbol formation and rational thought. One of several possible abnormal outcomes is that the individual may resort to obsessional, compulsive acts to put right the imagined damage. For example, a patient of mine found it necessary to destroy several of his son's books and replace them with new copies because the books were on his desk at a moment when he had a sudden image of his son lying dead in the road following an accident. He believed the books now contained his image of his son's death and that the image had to be eradicated.

In order to understand why this took such a concrete form and required physical acts it is necessary to realise that in some people the development of symbolic capacity is not fully achieved or sustained. Klein linked the development of the capacity to symbolise to the working through of the fundamental anxieties she had described, but it was Hanna Segal who was in later years to show that the capacity to symbolise, and therefore to make symbolic reparation, was a consequence of working through the depressive position (Segal 1957).

What I have emphasised is that the depressive position and the Oedipus situation are never finished but have to be reworked in each new life situation, at each stage of development and with each major addition to experience or knowledge. The depressive position arises inevitably and naturally in infancy as a consequence of the developing capacities of the child: to perceive, to recognise, to remember, to locate and to anticipate experience. This does not simply enlarge the awareness and knowledge of

32

the infant, but also disrupts its existing psychic world. What had previously been the separate world of timeless bliss in one ideal universe and the terror and persecution of another now turns into one world. And they come, these contrasting experiences of bliss and horror, from one source. The fount of all goodness, loved in phantasy as an ideal breast, turns out to be the same object as the hated bad breast previously perceived as the source of all things bad and the essence of evil. Innocence is lost, then, in its two senses. We are no longer innocent of knowledge and we have lost our innocence in the sense of becoming capable of guilt, because we now know we hate that which we love and which we regard as good. We have eaten of the fruit of the tree of knowledge of good and evil, and therefore we can no longer live in Eden.

The depressive position is provoked by, and establishes, that greater knowledge of the object which includes awareness of its continuity of existence in time and space, and also therefore of the other relationships of the object implied by that realisation. The Oedipus situation exemplifies that knowledge. Hence the depressive position cannot be worked through without the Oedipus complex being worked through, and vice versa. Freud made clear that repression of the complex intact was a foundation for neurosis and that something else was needed, which he called its dissolution, for healthy development. Something had to be given up (Freud 1924a). In 'Mourning and melancholia' (1917c), Freud had linked the preservation of sanity and attachment to reality with the relinquishment of the permanent possession of the love object after its loss. But he did not apply this to the dissolution of the Oedipus complex.

Following Freud's ideas in 'Mourning and melancholia', Klein linked giving something up in the external world – as we do in weaning, for example – with the process of mourning. This is a process which necessitates once again that we give up the expectation of finding an ideal world which might be realised in the material world, and that we recognise the distinction between aspiration and expectation, the distinction between the psychic and the material. She saw this as a process of repeatedly anticipating something and then discovering it to be absent. She considered it to be a means of relinquishing the object in the material world and simultaneously installing it in the psychic, or inner, world (Klein 1935, 1940). In Bion's language, a pre-conception which is followed by a negative realisation gives a thought, though only if one can bear the frustration following the realisation that it does not give the thing one wants (Bion 1962b). If the frustration cannot be tolerated the negative realisation (that is, the absence of something) is perceived as the presence of something bad – '*a no-thing*' – and with this goes the notion that it can be got rid of; hence the belief that a state of deprivation can be remedied by abolishing things. If because of this there is in phantasy a bad object inside with material rather than

33

*different from Klein's
ideas of absent breast
becomes the bad breast'*

ideational qualities, a state of mind exists which underlies some psychotic and severe obsessional states. For example, a patient of mine, prior to seeking psychiatric help, had actually sought the help of a surgeon to have removed a black, bad thing inside her, which she was convinced made her have bad thoughts.

An essential element in the depressive position is the growth of the sense of distinction between self and object, and between the real and the ideal object. Hanna Segal has suggested that failure to make such distinctions results in failure of symbolisation and the production of 'symbolic equations' – that is, symbolic objects experienced as identical with the original object (Segal 1957). A similar state of affairs is implicit in Freud's account of the neurotic patient's treatment of all subsequent love relations as if they were with the original Oedipal object. Just as in the depressive position the idea of the permanent possession has to be given up, so in confronting the parental relationship the ideal of one's sole possession of the desired parent has to be relinquished. The Oedipal phantasy may become an effort to reinstate it, to deny the reality of the parental sexual relationship. If this denial threatens to sever the individual's hold on reality the Oedipal romance may be preserved by splitting it off into an area of thinking protected from reality where the *pleasure principle* is preserved, as Freud described, in a *reservation* (Freud 1924b). This reservation may be an area of daydream or masturbatory phantasy, or as I suggest later it may be the basis of escapist fiction. William Blake described it in his prophetic verse as Beulah (Keynes 1959: 518), which I discuss in Chapter 14. It can become the place where some people spend most of their lives, in which case their external relationships are used to enact these dramas only in order to give a spurious claim of reality to their phantasies. In others the reservation may be preserved as an island of activity, such as a perversion, separated from the mainstream of the individual's life.

I am making a distinction here by claiming that some phantasies possess psychic reality, not by their correspondence with an external reality, but by the sense of truth, which Bion suggested has a similar quality in relation to the inner world as the sense of reality possesses in relation to the external world (Bion 1962a: 119). He proposes that a sense of reality comes from our combining data derived from different sensory modalities, such as sight, hearing, touch and so on, to give us common sense. In a similar way, he suggests that a sense of truth comes from our combining different emotional views of the same object. Thus when we acknowledge we hate what we feel to be the same person as someone we love we feel ourselves to be truthful and our relationship to be substantial. If this recognition of ambivalence is evaded by, for example, using the Oedipal configuration to perpetuate our divided universe by having one permanently good parent and one permanently bad, then this reliable sense of the truth of things is lacking, and this, I think, often leads to repetitious patterns of behaviour designed to assert a reality that lacks inner conviction – for example to repeated re-enactments of stereotyped Oedipal situations in life. One such form might be the initiation of incest with a child to actualise by projective identification the Oedipal illusion.

If in order to achieve integration the common view of the object has to be established and tolerated, it means that the mother perceived as a feeding and loving mother has to be perceived as the same person as the sexual mother – that is, in the first instance as father's sexual partner. This poses great difficulty for many people. It often seems to be represented by images of women as degenerate or, as a male patient of mine described them, blemished. He recently had begun an affair with a romantically idealised woman and he described with lyrical intensity the meal they had together, which was flawed only by her mentioning her former husband at the end of the meal. Then something began to go wrong for him and he noticed a small scar like a blemish on her leg. He then became impotent and subsequently could not bring himself to contact her. Having cut himself off from her he then developed a state of alarm about her, convinced she must be severely depressed and possibly suicidal. I was familiar with this pattern in this patient and it recurrently manifested itself in the transference. What seemed to happen was that his aversion to the thought of parental sexuality was represented by the image of a disgusting woman, and the hostility provoked by his envy and jealousy led him to cut himself off from her, an act which he felt mutilated those to whom he subjected it. His subsequent anxieties about the fate of the woman are typical of those Klein designated as depressive anxieties.

This sort of reaction was a relatively recent development in this patient. When he first came into analysis women were for him either pure and remote or the objects of pornographic study and perverse scopophilia as excitingly degraded figures. He had secret states of grandeur and elation when he assumed the characteristics in his mind, by projective identification, of a magical, omnipotent father. At other times he suffered paranoid anxieties. Prior to his analysis he was usually in a state of mind resulting from his sojourn in a pathological organisation which had manic and perverse characteristics, and whenever this broke down he was assailed by persecutory anxieties. It was these that drove him into analysis. The episode I have described was the consequence of a move into the depressive position and the Oedipus situation.

The patient in a paranoid-schizoid mode has buried his unacknowledged thoughts in others, in his actions or in his perceptions, and though they are symbolic in form they are treated as things. As Betty Joseph pointed out in her paper on 'Different types of anxiety and their handling in the analytic situation', analysis in such cases is likely to be a scene for action rather than thought (Joseph 1989b). It is then the analyst's task to reclaim for thought what may otherwise be dispersed in action and reaction.

Oedipal illusions

In Sophocles' *Oedipus Rex* Jocasta, before the truth is finally exposed to her that her husband is her son and that he has killed his father, reassures her husband Oedipus:

> *Jocasta*: 'Fear? What has a man to do with fear?
> . . . Nor need this mother-marrying frighten you;
> Many a man has dreamt as much.
> (Sophocles, cited in Watling 1947: 52)

This apparent license for incestuous dreams may have been too much for W. B. Yeats because he left Jocasta's speech out of his translation of Sophocles play, or perhaps he thought it gave the game away. The game I have in mind is that of Oedipal illusions, the unconscious claim that it is not just a dream but a real and delightful or dangerous possibility. With some people, life, instead of being lived, can become the vehicle for the reinstatement of Oedipal illusions, and the relationships of the external world are used only as stage props for an insistent internal drama whose function is to deny the psychic reality of the depressive position and the pains of the real Oedipus situation. It was with such patients that psychoanalysis began, in the *Studies on Hysteria* (Freud 1893–5). In this sense the so-called classical Oedipus complex is a defence against the Oedipus situation.

I would like to clarify my view of the normal development of the complex by describing it in terms of the Oedipus myth. It begins with the nature of the parental relationship and the child's phantasies about it. In the Oedipus myth this would be represented by the story of the infant Oedipus abandoned on the hillside by his mother at his father's instigation, a tragic version in the child's phantasy of being put out to die so that the parents can sleep together. Psychically, the complex unfolds further with the development of the child's rivalry with one parent for absolute possession of the other. This I see exemplified in the myth by the meeting at the crossroads where Laius bars the way, as if representing the father's obstruction of the child's wish to re-enter mother through her genitals. This is what I regard as the psychic reality of the Oedipus complex, as are the fears of personal or parental death as imagined consequences of self-assertion.

What I have called *Oedipal illusions* are defensive phantasies meant to occlude these psychic realities. In the myth I see the Oedipal illusion as the state in which Oedipus is on the throne with his wife-mother, surrounded by his court, whose members are turning a blind eye, as John Steiner has put it, to what they already half-know but choose to ignore (Steiner 1985). In this situation, where illusion reigns supreme, curiosity is felt to spell disaster. In the phantasised tragic version of the Oedipus complex the discovery of the oedipal triangle is felt to be the death of the couple, the nursing couple or the parental couple. In this phantasy the arrival of the notion of a third always murders the dyadic relationship.

I think this idea is entertained by all of us at times, but for some it appears to remain a settled conviction, and when it does it leads to psychopathology. It is through mourning for this lost exclusive relationship that one can realise that the Oedipal triangle does not spell the death of a relationship, but only the death of an idea. *essay*.

When Oedipal illusions are paramount the parental relationship is known but its full significance is evaded and its nature, which demonstrates the differences between the parental relationship and the parent–child relationship, is not acknowledged. The illusion is felt to protect the individual from his own phantasies of the Oedipal situation. I have found in such cases expectations of an endlessly humiliating exposure to parental triumphalism or a disastrous version of parental intercourse. The latter is perceived either as horrific sadomasochistic or murderous intercourse or as depressive images of a ruined couple in a ruined world. However, while such illusions are perpetuated as evasions of the underlying situation, the Oedipus complex cannot be resolved through the normal processes of rivalry and relinquishment.

I think that in normal development such illusions are frequent and transitory, producing cycles of illusionment and disillusionment that are the familiar features of everyday life and analysis. In some people, however, the persistence of an organised Oedipal illusion prevents the resolution of the complex, and in analysis prevents the full development of its transference counterpart.

These illusions are often conscious or almost-conscious versions of actual life situations. For example, I heard in supervision about a young woman musician who gave to her professional relationship with her music teacher the secret significance of a mutually intended love affair. Once she was in analysis her ideas about her analyst were suffused with the same erotic significance and the belief that analysis would end in marriage. Such wish-fulfilling ideas are often undisclosed in analysis, where they take the form of the patient's belief in a secret understanding between patient and analyst that transcends the formal relationship, as Freud points out in his paper 'Observations on transference-love' (1915). The illusory special relationship may take much less conspicuously sexual forms than the example I have quoted while still having an erotised basis.

The transference illusion is felt to protect the patient from what is imagined to be an unbearable transference situation; as such, it poses considerable technical problems. While it persists all the analyst's communications are interpreted by the patient in the light of the illusional context; if it is relinquished it exposes the patient to a persecutory or painful situation in the transference.

Daydreams

As the individual moves into the mode of the depressive position the sense of persecution is diminished and the theme of loss is more to the fore. As I said, it necessitates mourning, which may be evaded by the creation of an Oedipal illusion or by taking refuge in daydreams. In Chapters 12 and 13 I discuss this further in relation to the use of the imagination in a creative or escapist way, and describe a man, Mr D, whose habitual daydreaming was an established psychic refuge. Here I want to illustrate this form of evasion in a boy of 9, Peter, whom I treated, who was reacting to a loss that he experienced as a reactivation of his original loss in the Oedipal situation. His only sibling, Carol, with whom he had shared a room, was fourteen years older than Peter and had recently married, left the parental home and was now having a baby. Peter was doing badly at school as he spent most of his day in a dream. The content of these daydreams I was to discover in the course of his treatment. They were extremely elaborate stories which he illustrated in fine details or modelled in Plasticine. Their purpose was to provide him with the 'reservation' where he could reinstate old phantasies of omnipotent self-sufficiency based on his bodily functions. His favourite stories were about a primitive tribe he had invented, which he called the 'Wallies'. They had a mine with many underground levels and a central shaft. The 'Chief Wally' sat at the top of the shaft and was fed on food which was mined from the mud and brought up from below. He also received jewels from the mine. Peter confided that he thought of his body as like the mine, with little men inside. Later in his treatment he said that, although the Wallies *said* they were jewels that they found in the mud, *really* they were germs. In this elaborate fantasy Peter reinstated an old phantasy of feeding himself from his own faecal products, as he now fed his mind on his own daydreams and tried to ignore his teacher's words and mine; this was in order to turn from the painful conflicts he experienced in any dependent relationship to a fictional self-sufficiency.

The issues involved in this were illustrated in his first session following a holiday break after a year of treatment. He had begun to react to my leaving him and this was portrayed in his play. He began to draw the Wallies, who were preparing to resist the attempt of Baron von Wally to invade their territory. Baron von Wally was a character who had emerged to become the leader of the Wallies since Peter had been in treatment. Now, however, the Wallies had got rid of their leader for not feeding them; they fought him off and took possession of the mine. When I talked to Peter about his feelings of my having deserted him like the Baron and his turning away from me angrily as a result, he began to play with two rulers on the table. Then he said they were two ships, one British and one American. I felt there was some transference reference in this because my female colleague, who saw Peter's parents regularly, was American, a fact he had always remarked on. The two rulers in his game bumped their ends together and Peter said that when the two ships came together a little pug dog who was swimming in the water was crushed in between them.

This, I think, portrayed Peter's experience of two ruling parents coming together and of his finding it to be a crushing blow. He responded to the interpretation that I made along these lines by taking up the camel from among the animals. The camel had two humps and on top of each was a sort of protruding harness. Peter said this was a nipple and began to feed the little animals from it. Then he looked at the two humps intently and put his finger on them. When his finger came to the space between them he shuddered and said: 'Ugh. I don't like that bit in between; it makes me feel funny.' I linked this to his not liking gaps between sessions and the fact that it reminded him of what it would be like between feeds. Peter said: 'Daniel, my baby, drinks from a cup.' This was said defiantly, and he added: 'He used to drink from my sister's tits but he didn't like it so after about three weeks he gave it up, so now he drinks from a cup.' He looked at me very intently and then said: 'I think it was after one week.' My break had been for three weeks!

When, in the course of time, Peter's reaction was no longer to turn away but to express his anger more directly it also became clearer that he was worried about the effects of his anger on his parental objects, both at home and in the transference. His father's health and his mother's anxious nature lent some substance to his fears, but it was also clear that Peter was unwilling to give up the omnipotence that led to such depressive anxieties. When he began to do so in the transference he became assailed by a new thought, that I was going to start treating a new boy. Peter hated to think he did not know things, and so was apt to assert that if he believed something it was a fact. So it was with the putative new boy. Peter declared that the boy was going to come from his class at school. His intolerance of ignorance was linked to his feelings of exclusion from some parts of his parents' life, and now he faced it again with his sister's marriage, pregnancy and childbirth.

Peter's body-based system of self-feeding and self-production, represented by the Wallies' mine, was a rival organisation to the parents' feeding and reproductive capacity; it denied the differences of sex and generation that are the essence of the Oedipus situation. Peter's mine served the same purpose psychically as William Blake's Beulah. It was mitigated, however, by feelings of love and appreciation. Initially he tried to protect both by putting them alongside each other; his narcissistic daydream and his relationships with his family existed in parallel. His relinquishment of his belief in the efficacy of his psychic refuge led to pain and anxiety. It paid off, however, in the remission of his learning difficulties and the not inconsiderable academic success that followed.

Subjectivity, objectivity and triangular space

realism and idealism both go too far.
(Henri Bergson, *Matter and Memory*; in Ayer and O'Grady 1992: 51)

A first version of the present chapter was read as a paper at a conference on 'The Oedipus Complex Today' at University College London in 1987 and later published as a slightly modified paper called 'The missing link' (Britton 1989). I suggested that for some patients the emergence of the Oedipus situation is not simply unwanted because it is painful, but that it is dreaded as a catastrophe. This was so, I maintained, because these patients had encountered the primal scene in phantasy or fact without having previously established a securely based maternal object through the process of containment. As a consequence, belief in a good maternal object had been retained only by splitting off the experience of misunderstanding and attributing it to a third object, the father of the primitive Oedipus situation, the partner of mother in the primal scene. So the father in such cases becomes the incarnation of *malignant misunderstanding*. Then the phantasised union of the parents unites the understanding object with the malignant misunderstanding object, creating a combined figure that personifies contradiction, meaninglessness and chaos.

In normal development the perception by the child of the parents' coming together independently of him unites his psychic world. It creates one world in which different object relationships can occur, rather than monadic serial worlds each with its own object relationship.

The primal family triangle provides the child with two links connecting him or her separately with each parent and confronts the child with the link between the parents, which excludes the child. Initially this parental link is conceived in primitive part-object terms, and in the modes of the child's own oral, anal and genital desires, and in terms of his or her hatred expressed in oral, anal and genital terms. If the link between the parents

41

perceived in love and hate can be tolerated in the child's mind it provides the child with a prototype for an object relationship of a third kind in which he or she is a witness and not a participant. A *third position* then comes into existence from which object relationships can be observed. Given this, we can also envisage being observed. This provides us with a capacity for seeing ourselves in interaction with others and for entertaining another point of view while retaining our own – for observing ourselves while being ourselves. I called the mental freedom provided by this process *triangular space.* This is a capacity we hope to retain and to find in our patients in an analysis. There are analyses when for some time, or at certain times, this seems impossible for patient and analyst, and it is at these times that one realises what it means to lack the third position.

In my paper 'The missing link' (Britton 1989), which was based on experiences with a number of patients who showed the effects of lack of the third position in analysis, the patients did not risk envisaging a relationship between their analyst as their primary object with a third object because this would be catastrophic. This also applied to events in the analyst's mind as they might be imagined by the patient. Consequently it was intolerable for such patients to feel that I was communing with myself about them. The mental communion I might have with ideas from other sources, such as imagined colleagues, ancestors or psychoanalytic theory itself, would be for them the catastrophic union. Until the psychic situation changed, usually after a good number of years, I found that any attempt of mine to marry publicly my empathic understanding of the patient's subjective experience with my objective view of the situation could not be tolerated. Usually any attempt would provoke violence or withdrawal.

As a consequence of this situation it seemed impossible to disentangle myself within my own mind from the to and fro of the inter-subjective interaction and to know what was going on. Patient and analyst were to move along a single line and meet at a single point. There was to be no lateral movement. A sense of space could be achieved only by increasing the distance between us, a process the patients found hard to bear unless they initiated it. What I felt I needed desperately was a place in my mind that I could step sideways into and from which I could look at things.

I came to realise that these efforts of mine to consult my analytic self were detected by the patients and experienced as a form of internal intercourse of mine, which corresponded to parental intercourse. This was felt to threaten the patient's existence. The only way I discovered of finding a place to think that was helpful and not disruptive was to allow the evolution within myself of my own experience and to articulate this to myself while communicating to the patients my understanding of their point of view. This, I found, did enlarge the possibilities of co-existent thinking.

Since writing that paper I have added to my own experience and supervised many more such analyses. It appears to be the case in such clinical contexts that the patients fear that the analyst's psychic reality, if emergent, will destroy their own. The complementary counter-transference of the analyst is that if he or she adopts the psychic reality of the patient the analyst's own psychic reality will be annihilated. As I have said above, I believe that the only way out of this impasse is for the analyst to struggle to accommodate both the patient's and the analyst's own view of the situation. Otherwise the analyst tries to compel the patient to do this, which results in explosiveness or masochistic submission. If the analyst submits completely by sharing the patient's view and breaking his analytic links a collusive situation results and the analyst may become involved in some form of mutual analysis.

I think that in these cases it is the attempted integration of subjective and objective ways of thinking in the patient or the bringing together of empathic understanding and intellectual comprehension by the analyst that is believed to cause a catastrophe. The feared outcome, I suggest, is of Bion's *nameless dread*, which he regarded as a consequence of a failure of containment in the mother–infant relationship (Bion 1962a: 116). As it is an aim of psychoanalysis to integrate subjective experience and objective understanding, the very process of analysis is felt to be a threat to this group of patients. This makes for characteristic difficulties and raises considerable technical problems.

I am using the terms 'subjective' and 'objective' *ontologically*, that is, to mean the first-person point of view when I say subjective and the third-person point of view when I say objective. So 'I feel stupid' is subjective and 'he is stupid' is objective. In this usage subjective does not necessarily imply prejudiced and objective does not mean unprejudiced. This is the very useful distinction made by the philosopher John R. Searle (1995) between the use of the word 'objective' to mean simply third-person description, which he calls *ontological objectivity*, and the use of the word to denote dispassionate judgement, which he calls *epistemic objectivity*. Searle believes it is necessary to make this crucial distinction in the use of the word 'objective' in order to debate with mentalists such as D. C. Dennett who propose that any theory of mental life will *have* to be non-subjective in order to be scientific because science must be objective. Searle considers this to be 'a bad pun on the word objective' (*ibid.*: 61). Even in this clash of opinion, which has passion on both sides, we see subjectivity and objectivity embattled. In this paper I want to explore this latent conflict between the champions of subjectivity and objectivity as it manifests itself in analysis.

As I said earlier, in some analyses any effort on the analyst's part to introduce an objective (third-person) view into the place where the patient's subjective (first-person) experience lies exposed is felt to be catastrophic. It

43

was as a consequence of working in such analytic situations that I fully appreciated that in all analyses the basic Oedipus situation exists whenever the analyst exercises his or her mind independently of the inter-subjective relationship of patient and analyst. A link is made in the analyst's mind with an internal object, whether it be a person or an abstraction such as psycho-analytic theory. This is, in infantile phantasy, the parental relationship now being consummated within the privacy of the analyst's mind. If privacy of such a kind does not exist for the patient because containment does not exist, internal psychic intercourse of the analyst intrudes into the patient's psychic space and is felt to be destructive. If in other cases the privacy of the parental relationship is felt to be unbearably provocative the analyst's private thoughts are felt by the patient to be intolerable. In yet other cases where voyeurism has been a pronounced feature various strategies are employed in the analysis to spy on the analyst's thinking.

The crucial importance of the third person in the psychic triangle has been emphasised by analysts of other schools and in other countries, partic-ularly in France. Janine Chasseguet-Smirgel emphasised that the parental sexual relationship was the world of mature genital object relations and that denial of and rivalry with that reality could be manifest in a narcissistic, anal, perverse organisation (Chassequet-Smirgel 1974, 1981). Lacan's theory of *le symbolique*, as the world of the father with language as its medium, in contrast to *l'imaginaire*, the world shared with mother, has resemblances to the notion of the third position and triangular space that I have just described. Lacan suggests that the individual, from his shared world with mother, is inserted into a pre-existing symbolic order of the father (Lacan 1979). In a paper on fundamentalism and idolatry ('Fundamentalismus und Idolbildung', 1993) I put forward the suggestion that in some patients we find in the transference idolisation of the maternal presence and an aversion to paternal words, and in others we find worship of father's words and anathematisation of mother's flesh, and I linked this to recurrent religious divisions (Britton 1993). I arrived at these ideas and the theory of triangular space from particular clinical experiences informed by a background of theory taken mainly from Freud, Klein, Bion, Rosenfeld and Segal inde-pendently of the French school. If there is a common source, other than Freud, it could be Klein's writings, with which Lacan was familiar. My emphasis was on a failure of maternal containment leading to problems with meaning and impediments to negotiating the depressive position and the Oedipus situation, which in turn limits the capacity for symbolisation and creates difficulties with father and his world of language (Britton 1989). The concept of symbolism I have drawn on is therefore different from that of Lacan's *le symbolique*, which is based on the structuralism of Lévi-Strauss and the linguistic theories of de Saussure (Lacan 1979). Nevertheless, as clinical theories they have resemblances. That ideas derived from psychoanalytic practice in the British Kleinian school of thought should lead to theoretical formulations with a resemblance to those of the French school, with its different tradition, encourages me to think that such theories might correspond to clinical reality.

Having written about triangular space and its relationship to the primal scene in 'The missing link', I was struck on finding, or re-finding, that Jean-Paul Sartre in *Being and Nothingness* (1943) had described the observing object as the source of self-consciousness and that his imaginary setting for this was the witnessing of a primal scene:

> Let us imagine that moved by jealousy, curiosity, or vice I have just glued my ear to the door and looked through the keyhole. I am alone and on the level of a non-thetic self-consciousness. This means first of all that ... I am a pure consciousness of things. ... But all of a sudden I hear footsteps in the hall. Someone is looking at me! What does this mean?
>
> ... I now exist as myself for my unreflective consciousness. It is this irruption of the self which has most often been described: I see myself because somebody sees me.
>
> (Sartre 1943; quoted in Ayer and O'Grady 1992: 404)

Like the group of patients that I am concerned with in this discussion, Sartre took this situation to be persecutory and destructive of the essential identity of the self. He wrote: 'The other looks at me and as such he holds the secret of my being, he knows what I am. Thus the profound meaning of my being is outside of me, imprisoned in an absence.' Sartre felt that 'The other's look as the necessary condition of my objectivity is the destruction of all objectivity for me' (*ibid.*). The patients I refer to fear that an objective description of them will be destructive of their own subjectivity. As our French analytic colleagues remind us, the term 'the other' (a term signifying something dialectically opposed to the subjective self) is not synonymous with 'the object' as used by Klein and others. Nevertheless I think that *otherness* can be a characteristic of the object or not, and in the group of patients I am considering it is the *otherness* of the observing object that is the trouble. Internally, this quality of *otherness* also can apply to an internal object which, though incorporated, is not assimilated. If this is felt to be a bad object it is experienced as a foreign body embedded in the self (Heimann 1942). If it is worshipped it impoverishes the sense of self: 'with an unassimilated idealised object there goes a feeling that the ego has no life and no value of its own' (Klein 1946: 9). I would add to this that 'the ego' fears having no beliefs of its own and of being condemned to act as a host to alien ideas.

I think it is hard to designate the group of patients in whom this hyper-subjectivity is conspicuous. I find it hard to find an agreed name for them, although it is not difficult to describe them or to recognise them clinically. I refer to them as suffering from the *borderline syndrome*, but that term tends to be applied by others to many patients of varying character. Herbert Rosenfeld (1987) eventually classified what he called *narcissistic patients* as *thin-skinned* or *thick-skinned*. And the patients I am describing who find the analyst's objectivity intolerable he would have called thin-skinned, in contrast with thick-skinned narcissistic patients, who appear immune to interpretative comments. There are those, he wrote:

> whose narcissistic structure provides them with such a 'thick skin' that they have become insensitive to deeper feelings, . . . to avoid impasse these patients have to be treated in analysis very firmly. . . . When interpretations at last manage to touch them they are relieved, even if it is painful to them. . . . By contrast . . . the thin skinned patients are hypersensitive and easily hurt in everyday life and analysis. Moreover, when the sensitive narcissistic patient is treated in analysis as if he is the thick skinned patient he will be severely traumatised.
>
> (Rosenfeld 1987: 274)

What I have found in my work is that inside every thick-skinned patient is a thin-skinned patient trying not to get out, and in every thin-skinned patient is a thick-skinned patient who is usually giving himself a hard time and periodically gives the analyst a hard time. There are some analyses where thick-skinnedness and thin-skinnedness alternate from session to session, and some where the two qualities alternate in a reciprocal manner between patient and analyst.

What I suggest is that these two clinical states, thin-skinnedness and thick-skinnedness, are the result of two different relationships of the *subjective self* with the *third object* within the internal Oedipus situation. In both states the third object is alien to the subjective, sensitive self. In the thin-skinned mode the self seeks to avoid the objectivity of the third object and cling to subjectivity; in the thick-skinned situation the self identifies with the third object, adopts its mode of objectivity and renounces its own subjectivity. Some people live in one mode or the other and some oscillate between them. Where the first, thin-skinned, mode is dominant I describe the patient as borderline, and where the latter, thick-skinned, mode is predominant I use the term schizoid. In the hyper-subjective mode the patient seeks to incorporate the analyst within his or her subjective world. To do that, any difference between the patient's version of the analyst and the analyst's person has to be eliminated. In the hyper-objective mode the alliance with the analyst is sought in a world of reasoned understanding based on a denial of their subjectively experienced relationship.

The thin-skinned syndrome

What characterises this group of cases clinically is their *difficulty*. They find life with others difficult; they find tolerating themselves difficult; they find being in analysis difficult; and, in a characteristic way, their analysts find working with them difficult. When analysts bring such cases for consultation they almost always begin by saying 'I want to talk to you about my difficult patient' or 'I seem to have particular difficulty with this case'. This is often accompanied by a sense of shame in the analysts, who feel either that they have let the patient down or that they have become involved with their patient in a way they are reluctant to acknowledge to colleagues. Recently an analyst began a consultation by saying 'I want to discuss my most difficult patient. It has been difficult from the beginning – the patient did not want me to speak at all for the first year. She said my words removed her skin. Now at times she is terrified of what I might say.'

Of course, many analytic patients pose considerable technical and counter-transference problems, but the characteristic problem that leads analysts to use the word *difficult* is of a particular kind. It is the way that the analytic method itself is felt by the patient to be a threat: its structure, its method, its boundaries. The corollary of that in the analyst is a feeling that he or she has never properly established an analytic setting. This has been used by some analysts to promote an alternative strategy as a superior method, whereas it has really been dictated by the patient as a necessary condition for the patient. This, I think, corresponds with a belief of the patient, secret or not, that his or her atypical method of growing up was a more authentic way, and that ordinary children and more tractable analytic patients are either victims of oppression or collaborators.

A simple but typical example of this syndrome at the beginning of an analysis that I supervised was of a young woman somewhat at a loss in her life. She was not sure whether she ought to stay in the relationship she was in, but she did not know how such things could ever be decided. At her work she felt oppressed because she thought things were expected of her which she felt were unreasonable, but she was not sure whether she was right to feel like that. In the home which she had shared with her brother and her parents she thought her father was always wrong, but she also thought it might be because she was argumentative, since she disagreed with everything he said. She also thought he was too fond of her and familiar with her physically when she was adolescent, but he said she was too cold and perhaps, she thought, he might be right.

The analyst felt he had two problems when he consulted me. The patient could not use the couch and he found that he could not think freely at all in the sessions but simply followed what she was saying, commenting on it without adding anything very many of his own ideas.

47

When she had initially contemplated getting on to the couch she had rapidly pulled away from the idea, saying that if she was on the couch and the analyst spoke it would be like God speaking; if she sat up it was not so frightening. The analyst worked patiently and sensitively with this situation, expressing as best he could what he thought was her view of the situation. He was rewarded by being given, from time to time, associations about her family which gave some insight into the past, her inner world and the unconscious aspects of the transference. For example, he had interpreted that she felt that she had to explain and justify to him in detail everything that she did or said. Having concurred with this, she said spontaneously:

> My mother doesn't really exist; she is only there to look after my father. My father advances suggestions to me and if I differ from him he says I am cold. There was this strange business of my signature. He wanted me to have a signature the way he thought a signature ought to be, so I used to practice doing my signature as he would want it.

I give this brief picture of the beginning of an analysis because it is very like a number of others on which I have been consulted because the analyst finds them so difficult. The patient also resembles patients of my own whom I found difficult; they found ordinary analysis very difficult and at times were unable to tolerate the analyst in the third position. I think we can see the usual configuration in the small fragment of a family picture produced by the patient. While he is working empathically with the patient and validating her subjective experience in a way she finds helpful, the analyst finds himself to be like the mother, who does not really exist in her own right. The patient feels very reliant on this function and on the analyst as this receptive figure, but the analyst fears he has lost his analytic identity. If, however, the analyst asserts himself and produces objectively based interpretations she will feel persecuted and then either submit in a masochistic way or explode. She will, one way or another, eliminate what he says or eradicate the elements in it of difference. She may feel the need to remove her mind from his presence by psychic withdrawal, and some patients find it necessary to remove their bodies in order to remove their minds and so break off analysis. These patients are inclined to leave some analysts or stay in an impasse with others. The risks are of analytic abortion or interminable analysis. This arises, I believe, where subjective and objective realities are believed to be more than simply incompatible, to be, in fact, mutually destructive. Objectivity appears to be associated with gaze. There is a fear of being seen, just as there is a fear of being described. Merleau-Ponty took issue with Sartre's assertion that 'The other's gaze transforms me into an object and denies me, I transform him into an object and deny him'

(Merleau-Ponty paraphrasing Sartre; quoted in Ayer and O'Grady 1992: 300). He wrote in *Phenomenology of Perception*:

> In fact the other's gaze transforms me into an object, and mine him, only if both of us withdraw into the core of our thinking nature, if we both make ourselves into an inhuman gaze, if each of us feels his actions to be not taken up and understood, but observed as if they were an insect's.
>
> (Merleau-Ponty; quoted in Ayer and O'Grady 1992: 300)

I agree with Merleau-Ponty's robust defence of the phenomenology of normal life and his rebuttal of Sartre's assertion about objectivity. However, Sartre's description fits precisely the experience of the hyper-subjective individual, particularly in analysis. A child with similar problems in treatment serves well as an example because of the directness of the exchange with the psychotherapist.

In a case I supervised a 7-year-old girl was clearly very persecuted simply by being in the therapist's room and screamed whenever he tried to speak. Eventually, with his help, she managed to make it clear to him that if she blindfolded and gagged him so that he could not see or speak, but only listen, then she would talk to him. When he was able to say to her that she believed his words would spoil and mess up her thoughts she burst out: 'They will, they will! So shut up!'

Such situations in their adult versions can evoke existential anxieties in analysts because their empathic identification with the patient seems incompatible with their objective clinical view of the situation and their ideas of what is necessary. Therefore analysts feel cut off from the theories that link them to their colleagues and that give them their professional identity. This also manifests itself as a difficulty for analysts in using their general experience or their general ideas, as this appears to intrude on the singularity of the encounter with the patient and the particularity of the patient's psychology. Particularity seems to be at war with generality in much the same way as subjectivity is with objectivity. In terms of the figures of the Oedipal triangle, while the analyst is able to follow and enhance the patient's emergent thoughts he or she is identified as an understanding maternal object. When introducing thoughts of his or her own derived from general experience and analytic theories the analyst is identified as a father who is either intruding into the patient's innermost self or pulling the patient out of his or her subjective psychic context into one of the analyst's own.

So we have a defensively organised Oedipal situation with the phantasy of a totally empathic, passively understanding maternal object and an aggressive paternal figure who is objectivity personified as seeking to impose meaning. This configuration serves as a guarantee that reintegration will never take place between the understanding object and the misunderstanding object, as this would result, it is believed, in the annihilation of understanding. While this split is preserved, subjectivity and objectivity are felt to be mutually incompatible.

In order to consider this further I will first recapitulate the two clinical syndromes that I referred to earlier, the thin-skinned and the thick-skinned. In them the Oedipus situation is defensively divided in such a way as to produce two different and characteristic transferences. In the thin-skinned case the inter-subjective (maternal) transference is paramount and the transference is sought solely in the empathic receptive mode. The alternative organisation of this split situation underlies the thick-skinned syndrome; an inter-subjective relationship with the primary object of an empathic kind is avoided and the third object, personifying objective knowledge, is sought as the source of understanding. In the transference subjectivity is evaded and objectivity is pursued.

In the thin-skinned, hyper-subjective mode the positive transference expresses its energy, not by penetration, but by extrapolation. Its intensity is expressed by extension. It encompasses the object and invests everything it covers with heightened significance. The physical person of the analyst and, by extension, the contextual details of the analysis are given great importance – for example the minutiae of sessions, the room and its contents and so on. Patients may collect and retain remnants of the analysis such as bills, paper tissues, etc., which serve a similar function to religious relics. The negative transference is with a penetrating object. Objective knowledge is equated with vision and cognition, and is attributed to the third observing/penetrating object, while feeling understood is attributed to the primary object.

The encompassing, embracing transference figure is regarded as positive, and the figure with penetrating understanding is the object of the negative transference. Both positive and negative transferences are in play: one craved for and sought after; the other dreaded and evaded. The desired transference is skin-deep and enveloping. Its epistemological mode is empathy, its physical expression is touch and its emotional qualities are erotic or aesthetic. What I am describing has much in common with Esther Bick's description of *adhesive identification* (Bick 1968: 187–91). There is a hypertrophy of touch and its psychic counterparts, resembling Freud's description of skin erotism. It leads to an erotic or aesthetic idealised transference. The analyst's words are valued for their tone, not their content. The parallel penetrating negative transference is to the third object, which is felt to be an intruder in the analysis. The affective quality of the phantasised third object, in Bion's terms, is pure K divested of L and of H. A scrutinising object is envisaged, personifying curiosity, which seeks knowledge without sympathy, penetration without desire and possession without love. What is dreaded most is the conjunction of the encompassing transference with the penetrating transference, that is, of subjectivity with objectivity.

Thick-skinned narcissism: hyper-objectivity

I turn now to the thick-skinned hyper-objective syndrome. In an analysis of this kind enlightenment seems possible but directly experienced desire or antipathy is not. To illustrate what I mean I will offer an example of a case that I supervised that was similar to some of my own cases. The analyst consulted me because he felt stuck in his work with the patient. Despite the patient's cooperativeness and readiness to listen the analyst was left feeling that his work was sterile, unconvincing and futile. The patient, an unmarried woman in her late thirties, was a professor of mathematics in another European country. The breakdown of her previous steady state, which led to her seeking analysis, was precipitated by the recent marriage and departure of her brother, with whom she had shared a house. Her previous calm reasonableness was now interrupted by anxiety, and her usual optimism periodically shattered by episodes of 'blackness of vision and boundless terrifying emptiness' in which she could no longer reason but only dread. She referred to these episodes as 'the dark night of the soul' and the place she felt she was in as 'the void'. She longed to escape from them into sleep or, even better, into death.

Though at the commencement of analysis both her parents were dead, this woman quickly made clear that she had, throughout her life, oriented herself by knowing that she hated her mother and loved her father. In particular, she was averse to her mother physically and any thought of contact with her made her feel nauseous. She feared chaos if anything to do with her maternal relationship should ever enter into the world of order provided by her own systematic thinking, which she identified with her father, who had been a mathematician. Initially, she organised her relationship with analysis along systematic lines. Her relationship with her analyst was to do with logic and empirical observation; ideas were abstract and perceptions objective; common sense prevailed. In contrast to the other patient in the 'difficult' category, this patient found the externals and conventions of analysis very easy to accept and the restriction of analysis to verbal contact congenial. Her references to herself were all objective, and she expected objective explanatory interpretations. The emotional difficulties were in the counter-transference. The analyst felt himself to be isolated, personally insignificant, and since he was deprived of empathic contact he lacked emotional conviction in his work. I pointed out to the analyst that whatever he said was transformed by the patient into an objective statement about herself and that how or what she felt in the transference was immaterial, other than a wish for guidance. If the analyst made efforts to suggest that he had emotional importance for her as a physical being his suggestion was politely rebuffed; if he persisted he became a threat. He then became, she said, like her mother; the patient believed that he was going to insist on telling her how she felt, and claiming that he knew that she loved him really and that it was only her wickedness that made her deny it. This, I should say, was always a transference possibility since he might well have embarked on the interpretative equivalent of this in a fit of analytic zeal and fundamental belief that he should assert his transference importance. The patient made it clear that if he were to acquire these characteristics of her mother and insist on some emotional intimacy she would have no choice but to leave. In the early periods of analysis anything which drew attention to his physical presence and her physical presence disturbed her. She was usually able to accommodate his existence by endowing him with analytic anonymity. 'But, of course,' she would say, 'I know that as an analyst you feel nothing.' The relationship between patient and analyst was between two collaborating, objective observers of the subject patient. The material of the sessions might include objective accounts by the patient of her own recent emotional experiences; what was missing was the patient's subjective voice articulating current feeling or impulse. The private, subjective experience of the analyst was of depersonalisation, and it is of some interest that the patient suffered from depersonalisation as a symptom intermittently outside the sessions.

Interpersonal relating did exist for this woman in a sensuous mode in the form of wordless, predominantly tactile exchanges with either sex and she enjoyed heterosexual relations. From the time she began she had accompanied the analysis with a variety of physical therapies in parallel: yoga, massage, osteopathy, special movement classes, all of which were of some importance to her but interchangeable. The person administrating these had to be anonymous and relatively silent. When one enthusiastic physical therapist offered a psychological interpretation during treatment she promptly left.

This syndrome is not gender-related. I have also found some male patients with a non-verbal, sensuous, sexual life outside analysis in parallel with a spiritual, oracular, non-physical transference inside analysis. Nor is the gender of the analyst a significant factor with either the thick-skinned or thin-skinned patients. I wish to use the case of the woman mathematician to make one point. She sought an explanatory experience in analysis and wanted to avoid emotional experience in conjunction with it; she was seeking in the transference an epistemically dependent relationship with verbal guidance or instruction while avoiding a feeling of emotional dependence. In historical terms, as a child she had an aversion to her mother and hero-worshipped her rather distant father. This gave the misleading appearance of being a classical, positive Oedipus complex simply based on rivalry with mother for the love of father. The transference told another tale; the love of her father, which was echoed later in her relationship with her brother, was expressed in shared intellectual interests and provided a refuge from maternal love. Physical pleasure and sexual desire were unpersonified. The familiar split configuration of the positive Oedipal configuration, which is usually used to separate love and hate, in this instance was used to provide a structure to segregate any desire for subjective understanding and love from the wish for objective knowledge and a shared intellectual identity.

The fears of these thick-skinned or schizoid patients, when they emerge, have something in common with those of the thin-skinned patients, who otherwise appear to be so different. What they share is the fear of a psychic state that resembles mythic and literary descriptions of primordial chaos, with its two characteristics of confusion and boundlessness. If there is a difference in the state dreaded by the two groups it is a difference in emphasis. In the *objectivity-seeking* group, the thick-skinned patients, it seems that the fear is mainly of the total emptiness, bottomlessness and darkness of chaos. Several patients have referred to it as *the void*, a place of blackness and endlessness. The *objectivity-avoiding* group, the thin-skinned patients, appear menaced more by the destruction of meaning and the incomprehensibility of chaos. However, there are patients who are, at different times, fearful of either of these states of mind.

In order to take further an examination of these fears and their origins I would like to return to the clinical syndrome described by Rosenfeld as thin-skinned narcissism. These are people, I have suggested, who are afraid of abuse by objective interpretation. In 'The missing link' (Britton 1989), in an attempt to understand this clinical situation, I used Bion's concept of the container and the contained. Bion (1959) made clear that the inability of the mother to take in her infant's projections is experienced by the child, not simply as a failure, but as a destructive attack by her on the infant's link and communication with her as his or her good object. I suggested that in these circumstances the mother can be retained as a good object in the child's mind only by the child denying the experience of her impermeability and attributing the interference with understanding to another object. This creates a phantasy of a hostile object, or third force, which always threatens to attack the child's communicative link with the mother. In the Oedipal situation the hostile force becomes equated with the father. In this circumstance, if a link joining the parents is perceived or imagined it is felt to reconstitute mother as a non-receptive, malignantly misunderstanding maternal object. As imagining the primal scene is tantamount to the event taking place in phantasy, bringing the parents together in the mind is felt to initiate a mental catastrophe. A dream of a patient whose psychic organisation was deeply committed to segregating the parental couple and the different mental functions they personified might illustrate this point. In the dream he was holding in one hand a vase and in the other a candleholder. If the two hands should come together something terrible would happen. The two objects touched and each of them was shattered into thousands of fragments. His association with the vase was that it was a family heirloom of his mother's, and with the candleholder that it was usually on his father's organ; his father was a professional musician. The dream seemed to relate to a comment in the previous day's session by me about his left hand having to remain uninformed as to what his right hand was doing.

Malignant misunderstanding and fear of chaos

I would like to try to explore further the mental catastrophe that is antici-pated should the primary object of love *and* understanding be reconstituted. From the transference it seems that the basic fear is of malig-nant misunderstanding. By this I mean an experience of being so *misunderstood* in such a fundamental and powerful way that one's experience of oneself would be eliminated and thus the possibility of the self estab-lishing meaning would be annihilated. It is, I think, fear of a return to primordial chaos, which I think corresponds to Bion's notion of nameless dread.

In the ancient religions, from which Judaism and Christianity built their creation story, the belief was that before there was World there was Chaos, a permanent state of contradiction, formlessness, darkness, endlessness before there were two of anything (Cohn 1993). Freud located primordial Chaos in the id. He wrote: 'We approach the id with analogies: we call it chaos, a cauldron full of seething excitations. . . . The logical laws of thought do not apply in the id, and this is true above all of the law of contradiction' (Freud 1933a: 75). Freud wrote of *fear of the id* as fundamental, but he was tentative in describing it. He wrote that 'we know that the fear is of being over-whelmed or annihilated, but it cannot be grasped analytically' (*ibid.*: 57). I think there is now more possibility of understanding this analytically and aetiologically, with the aid of Bion's concept of nameless dread (Bion 1962a: 117), as a fear of being overwhelmed by uncontained, untrans-formed, psychic elements or of living in the aftermath of their annihilation.

The principles of order, truth and meaning are delineated in all the ancient cosmologies, where they are represented under different names. In the case of Egypt they were called *Ma'at*. *Ma'at*, it seems to me corre-sponds, with that function of the primary object, as perceived by the infant, that gives understanding, order and meaning to the world. Its demise there-fore returns the world to chaos. Other Ancient cultures had similar principles; for example, the Vedic Indians called it *Rita*, the force that regu-lated the stars, the cycle of the day, the way the rivers ran and how the cows gave milk. Like *Ma'at* it was always threatened by a counter-force. in the case of *Ma'at* this counter-force was called *Isfet*; in the case of *Rita* it was called *Anrita*. *Ma'at* came to be personified as a goddess and *Isfet* was personified by the Chaos monsters, such as *Apophis*; he, they said, ran counter to the rightness of the world. 'Apophis was an embodiment of primordial chaos. He had no sense-organs, he could neither hear nor see, he could only scream. And he operated always in darkness' (Cohn 1993: 21).

Here, I think, are mythic descriptions that correspond to Bion's K and −K. In this Egyptian account naming produces order and provides some-thing on which the world can stand. The return of namelessness would seem to be an incursion of chaos into the ordered, differentiated world, and so in the old cosmology we seem to find Bion's concept of nameless dread represented as a Chaos monster, the personification of −K. If *Ma'at* could be displaced by *Isfet*, if the throne of God could be occupied by the Chaos monster, bounded space would be replaced by the void and meaning by meaninglessness. In intrapsychic terms the occupant of the third position, the super-ego, would be a Chaos monster. This monster, I think, resembles what Bion called the 'Ego destructive Super-Ego' (Bion 1959: 107). In Oedipal terms we then have father as psychic anarchist and the death of the mother of meaning.

In one of her last papers, 'On the development of mental functioning' (1958), Melanie Klein reintroduced into her post-depressive-position scheme of things her original monsters of the deep unconscious. In this paper she reinstated her earlier view that 'terrifying figures' remained in 'the deep layers of the unconscious' despite any amount of working through of the depressive position:

> I assume, however, that even under such favourable conditions, terri-fying figures in the deep layers of the unconscious make themselves felt when internal or external pressure is extreme. People who are on the whole stable . . . can overcome this intrusion of the deeper uncon-scious into their ego and regain their stability. In neurotic, and still more in psychotic individuals, the struggle against such dangers threat-ening from the deeper layers of the unconscious is to some extent constant and part of their instability or their illness.
>
> (Klein 1958: 243)

Bion gives two accounts of the production of nameless dread from a failure of maternal containment in infancy (Bion 1962a, 1962b). In both the infant's as yet unformulated fear of death is transformed by the failure of containment into nameless dread. In other words, it is not transformed into a less intense, because now identifiable, fear, but into something worse. The uncomprehended has become the incomprehensible. In his first account, in 'A theory of thinking' (Bion 1962a), he described the transformation of the fear of death into nameless dread. He wrote: 'the projection is not accepted by the mother the infant feels that its fear of dying is stripped of such meaning as it has. It therefore reintrojects, not a fear of dying made tolerable, but a nameless dread' (*ibid.*: 116). I want to enlarge this notion to include *any* projection by the infant of an undefined state into a mother who either does not allow its ingress or distorts the projection by her own preoccupying phantasies, thus invalidating the infant's experience. In all these situations the uncomprehended is transformed for the infant into the incomprehensible. One could say there is then a dread of the namelessness of everything. If in a paranoid-schizoid mode this misunderstanding is experienced by the infant as an attack rather than as a deficiency, a force is felt to exist destroying the possibility of self-knowledge and the possibility of finding meaning. One sees this repeated in the transference when the failure of the analyst to understand the patient precisely is experienced by the patient, not simply as a deficiency of the analyst, but as an attack on the patient's psychic integrity.

If this propensity for malignant misunderstanding remains or returns to the primary (maternal) object she becomes the prototype of an object of desire that is at the same time a menace to individual integrity. Then love itself is felt to be the harbinger of existential anxiety. Such was the case for the poet Rilke, who described having to divest himself of any affectional contact, even including a dog, for the winter of 1921/2, in order to complete, after ten years, his major work *The Duino Elegies*. I describe this situation in Chapter 12.

However, in the cases for whom I have used the term 'thin-skinned narcissism' or 'borderline disorder' the primary object of desire is preserved as an object devoted to empathic understanding, by splitting, so that love is then possible if it remains free of objective appraisal. This, however, creates in phantasy the third object as the source of malignant misunderstanding forever threatening the mutual, empathic understanding between the self and the primary object. As it is based on splitting, the third object is always a potential intruder, and remains a threat, even though it can be kept out of the dyadic inter-subjective interaction by denial supported by transference–counter-transference enactment. When at certain points the denial breaks down the patient feels objectively perceived while simultane-ously subjectively experiencing him- or herself; it is then the analyst's gaze that is feared. It gives rise to feelings of exposure, shame, humiliation and isolation; or there is an escape from this into subjugation by becoming a

creature of the analyst. As Sartre described it: 'The *other's* look as the necessary condition of my objectivity is the destruction of all objectivity for me'
(Sartre; quoted in Ayer and O'Grady 1992: 404). Some patients are unable
to bear being seen by the analyst at these times. Both parents are taken to
be present in the person of the analyst, and the analyst's objective view of
the patient is now coupled with subjective or empathic understanding in a
monstrous combined object.

The need for agreement

When there is a desire for understanding from the primary object, with a
dread of misunderstanding, there is an insistent, desperate need for agreement in the analysis and annihilation of disagreement – or, to put it more
strongly, the annihilation of disagreement. I have come to believe that there
is a general rule arising from anxiety about misunderstanding which applies
in all analyses; it is that *the need for agreement is inversely proportional to the
expectation of understanding*. When expectation of understanding is high,
difference of opinion is tolerable; where expectation of understanding is
fairly high, difference is fairly tolerable; when there is no expectation of
understanding, the need for agreement is absolute. In analyses, where the
need for agreement is felt to be absolute and paramount it can be achieved
only by obedience or tyranny; then submission, not understanding is
required. This is achieved by the patient either slavishly submitting or
tyrannically controlling. Some patients practice both methods: at some
moments tyranny; at others submission. In the case of the young woman
described earlier in this chapter (p. 48) one can see that she perceives the
situation as having only these two alternatives. The analyst will follow her,
dutifully putting into words her subjective experience while feeling
constrained from making any other comments, or she will feel impelled to
sacrifice her own subjective experience and incorporate instead his description of herself. This she will then take in like a foreign body implanted in
the place of her own soul. Then her signature will become a replica of
father's idea of what her signature should be.

Herbert Rosenfeld emphasised a history of trauma in these thin-skinned
narcissistic patients (Rosenfeld 1989: 294), and in severe cases I have always
found there to be a traumatic background. But I have found this syndrome
in milder form and in these cases severe trauma was not evident, and I
believe that adverse infantile and childhood circumstances do not always
produce this result. So is there something in *the temperament* of some individuals that *predisposes* them to this particular development or response to
trauma? Is there anything in the endowment of the individual that might
encourage the individual to believe that an independently existing object

will destructively misunderstand him or her? Is there *an innate factor* in the infant that increases the risk of a *failure of maternal containment*, and, if so, what might it be? I believe there is and I have come to think of it as a kind of *psychic atopia*, a hypersensitivity to psychic difference, an allergy to the products of other minds.

My analogy would be with the body's immune system; just as recognition and response are central to our physiological functioning, so they might be to our psychic functioning. The *not me* or *not like me* recognition and response might be regarded as fulfilling a similar psychic function to that which it does in the somatic. And just as the immune system makes possible allergic reactions and even auto-immunity in the somatic sphere, so might there be psychic equivalents. Some individuals might be hypersensitive, some, as it were, suffering from psychic atopia. In analysis this sensitivity applies not only to minute variations in the analyst but also to approximations in understanding. Where this sensitivity is considerable what is required in the way of understanding is perfect understanding. Less than *perfect understanding* might therefore be perceived as *misunderstanding*.

I have described the first account Bion gave of nameless dread, in which he emphasised its origins in the mother's failure to introject the infant's experience. In his second description of this failure of containment, in *Learning from Experience* (Bion 1962b), he emphasised a factor in the infant that he called $-K$, an innate opposition to containment by maternal understanding. This he equated with Klein's concept of *envy*. I find the developmental and clinical significance of envy as an individually variant personality factor in children and adults completely convincing. However, I find its description in infancy as an irreducible element less satisfactory. I think of it more as a result of a number of factors, not so much an atom as a molecule, so to speak. Therefore I find Bion's equation of $-K$ with envy less helpful than regarding $-K$ as a variable factor that joins together with other factors to produce envy. This may seem to some like splitting hairs, but I have a suggestion as to what $-K$ might be, namely that which underlies what I have called psychic atopia – an antipathy to knowing anything that is different. I believe this variable in the individual constitution, the psychic counterpart to the tolerance and intolerance of the somatic immune system, may contribute to difficulties in infantile containment

Perhaps, then, we can posit factors on both sides of the infant–mother interaction in their mutual problems of containment and the establishment of an expectation of understanding: on the maternal side an inadequate capacity to internalise and process accurately the infant's projections; on the infant's side an inadequate tolerance of the mother's approximations to understanding. As, on the whole, we proceed by a series of approximations in analysis, if we have a patient who experiences approximation as traumatic or aggressive we are engaged in a difficult analysis.

5

The suspension of belief and the 'as-if' syndrome

> She knew that this silent, motionless portal opened into the street. . . .
> But she had no wish to look out, for this would have interfered with
> her theory that there was a strange unseen place on the other side.
>
> (James 1981: 23)

In a footnote in the *Studies on Hysteria* Freud drew attention to a state of
mind which he described as the 'blindness of the seeing eye', in which 'one
knows and does not know a thing at the same time' (Freud 1893–5: 117).
Later he was to use the noun *Verleugnung*, which Strachey translated as
'disavowal', to describe this non-psychotic form of denial (Freud 1924b,
1927b, 1938). In 1938 he wrote of it as a 'half measure' in which 'the
disavowal is always supplemented by an acknowledgement; two contrary
and independent attitudes arise and result in . . . a splitting of the ego'
(Freud 1938: 204). Basch (1983) has suggested that, unlike psychotic denial,
disavowal obliterates only the significance of things, and not their perception. Steiner (1985) used the phrase 'turning a blind eye' for this defence,
relating it to the Oedipus complex in particular. In Chapter 1 I described it
as 'the willing suspension of belief', which results in facts being known but
not believed.

Freud describes disavowal in two clinical conditions, perversion and
obsessional neurosis (Freud 1927b). However, there is another syndrome in
which disavowal is not partial but all-pervasive, what Helene Deutsch
(1942) called the 'as-if' personality. In this pathological organisation
disavowal is placed at the centre of the individual's mental life and characterises his or her whole relationship to the world. Deutsch emphasised the
pervasive sense of unreality of such a person's relationship with the world
and with themselves, the complete lack of conflict, and the contrast
between apparent sensitive emotional capacity and the apparent absence of
inner experience. Deutsch says the 'as-if' personalities neither fly to

external reality to escape their minds nor withdraw into an inner world to avoid fears of the outside, which, as Ferenczi (1926) suggested, are alternative defensive strategies. I think that these people cannot take either of these defensive steps because they are terrified of both internal and external reality. Therefore they seek refuge in a state of unreality, which characterises all their relationships. The 'blind but seeing eye' is directed not only outwards but also inwards, so that it is not only the things of this world that are known and not known, but also all thoughts and feelings: their external perceptions lack significance and their inner experience lacks substance.

The term 'as-if' is especially apt as a name for this defensive organisation, not only because it results in a clinical presentation like that described by Deutsch, but also because it epitomises Vaihinger's (1912) 'as-if' philosophy, from which she borrowed the name. This philosophy, as I described above in chapter 1, proposed that faced with scientific facts which make certain religious beliefs untenable we should nevertheless retain these: 'they perish only as theoretical truths; as practical fictions we leave them all intact' (Vaihinger 1912; quoted in Freud 1927a: 29, fn). These patients regard the unacceptable facts of their daily life as 'only theoretically true', and the manifestly untenable beliefs they wish to retain they treat as 'practical fictions'.

Normally, I think, a sense that the external world has *significance* comes from its investment with *psychic reality* by projection. In a complementary way, a sense of internal *substance* derives from the introjection of some of the 'real' qualities of the external object. Projection and re-introjection constitute a continuous cyclical process in life and are manifest in the interplay between patient and analyst. In the patients I am about to discuss in this chapter the flow of traffic between internal and external is stopped and something else is substituted for it. In analysis normal projective identification and re-introjection are replaced by something more solipsistic, in which the interplay with the analyst results in what Sohn (1985) called an 'Identificate', an ersatz personality composed of some aspects of the analyst and some of the patient knitted together. This process, which mimics projection and re-introjection, has the characteristic of alternation but is static, not dynamic; it is like running on the spot. I will call it 'oscillation'. It corresponds to what Bion termed 'reversible perspective' (Bion 1963: 58). Bion took his term from those pictures in which foreground and background are reversible so that two different images, a vase or two facial profiles, can be perceived as alternative possibilities. This, he thought, was what was obtained in some analyses. Whichever foreground the analyst selected, the patient saw it the other way round while ostensibly seeing the same picture; thus the patient could alternate positions while remaining in basically the same situation. The one perspective was simply the inverse reciprocal of the other (*ibid.*). Bion considered that it was the Oedipus situation appearing in the patient's thoughts which made him reverse perspective. In the case I use to illustrate this phenomenon, for reasons which I hope will become obvious, I want to describe it as 'negative, or inverse, symmetry'. There is no ultimate outcome and therefore there are no consequences. No firm belief is established that cannot immediately be reversed. *Either/and* rather than *either/or* is the mode and inconsequentiality is the result. As I said, one could characterise the whole organisation as sustaining inconsequence by suspending belief.

The patient I will principally refer to was typical of 'as-if' patients in that his unconscious conviction was that any *real* consequences would be dire consequences, that *any* outcome would be catastrophic. Ruth Riesenberg Malcolm has suggested that 'as-if' patients avoid psychic change in analysis to avoid learning about what they believe to be their irreparably damaged internal objects (Riesenberg Malcolm 1992). I think that they also believe that they cannot afford to know the reality of their external objects, which they expect to find devastated or horrifying. They therefore remain poised between what they fear in their own minds and what they fear in the world outside them. As a consequence they remain afraid of both true projection and true introjection. They are refugees from the external and internal world. Their refuge is that 'domain' which Freud described as provided by secret beliefs, hidden in neuroses or perversions 'a domain kept free from the exigencies of life, like a kind of reservation' (Freud 1924b: 187). It is, I think, what Winnicott called *transitional space*, which, in a letter to his translator, he described as 'the resting place of illusion', a rest from 'the constant struggle, distinguishing fact from fantasy, external from psychic reality' (Rodman 1987: 123). The personalities I am describing attempt to make this resting place or reservation a permanent home.

Klein pointed out in her paper on 'The theory of anxiety and guilt' that normally 'external experiences which rouse anxiety activate anxieties derived from intrapsychic sources' (Klein 1948: 40). She comments that 'the interaction between anxiety arising from internal and external sources corresponds to the interaction between external reality and psychic reality' (*ibid.*). As in other contexts, she implies that anxiety in moderation acts as a spur and facilitator but if it is excessive it disrupts learning. An illustration of how this disruption might lead, at least temporarily, to a cessation of the exchange between daily life and phantasy life is given by some material from analysis with a young child whom I will call Tracy.

Tracy was a 4-year-old girl in treatment, who came to her regular session, in a clinic, after a traumatic episode in her family had taken place the previous night. The episode was described by the 'escort' who regularly brought her to the clinic. Tracy had been present with her infant sibling during a violent quarrel between her parents in which her father had physically attacked her mother, who subsequently attempted suicide and was taken to hospital in an ambulance.

The girl began her session in silence by taking out the toy animals and carefully placing them in two groups: the domestic animals in one group and the wild animals in the other. She then made a barrier between them. On one side she arranged the pig family so that it consisted, like her own, of a father, a mother and two little pigs. The pig family then played out the scene reported from the night before. The father pig attacked the mother pig while she was feeding the baby pig and the other little pig was looking on. An ambulance was brought to the scene and the mother pig was taken away. During this time, Tracy built the barrier higher and higher between the wild animals and the pigs, and briefly fingered the crocodile. The complete segregation changed after an interpretation that Tracy was afraid that her bad dreams and wild thoughts might get mixed up with what happened at home and that what she liked to play in her sessions might get mixed up with what happened to her family in her mind. She took the crocodile and made it crawl over the barrier. It attacked the mother pig and the little feeding pig. In the next session Tracy reconstructed her divided world but a little human climbed the barrier and joined the wild animals.

If we take the wild animals to represent Tracy's inner phantasy world and the pig family to represent the figures of everyday life, as wild and domestic animals tend to, her play suggests that the traumatic episode temporarily put a stop to the continuity of interchange between her inner and outer life.

This glimpse of the effect of recent trauma gives rise to interesting speculations on the sequestrated nature of unassimilated experience in mental life. However, I mention it now to illustrate the interruption in the flow of projection and introjection that may follow external trauma. If such dislocations become chronic I suggest that substitutes are formed for the normal cycles and that oscillation arises to simulate the natural interflow between the inside and outside world, as a form of pseudo-projection and pseudo-introjection.

I would like to begin my discussion of just such a defensive organisation with a dream from the analysis of a patient, Mr B, whom I shall discuss at greater length because his material provides an image for the mental posture of someone seeking refuge from the external world created by projection and the internal world resulting from introjection. He suffered some hunger as an infant, which, in conjunction with his own aggression, appeared to provide him with fierce biting internal objects, often represented as tigers in his dreams. He experienced harshness at the hands of his parents and at times was afraid of them; in addition he suffered some night terrors as a child and could be fearful of projected terrors such as monsters. The dream shows his fear of projection because of the terrifying, inescapable external world he would create if he amalgamated his inner objects with external objects. His fear of introjection was as great because of the substantive reality it would give to his phantasised internal savagely consuming objects.

His dream was set in Hyde Park in London. Someone had released the tigers from their cage. In Hyde Park he was very afraid: the tigers were attacking and eating people in the park; he felt very distressed and in some way responsible for it. He took flight into the adjoining park, Kensington Gardens, but he found the tigers had also moved there. Now he was afraid for himself, that they would attack and eat him. So he got under the fence which divided the two parks, where no one could see him or harm him.

After telling me the dream, Mr B was thoughtful; he told me he was struggling to think of some famous statue which he thought was near the boundary between the two parks – 'A fairy or something,' he said. Then, with surprise, he exclaimed: 'Peter Pan.' After another pause, he murmured: 'Never-Never Land.' My patient also took refuge in the unconscious notion that he lived permanently in the 'anteroom' of life, where the things that occupied his mind were given a double guarantee of unreality: they had never really happened and never would happen.

'Under the fence' Mr B appeared to be sheltering from paranoia on one side and melancholia on the other. What might have been a straddling posture of equivocation – 'sitting on the fence' – had become a permanent position of refuge – 'under the fence' – a sort of sustained internal prevarication provided as an illusion of infinite postponement.

Mr B fitted Deutsch's description; my initial experience of him was of unreality and I also had a sense of unreality about everything I did in the analysis. His manner was pleasant and he gave the impression that his experience of the world was vaguely benevolent, but with a distant sense that all was not well. His clothes were informal, of soft material and of such design that they adhered to his shape. He never used an active form of speech in the present tense, so that 'I think', 'I feel', 'I will' or 'I want' never occurred in his communication. Anger and conflict were absent, but he did not lack affect. What was missing was any link between his emotional state and the ideas which provoked it. His sole aim in analysis was to find agreement with me. His technique was either to find a way to stimulate an interpretation corresponding to his existing idea or to tread water with vague, verbose material until I made an interpretation which he could then illustrate with his associations. We were like the pantomime horse, two men in one skin. He had dream images which illustrated the relationship, for example two men in one shirt with one arm each in each sleeve. In another dream he and his mother were driving a car, each with a hand on either side of the steering wheel. Alternating with this was another car that had the same arrangement, but in this car he was with his father.

Mr B was the oldest of three children and the birth of his two sisters came as a great shock to him. He was 8 years old when his second sister was born. During his mother's pregnancy he suffered an unusual symptom: he developed intermittent micropsia. He would wake to find that everything in his room had become tiny. This frightened him considerably, but he did not disclose it to anyone.

When he first came to analysis he had virtually no childhood memories but made a few fixed statements about the past, which were invariant; his accounts of them were always couched in the same phrases. One such statement was that throughout his childhood his parents lived in the same house but on different floors. Subsequently it became clear that the reality of their relationship gave some substance to this account but that it was a caricature. It served to structure his phantasy that he was involved with each parent separately. In all his phantasies the positive and negative versions of the Oedipus complex were treated as reversible, inverse parallels which would never converge. This appeared to form a prototype for the organisation of his internal object world. They existed like alternative universes in which all qualities and directions were simply reversed. The two parents were like two opposite magnetic poles which alternately oriented him. Thus ambivalence was evaded while these alternatives existed and convergence was replaced by negative symmetry.

A dream will illustrate what I mean. In the dream Mr B had gone to see his male dentist; at the surgery he met an attractive woman receptionist, with whom he developed a relationship instead of seeing the dentist. His associations to the dream made it clear that the woman represented my wife. The scene changed in the dream, and he found himself on the analytic couch lying between the woman and myself on the couch. The arrangement was such that the woman's head was at the end of the couch where my feet were, so that Mr B had to change from one end of the couch to the other in order to lie beside either. He was continually oscillating from one position to the other between the two figures in the course of the dream, and there was something sexual about this movement.

I would suggest that it represented the insertion of Mr B into the primal scene so that he took over the sexual movement of the parents by his oscillating movement between them and dismantled the primal scene into his two inverse relationships. These then formed the basis for the 'cleavage of his ego' – two diametrically opposed identifications. By this means he formed a half-identity in projective identification with one object and another with its negative. This arrangement, while giving expression to a fundamental antipathy to objects, also enabled him to secure object attachment while maintaining internal coherence. This was, I think, the basis of his defensive or pathological organisation, in which he hoped to evade the natural convergence of the depressive position. He found the means of binding his internal object relations and therefore his ego while indulging his opposition to all links – by using a negative link. In his paper on

'Negation' Freud comments that 'Affirmation – as a substitute for uniting – belongs to Eros; negation – the successor to expulsion – belongs to the instinct of destruction' (Freud 1925: 239).

By using negation in forming a link, such a patient appears to find a way of binding the *death instinct*. Thus there is always silent opposition to every agreement and this silent opposition is the unexpressed obverse of what is agreed. This inverse symmetry provides *balance*, which is what is sought in lieu of integration.

My patient dreamt profusely, producing the most illuminating dreams. These provided me with a great deal of intellectual understanding but served Mr B in another way. I realised after a time that he rid himself of insight by this method; that is, that the dreams were a means of evacuating knowledge so that through my interpretations of his dreams his self-awareness was coming from outside not inside. Therefore instead of having insight he felt he was agreeing with his analyst. Our two minds had a single 'mental skin' of comprehension. I realised that he was content that I should produce a character shape for him into which he could fit himself from the material he provided. The pictorial images I am using as metaphors in this paper – such as 'mental skin' – were all provided by his dream imagery.

How is it possible in such circumstances to communicate in a way that can establish real contact? There were many times when I could not reach my patient, but there was no dramatic solution to the problem. I persisted in drawing his attention to the phenomena I have been describing and to his reactions to my interpretations. This tended to produce discomfort in my patient, which he would try to reduce by accommodating himself to the new interpretation, usually by illustrating it with associations, after which he felt we were in agreement again. Nevertheless, after a fairly considerable period things did begin to change in the analysis. The fixity of the organisation, with its all-pervasive symmetry, began to give way to more transient defences and different, affective object relationships. One could say that the analysis felt more normal while the patient felt more disturbed.

The counter-transference then began to include the fluctuating states of mind usually felt in analysis. Instead of a persistent sense of unreality, detachment and preoccupation, I had livelier and more varied feelings, such as anxiety, frustration, pleasure, guilt, hostility, sadness and helplessness – feelings that one expects to encounter in the course of analytic work. It marked, I think, the patient's increasing use of normal projective identification and introjective identification in his analysis, and hence a more natural flow of transference and counter-transference.

Together with this improvement came a clearer view of the terrors which had been held in check by this organisation; the latent grandiosity curbed by it; and the conflict between narcissistic self-regard and object hunger concealed by it. I also learnt much more of the unhappiness of my patient's childhood and the degree of his parents' psychological disturbance. The anxieties which emerged in his analysis when his defensive organisation disintegrated were 'psychotic anxieties', as described by Melanie Klein (1946). I have found this to be the case in all the patients of this kind I have encountered.

To conclude this section on the clinical features of this syndrome I will recapitulate and enlarge a little on the transference and counter-transference which obtain while this defensive organisation remains ascendant. Although the patient does not lack feeling and produces ideas, the analysis has an insubstantial quality and lacks real development. There is a marked absence of conflict in the interaction between patient and analyst as well as internally within the patient. The transactions and communications within the analysis, like the patient's thoughts, do not have consequences. There is therefore an overall sense of unreality and *inconsequentiality*.

On closer scrutiny an echo of contradiction can be heard to every profession of belief, or an unstated negation detected where overt contradiction is not evident. Even where 'negation' is manifest it is in the form of a 'post-lude' which subtly contradicts what has gone before.

I consider the most significant clinical feature to be the counter-transference. I believe the most characteristic experience of the analyst to be the consequence of an absence of the normal flow of projective and introjective identification which runs through an analysis. The patient does not make use of the analyst as a container of his projected feelings in an ordinary sense and therefore deprives him of projected emotional significance. What is missing is the normal counter-transference resonance to the patient. The analyst lacks a sense of the patient inside him, and feels deprived of his customary empathic and sympathetic response. Conscientiousness has to substitute for spontaneity. As a consequence the analyst loses conviction and may, in extreme passages, feel denuded of his analytic identity. When the defensive organisation breaks down, the counter-transference, in contrast, may feel very intense.

I suggest that 'disavowal', knowing and not knowing, is central to the characteristic relationship of some personalities with both material and psychic reality. For some people it forms the basis of a 'defensive organisation' the purpose of which is to protect them from the phantasies they have about the external world and the phantasies they have about their internal world. Such people appear to possess knowledge of the facts of life but also not to know anything of them. Similarly, they appear to know a good deal about themselves but also to know nothing about themselves. I suggest that the defensive state of knowing/not knowing which protects the patient from the emotional consequences of his or her knowledge is achieved by treating these alternatives as if they were simply an inverse-symmetrical pair. In this way, what is known is not believed because belief involves

continuous adherence. My assertion is that only belief produces consequences and therefore, despite the encounter with disturbing knowledge, a
state of inconsequentiality is preserved.

Other crucial distinctions which are in reality *asymmetrical* are treated as
if they were *symmetrical* inversions. True/false, love/hate, child/adult,
psychic/material are all antitheses which are not symmetrical but asymmetrical. In this they are unlike up/down, left/right, front/back,
clockwise/anti-clockwise, which are symmetrical inversions.

The patient Mr B exemplified this elision of the distinction between
symmetrical and asymmetrical antithesis. From an accumulation of material
I realised that underpinning this inversely symmetrical mode he had a
phantasy of himself as having two surfaces, one facing an outer world and
another facing an inner world, as if he lived between two skins. He dreamt
of reversible situations and of objects that could turn themselves inside out
so that their 'inside skin' became their 'outside skin'. Such was the structure
of his psychic organisation that these two worlds were simply antitheses of
each other, like two sides of a mirror. Reversible or inversible paired states
proliferated, so that every situation was reduced to duality and symmetry.
The asymmetrical non-reversible distinction that exists between material
and psychic was treated as an inverse reversible symmetry of inside and
outside. Similarly, categorical distinctions between such things as right and
wrong were transformed into paired opposites like right and left, up and
down, or north and south. Fact and fiction were similarly treated as inverse
symmetries. His perceptions were often treated as reversibly interchangeable
with ideas which contradicted them, as if they had the same claim on his
belief. In his dreams top might become bottom, right become left, north
become south, bass become treble, white notes become black notes, back
become front.

The notions of *symmetry* and *asymmetry* which I am using correspond to
those of Matte-Blanco (1988). He distinguished between symmetrical logic
(which, roughly speaking, follows Freud's pleasure principle) and asymmetrical or classical logic (which roughly follows Freud's reality principle). In a
statement based on symmetrical logic any statement about one side of a
relationship holds true in reverse. An example from *Alice's Adventures in
Wonderland* will make it clear: the Mad Hatter says to Alice, 'you might just
as well say . . . that I like what I get is the same thing as I get what I like'
(Gardner 1960:95).

In symmetrical logic subject and object are interchangeable. The
exchange of subject for object inverts the situation. I think it is based on a
particular form of projective identification which in dynamic terms is
continuously oscillating or in terms of an image would be represented by a
half-subject/half-object figure. A sort of coherence is provided by such
means without the true integration of the depressive position, which is

evaded because it is thought to spell disaster. In this pathological organisation parallelism has been substituted for triangularity in the Oedipal situation and every other situation. All relationships based on this are seen as essentially the same and owe their partiality, not to the integration of other perceived relationships, such as that between the parents, but only to a splitting in the subjective self, with a partial identification with each parent and oscillation between them. A true capacity for subjective and objective experience of the self is therefore not achieved but, rather, a mechanical, alternating subjectivism which offers balance instead of stability – equilibrium, as Betty Joseph describes it, rather than change (Joseph 1989).

In this 'balance' the internal distinction between objective and subjective positions is not properly made; instead, one half-objective/half-subjective mode alternates with another half-objective/half-subjective mode. It may be intellectually rationalised as a sort of universal relativism, but a close examination will reveal that what unites all beliefs is that they are all half-beliefs. The organisation I have been describing is meant to function as a substitute container because of an inhibition in using the normal method of containment which involves repeated projection and re-introjection. It has to accommodate opposing ideas without reconciling them: conflicting impulses without conflict; and the expression of a schismatic tendency without disintegration. The solution seems to be to use the negative impulse itself to form a link in the form of negation, and to half-oppose the 'reality principle' through inverse symmetry. In *Through the Looking Glass* the characters apparently know about such things: ' "She's in that state of mind," said the White Queen, "that she wants to deny something – only she doesn't know what to deny" ' (Gardner 1960: 319).

6

Before and after the depressive position

Ps(n)→D(n)→Ps(n+1)

My hopes no more must change their name,
I long for a repose which ever is the same.

(Wordsworth 1984: 296)

We are familiar with the fact that Bion took Melanie Klein's concept of projective identification and extended it to produce his theory of *containment*. He introduced the notion of normal projective identification as essential to development and distinguished this from pathological projective identification. However, we have not so clearly adjusted to the fact that Bion did something similar to Klein's theory of the paranoid–schizoid and depressive positions. If we follow the implications of Bion's alternating Ps←→D and equate Ps and D with these two positions, then movement *from* the depressive position *to* the paranoid–schizoid position, as well as the other way round, is to be seen as part of a normal process of development. He wrote that where material emerges related to things unknown 'Any attempt to cling to what [is known] must be resisted for the sake of achieving a state of mind analogous to the paranoid–schizoid position' (Bion 1970: 124). He was emphatic that this Ps state should be tolerated 'until a pattern evolves'. This 'evolved state' he called D, 'the analogue to the depressive position', and he added that 'the passage from one to the other may be very short . . . or it may be long' (*ibid.*). He was concerned to distinguish his Ps from the pathological paranoid–schizoid position that Melanie Klein had described. To this end he suggested calling Ps patience and D security; neither of these terms has caught on.

This chapter is an attempt to produce a model that makes this distinction. It is based on a modification of Bion's formula and makes use of John Steiner's concept of pathological organisations (Steiner 1987). My model describes the movement through each position in turn as part of a continuous, lifelong, cyclical development and limits the word 'regression' to descriptions of a retreat to a pathological organisation.

If we look closely at Melanie Klein's own writings we find that she described the paranoid-schizoid position sometimes as a defence, sometimes as a regression and sometimes as part of development.

If we describe *any* move from a depressive position, with its sense of psychic order, to a paranoid-schizoid position, with its quality of disorder, as regressive, then Bion's D→Ps could be seen as a form of regression necessary for development. This would mean it had something in common with the ideas put forward by several authors that there was a sort of regression in analysis that was helpful. Kris's (1935) concept of *regression in the service of the ego* was probably the first of these. Balint's (1968) *regression for the sake of recognition* seems to be a similar notion and Rosenfeld's (1964) *partial acting out* as a 'necessary part of any analysis' has some resemblance to it. Winnicott, in the 1950s and 1960s, was probably the analyst who emphasised most the therapeutic use of what he called *organised regression* (Winnicott 1954). In the context in which he first introduced this it is a complex question, and it became a controversial issue. I suspect the different uses of the term 'regression' have contributed to it being dropped from the clinical vocabulary of many psychoanalysts. Before using it in this model I need briefly to discuss the history of the concept of regression.

Regression

Freud took the view that every mental illness involves some degree and some form of regression to early fixation points. He distinguished between topographical, temporal and formal regression. In other words, he saw regression as a return to an earlier pattern of object relating, to more primitive emotional expression and a style of thinking closer to perceiving than thinking (Freud 1900b: 548).

In 1943, as part of the 'Controversial Discussions', Susan Isaacs and Paula Heimann wrote a paper on the changes in the theory of regression in the light of Melanie Klein's work (Heimann and Isaacs 1952). They pointed out that parallel with the regression of libido was the regression of the destructive instinct and that this was of more significance in producing psychopathology. It made regression seem more dangerous and less benign. In 1946 the concept of the paranoid-schizoid position was launched by Melanie Klein and formed, together with the depressive position, what was then seen as 'a coherent and comprehensive theory of psychological development and its pathology' (Segal 1980: 125). From this point onwards regression was usually taken by Kleinians to mean a backwards movement from the depressive position to the paranoid-schizoid position. The words 'fixation' and 'regression' continued to be part of Melanie Klein's personal psychoanalytic vocabulary and that of Herbert Rosenfeld, but other Kleinian writers have hardly used either word. Betty Joseph, in a relatively rare use of the term, wrote: 'we see a patient . . . , better able to face depressive pain, now temporarily regressing in the face of anxieties about the past holiday and particularly the planning of terminating analysis. *She regresses to an earlier defensive system*, using mechanisms belonging more to the paranoid-schizoid position, splitting, projective identification, and so on' (Joseph 1989: 125; emphasis mine). I would ask you to note that Betty Joseph describes the patient as *regressing to an earlier defensive system*, *not* to an earlier phase, and she adds that this defensive system uses mechanisms belonging more to the paranoid-schizoid. In this passage she uses another concept commonplace in Kleinian thinking by this time, namely that of the *defensive system*, first introduced by Joan Riviere (1936). It is clear that in this passage Betty Joseph equates regression with a retreat from the depressive position to a defensive system using mechanisms characteristic of the paranoid-schizoid position. This is usually what is implied by the term 'regression' in Kleinian writing after 1952.

Meanwhile, as I mentioned earlier, others such as Winnicott and Balint had been speaking of the desirability of regression in analysis. However, whereas Winnicott wrote positively of protracted and extensive regression, Balint warned against a kind of wholesale regression that was malignant (Balint 1968: 141). Bion, like most other Kleinians after 1952, did not use the term 'regression' in his writings. However, in 1960, when the subject of regression in analysis was a contentious subject in the British Society, he wrote in his notebook: 'Winnicott says patients *need* to regress: Melanie Klein says they *must not*: I say they *are* regressed' (Bion 1992: 166).

I do not want to enter into that debate in this chapter, but for my own purposes I would just like to emphasise a distinction Winnicott made in his paper on 'Metapsychological and clinical aspects of regression within the psycho-analytical set-up' (1954), in which he advocated organised regression. He wrote 'an organised regression is sometimes confused with pathological withdrawal and defensive splittings of various kinds. These states are related to regression in the sense that they are defensive organisations' (*ibid.*: 283). In contrast to this withdrawal into defensive organisations, he refers to a kind of regression that provides a 'new opportunity for an unfreezing of the frozen situation' (*ibid.*). As I would see it, the 'frozen situation' would be a pathological organisation, and therefore the patient in it already regressed, as Bion commented. I would not use the word 'regression' to describe any developmental move from such a situation towards new opportunities, even if it involved more obvious disturbance and dependence.

In order to escape from the language trap of describing good regression and bad regression I want to reserve the term for a retreat into a pathological organisation that reiterates the past and evades the future. I prefer *not* to use the word 'regression' to describe *any* forward movement in analysis, even if it includes more disturbed behaviour and primitive expression. If it really is a means of making progress I still think of it as a necessary developmental step. Often in analysis it describes the inclusion of hitherto excluded or repressed psychic material that necessarily leads to the loss of the previously achieved psychic organisation and loss of cohesive functioning. I would see this as distinctly different from the regression that takes place in a negative therapeutic reaction, for example. The problem remains with us of distinguishing clinically and metapsychologically between a positive psychic development that produces turmoil and a pathological regression.

Pathological regression in this sense is commonplace, and it is often benign and short-lived, i.e. sunburn and the common cold it is, however, no less pathological for that. Regression may be a short-lived, unavoidable hiccup in analysis; it may be severe and recurrent, as in some negative therapeutic reactions; or it may be chronic and disabling, resulting in psychiatric disorder.

I want to emphasise two things in this chapter. One is the normality of the movement from a depressive into a post-depressive paranoid-schizoid position (D→Ps) and the other is that regression may occur from a normal post-depressive Ps position to a quasi-depressive position, a pathological organisation which I call D(path).

Towards a model of psychic development and regression

The regression from the depressive position into a paranoid-schizoid mode is very familiar in the Kleinian literature. In the model I am describing I refer to the pathological organisation of this regression as Ps(path) to distinguish it from the normal paranoid-schizoid positions of the developmental line.

What I wish to emphasise is the regression from a new paranoid-schizoid position Ps(n+1) into a defensive organisation in the depressive-position mode, D(path); that is, from an emergent position of uncertainty and incoherence, Ps(n+1), to a ready-made, previously espoused coherent belief system, D(path) – a move prompted by a wish to end uncertainty and the fears associated with fragmentation. The defensive state resembles the depressive position in its coherence, self-cognisant mode and moral rectitude but is without its anguish and sense of loss. Though it is sometimes hidden, there is always some degree of omniscience in D(path).

I refer in this model to the normal paranoid-schizoid position as Ps(n) when it precedes D(n) and Ps(n+1) when it follows D(n). The critical clinical difference is that in the *pre-depressive position*, Ps(n), the crisis is the

72

approach of the depressive position, while in the *post-depressive position*, Ps(n+1), the crisis is the relinquishment of cognitive and moral confidence for incoherence and uncertainty. It is the second of these crises that leads to refuge in a pathological organisation which offers coherence on a basis of dogma or delusion. In my new diagram I call this D(path) (see p. 72). What characterises it is an omniscient belief system. The configuration of this and the associated mood might be manic or melancholic.

The depressive position as described by Melanie Klein and explored and developed by Hanna Segal is a rich mine of clinical understanding. It encompasses developments in object relations, in the relationship with reality, in the capacity to make distinctions between internal and external, and it describes crucial developments in the cognitive and moral spheres. It is not surprising, then, that arriving at and working through the depressive position should be seen as a psychic achievement and should often be taken to be the aim of analysis and, quite possibly, of life itself. The elucidation of the development inherent in the move from paranoid-schizoid morality to depressive-position thinking, from *lex talionis* to reparation through love, has given the depressive position moral value. In addition, Hanna Segal has shown how the move from Ps to D makes symbolic thinking possible, which gives it reparative power and aesthetic value (Segal 1952, 1957).

However, the Kleinian theory of cognition as it has developed from the 1960s implies that the depressive position is no final resting place, that leaving the security of depressive-position coherence for a new round of fragmented, persecuting uncertainties is necessary for development. The only alternative to continuous development is regression; in a world of flux an attempt to stand still produces a retreat. Yesterday's depressive position becomes tomorrow's defensive organisation.

Reluctance to lose moral sensibility and sanity adds to the problem of relinquishing the depressive position. Once it is relinquished, triangular space and therefore reflective thinking are lost, only to be regained in a new depressive position, the form of which is not only unknown but unimaginable at this point. In Ps(n+1) the ability is gone to put ideas in perspective, to see round them rather than being inhabited by them or immersed within them. Such is the onward movement within an analysis; from integration to disintegration, followed by reintegration.

In order to clarify the model I am developing I will first put Klein and Bion's theories of the two positions into Ps and D nomenclature.

Klein's theory of the psychic positions expressed as Ps and D

In the beginning there is the infantile paranoid-schizoid position, which in time evolves into the infantile depressive position. This process can be represented as Ps(1)→D(1). Klein made it clear that they also represented characteristic psychic states and modes of object relating that recur repeatedly throughout life in whatever is the psychic currency of the day. The present-day version at any given time I designate as Ps(n)→D(n); the version destined to take place at some time in the future I signify as Ps(n+1)→D(n+1); n is a mathematical sign denoting the unknown number of Ps→D sequences leading to the present moment. Were it knowable a low number for n would indicate someone very young, mentally defective or emotionally immature.

[Ps(1)→D(1)→]	→Ps(n)→D(n)→	[Ps(n+1)→D(n+1)]
Past	Present	Future

In Klein's model the progressive movement is from Ps to D in each new situation, and further Ps and D positions lie in the future, waiting to be realised in the individual's object relationships of their day.

Bion's model Ps⟵⟶D

Bion proposed that thoughts arising required containing, naming and integrating. He saw D as producing a shape, and the process of *containment* as giving this shape meaning. For this to occur it was necessary to remain in the Ps position for a sufficient length of time to allow *the selected fact* to emerge and the configuration to crystallise, leading to D. He expressed this as Ps⟵⟶D.

I find Bion's formula suggests a chemical formula for dynamic equilibrium, with its implication of oscillation between two unchanging substances. As a psychological analogy this suggests reversible perspective more than psychic development and so I prefer to write it as:

Ps(n)→D(n)→Ps(n+1)→ . . . D(n+1)

The post depressive paranoid-schizoid position designated Ps(n+1) results from new knowledge or newly emergent previously segregated psychic material. It is not a point of arrival like the depressive position D(n), but a point of departure. If Ps(n+1) can be thought of as the wilderness the as yet unknown promised land is D(n+1).

Psychic growth through cycles of
$Ps(n)\rightarrow D(n)\rightarrow Ps(n+1)\rightarrow \ldots D(n+1)$

In this scheme I am putting forward $Ps(n)$, $D(n)$ and $Ps(n+1)$ represent actual states of mind but $D(n+1)$ represents only a future possibility. It exists only as hope resting on faith. In Bion's terms, $D(n+1)$ is a pre-conception which, when realised, will become the $D(n)$ of its day; in the meantime it is only an article of faith. As a new $D(n)$ becomes realisable $Ps(n+1)$, the post-depressive state, becomes the pre-depressive paranoid-schizoid position, or $Ps(n)$. Its character changes as a new resolution becomes imaginable, at first evoking alternating expectations of an ideal solution or a persecuting disappointment. The crisis is then integration and the approach to the depressive position that is so well described in the literature.

This is a state of mind tending towards a new D position; the cycle has moved on a step and $D(n+1)$, a pre-conception, will become $D(n)$, a conception. In other words, in order to describe an analysis we have to treat as static something that is moving. The diagram below is like a *still photograph* of a moving picture; it is not a photograph of still life.

$Ps(1)\rightarrow D(1)$ $\rightarrow Ps(n)\rightarrow D(n)\rightarrow Ps(n+1)\rightarrow$ $D(n+1)\rightarrow$

[__past__]   [_____present_____]   [_future_]

I emphasise this because apparent states of defensive stasis in analysis, as one can see clinically, require constant movement – even if it is only oscillation – to be maintained.

Development and regression using the concept of psychic retreats

Following the description in the work of Herbert Rosenfeld and others of a *narcissistic organisation* within the personality offering an alternative to reality and to object relating, John Steiner produced the concept of *pathological organisations* (Steiner 1987). He further developed this with his description of these providing a refuge from reality as *psychic retreats* (Steiner 1993). It is to such refuges that I see regression taking place. The model I offer below is an attempt to describe in abstract terms the forward movement of psychic development in life and in analysis, and the regression into psychic retreats organised either as quasi-paranoid-schizoid positions or as quasi-depressive positions.

The post-depressive position, that I am calling $Ps(n+1)$, is a psychic development that is necessarily accompanied by psychic discomfort and narcissistic loss. In some, it may produce panic and profound fears of chaos; in others, pride and envy may provoke regression.

The diagram below shows the movement that constitutes development from Ps(n), through D(n) and Ps(n+1) towards D(n+1); regression describes the backward movement into pathological organisations D(path) or Ps(path).

Development→

. . .
$$Ps(n)→D(n)→Ps(n+1)→ . . . D(n+1)$$

Regression ↓   ↓

$$Ps(path2)←D(path2)←Ps(path)←D(path)$$

Recovery   ↓   ↓

$$Ps(n)→D(n)→Ps(n+1)→ . . . D(n+1)$$

This diagram also illustrates the lines of regression and recovery. It is laid out in this way to emphasise that recovery entails the resumption of the developmental line by moving into a new normal paranoid-schizoid or depressive position.

Development and regression in practice

To try and show you how I think of these positions and the possible movements between them in practice I will simply give two brief sketches of different analytic situations. The first is one where the patient moves through analysis with brief episodes of regression and fairly rapid recovery such as one expects in an ordinary analysis. The second is one where severe regression both in terms of extent and duration is always a possibility.

In the first case the brief extract shows these movements on a small scale within the sessions of less than a week of analysis.

Cycles of development and regression in ordinary analysis

In the example I am about to give the frequently described and familiar movement from structured paranoid defence, through a more fluid paranoid-schizoid position to the depressive position is fairly rapidly traversed. The initial sticking place or point of regression in this analysis appeared to be at the point of development *from* the depressive position into a *post-depressive* position – from integrated understanding into a new situation of uncertainty and incoherence, from D→Ps(n+1).

The patient, a young woman social worker, had left the previous day's session, having been quite insightful, in a sad reflective mood. She arrived the next day five minutes late and in an angry mood, feeling persecuted but communicative. 'I don't know why I am late,' she said in an exasperated way. She then began talking angrily of a new woman colleague with whom she now shared an office in her department. This woman did not listen, she said; she had told her not to put her things in that area of the office they shared without agreement. But she went ahead and did so, and this made the office unbearable for my patient. 'This woman's things are horrible,' she said, implying that her own were pleasing and in good order. At some length she complained of the impossibility of her colleague and suspected her disruptiveness might be motivated. [I would describe my patient's movement overnight as from the depressive position D(n) into a pathological organisation organised on paranoid lines Ps(path).]

I commented: 'Where there is a difference in taste and when unfamiliar objects are introduced by someone else there is a problem, not just about physical space, but about shared mental space, and whose mental space is it anyway?'

'Yes! I have to *see* her things! They fill my mind!' the patient said. She continued to complain that her colleague's alien objects and different ways disrupted the pre-existing pristine harmony of the office. She could not see how such a situation could be solved except by getting rid of her. Her state was now one of persecutory feeling associated with a sense of intrusion and a desire to be rid of something, but it was more distressed than suspicious, and fragmentary rather than organised. I would describe this as a move to a normal pre-depressive paranoid-schizoid position Ps(n).

I then linked this situation to the transference. I spoke of the problem of the shared mental space of the analysis, and suggested that if I introduced anything new into it without her agreement and which did not accord with her way of looking at things it felt to her as though I had spoilt her way of seeing things.

There was a short silence; then she said, 'That's right!' After a longer silence, and in a quieter voice, the patient said, 'Dr Britton, how am I going to change?' After a short pause she continued: 'You see how I am. It's true, I persecute this poor woman. I'm intolerant, and I don't want to listen to you a lot of the time. It feels hopeless; how can anyone like that ever be the sort of person who can think of helping other people.' [This I would describe as a move into the depressive position D(n).]

I commented: 'You can see the need to change in some ways but you despair of doing so. You are ready to blame yourself for this, but I think you do not realise that it also indicates that you have no belief that analysis can do anything for you either.'

There was a long pause.

Then she said: 'That's true. . . . It is. . . . I hadn't realised it, but when I think about it I don't have any expectation that you will make any difference at all; I do think its all up to me that no one is capable of helping me.'

There was another pause.

'That is surprising. . . . I never realised that. How did you know I thought that? I didn't know. . . . How does one do that? It never occurred to me; I don't understand really, but its true,' she said, and then paused as if lost in thought. [This I would see as a move into a post-depressive paranoid-schizoid position, that I have termed Ps(n+1). The persecutory aspect of this advance rapidly became evident in the next shift in the session.]

After a short silence she resumed in a more decisive voice: 'Now I feel so discouraged . . . I will never be able to do that! . . . I will never learn to do that!' This then became a springboard for a familiar reaffirmation of inferiority, pessimism about her future, undervaluation of her abilities and overvaluation of mine, all in an omniscient mode. [This I would regard as regression to a familiar, somewhat masochistic, psychic retreat D(path).]

I said: 'Having discovered your lack of belief in me, you became anxious about what your scepticism might do to my self-belief, so now you are set on restoring it by attributing to me permanent possession of all the abilities you would like to have yourself. This puts you in the miserable but reassuringly familiar position of reproaching yourself for your inferiority while idealising me.'

The patient responded by saying, 'I remember now why I was late. I really didn't want to come. I was hating you a great deal before coming today.'

The patient finally ended the session speaking sadly of her mother, whose intrusiveness and imperviousness she frequently complained about and had hated as a child. But she now spoke of feeling guilty when she thought of her mother's lifelong depression. The patient remained thoughtful, rather sad, but now seemed quietly confident. I would describe her as in D(n) – that is, in the depressive position proper – at the point at which she left.

Coming to a new session having had an insightful dream which confronted her with unaccustomed thoughts and hence a move towards Ps(n+1), the patient then regressed. She arrived late for her session, full of self-reproach and absolutely sure she was disliked. I, she asserted, was superior in every way and above reproach; she was inferior, stupid and unable to learn. The mood was melancholic, the mental state omniscient. This I would describe as D(path), a quasi-depressive psychic retreat. This retreat was for her an uncomfortable but reassuringly familiar equilibrated state of mind, but one which for the analyst was frustrating and apparently impermeable. The patient stayed in this position for that session and then in the following session moved once again into a normal depressive position. After giving vivid expression to her envious feelings, her impatience, hatred of herself for knowing less and of me for knowing more, she moved into a state of sadness, resignation and guilt. By the end of that session a quiet sense of hope had emerged, which I would call the depressive position $D(n)$.

Further developments meant that patient and analyst had to confront new uncertainties in the analysis and the need once more to relinquish the coherence of $D(n)$ for the incoherence of $Ps(n+1)$. This was again to prove difficult. Thus there were to be further cycles of development and regression, which, to use another old term, I would call *working through*.

More prolonged severe regression

The second passage of analysis I want to refer to was very different. The patient could be said to belong to that group Rosenfeld (1987) described as *thin-skinned narcissistic*, the patients that I think of as people given to *a hypersensitive subjectivism*.

The episode is from a long analysis that took place some time ago, so I can speak from a position of hindsight. At the point where my brief account begins, the patient, a man, was in the state of mind I would characterise as the depressive position, $D(n)$. He was, after years of analysis which included much violence and considerable pain, in a state of mind of guilt, regret and sadness. This state of mind also included curiosity about me and conscious feelings of love and hate. He then inadvertently made a new discovery, namely the identity of another patient. It was a particularly significant discovery because the fellow patient was in the same field of the fine arts as the patient himself. To add to his provocation his newly discovered analytic sibling was undoubtedly gifted and more publicly established than the patient. The new discovery was like the birth of a new sibling. His reaction exposed the fact that his hard-won acceptance of life and analysis, his depressive position, was based on a belief that he was unique among my patients. This resembled his childhood belief about his family position, as the only boy, before the birth of a younger brother. Initially this fragmented his thinking and feelings. It moved him into a new paranoid-schizoid position, or $Ps(n+1)$.

This, I believe, would always be the case for anyone. It is what happens next that really matters. Is it going to be possible to move on to a new, as yet unimaginable, resolution, incorporating the new facts in what I have called $D(n+1)$, some depressive position of the future? Or is a regression to a pathological organisation likely to take place and, if it does, how long is that going to persist? A further possibility was demonstrated by this case, that the initial regression to a psychic retreat will not hold and further regression to more primitive pathological organisations might take place. I think this is the sort of sequence that Michael Balint (1968) meant by malignant regression.

To return to the moment in question in this analysis. The patient felt shattered by the new discovery. His previous sense of having a special, unique position in relation to the analyst was undone. He was no longer, even in his own mind, the only one. If he was not, then who was he, what was he and where was he in relation to me? Briefly he was in a new psychic situation with all his previous assumptions in fragments – Ps(n+1). Unable to bear the sense of fragmentation and associated fear of chaos in this, he rapidly regressed to a pathological organisation, D(path). This took a melancholic form: the patient asserted that he knew he was hopeless, someone contemptuously regarded by everyone; not only was he an unac-knowledged outcast, but he deserved to be. There was no doubt in his mind that I despised him.

Some patients might at this point work their way out of this by relin-quishing melancholic omniscience, and might find their way back from absolute worthlessness to a more realistic sense of their relative inferiority and the feelings accompanying that of jealousy and envy – in other words, moving towards a true depressive position. Others might remain in this place, D(path), by sustaining a steady state of moral masochism and might develop a chronic depression. Others might stay in the same moral zone while producing a manic reversal of roles and become by projective identi-fication a superior person contemptuous of all inferiors, such as those foolish enough to admire this new analytic sibling's work.

However, none of these things occurred. Melancholic and manic posi-tions rapidly alternated but neither was sustained; instead, unable to bear self-reproach and unable to achieve manic superiority, the patient regressed into a structured paranoid organisation, Ps(path). Now he was outraged, not simply enraged, and convinced that he had been exposed to something from which he should have been protected by me as his analyst. This was knowledge from which he should have been protected. It was, he implied, a conspiracy to humiliate him; first, by keeping him ignorant of it and not preparing him, and then by allowing him to be exposed to it. It sounds unconvincing as I say it, but it was not at the time, and the atmosphere in the sessions was that of a trial, with the analyst and analysis in the dock.

This self-righteous state of chronic grievance, which Michael Feldman has described (1995) as a defensive organisation, continued for a long time. It clearly functioned as a means of channelling hatred, while the grievance acted as a focus that functioned as a psychic organiser holding the patient's thinking together. In this way it provided him with a psychic container and protected him from his fears of fragmentation.

Whenever he moved out of this judicial mode it was first into a more generalised persecutory state, and then towards concern for the analyst and a reappraisal of himself. This move towards the depressive position would usually founder when he made adverse comparison of himself as an analytic patient with me or with other imaginary patients. Shame and humiliation would then displace guilt and remorse, and the restoration of pride took precedence over reconciliation, which moved him back into his paranoid organisation, Ps(path), for another round of grievance.

The problems in approaching or sustaining the depressive position have been well described, and it is not my intention to add to them here or to speculate on aetiology or psychopathology. I simply wanted to describe within the framework of this model the movement of a case in analysis where there was a marked tendency towards chronicity.

As quoted earlier, Bion stated, speaking of the move from Ps to D: 'the passage from one to the other may be very short, as in the terminal stages of analysis, or it may be long.' In this case the passage was not only very long but was complicated by many regressions, and sometimes compound regressions, into pathological organisations that removed it from the developmental line.

I would like to summarise what I have said in this chapter. I have suggested opening out Bion's formula to read: $Ps(n) \rightarrow D(n) \rightarrow Ps(n+1) \rightarrow \ldots D(n+1)$. I have described, in addition to the familiar pre-depressive position state, $Ps(n)$, which is characterised by the anxiety of integration, a post-depressive position of anxiety characterised by fears of disintegration, and I have called this $Ps(n+1)$. Although in $Ps(n+1)$ certain functions associated with the depressive position are temporarily lost, I regard it, not as regression, but as transition. I have reserved the term 'regression' to describe a retreat to a pathological organisation. This might be in the paranoid-schizoid or depressive mode, Ps(path) or D(path).

$Ps(n)$, $D(n)$ and $Ps(n+1)$ are all states of mind we experience in ourselves and meet in clinical practice. Unlike the other positions, $D(n+1)$ is not a state of mind that is realised, but a hope, based on faith, that future developments will bring coherence and meaning. It is, in Bion's terms, a pre-conception. To use a favourite device of Wilfred Bion's, if we put this in mythic terms $Ps(n+1)$ is the wilderness and $D(n+1)$ is the promised land. By the time this position is arrived at, $D(n+1)$ has become $D(n)$, the familiar depressive position; the promised land has become Israel and another struggle has begun.

81

7

Complacency in analysis and everyday life

One day everything will be well, that is our hope:
Everything's fine today, that is our illusion.
(Voltaire, *Poème sur le désastre de Lisbonne*, 1756)

The above lines relate to the disastrous earthquake of Lisbon in 1756, which resulted in great destruction and the death of many thousands; the Inquisition followed it by burning a number of people to death, since the University of Coimbra knew this to be a reliable method of preventing earthquakes. Both events feature in Voltaire's tale of 'Candide or the Optimist' (Voltaire 1759). In that story they provide further tests of Dr Pangloss's indestructible belief that all is for the best in the best of all possible worlds; this belief also remains unchanged by Dr Pangloss's subsequent hanging, which, owing to his executioner's incompetence, leads to the initiation of a post-mortem while he is still alive. In Candide and Dr Pangloss we have a literary antecedent to the complaisant patient and the complacent analyst. Candide, the complaisant, is happy to accept his mentor's dictum and remain his most agreeable pupil, and Pangloss, the complacent, while he can continue to teach his metaphysico-theologo-cosmolo-nigology to such a receptive person remains through all adversity convinced that this is the best of all possible worlds. 'Observe, for instance,' he comments, 'the nose is formed for spectacles therefore we wear spectacles. The legs are visibly designed for stockings, accordingly we wear stockings' (*ibid.*: 108). We must note, however, that Dr Pangloss does not say that things are right or good, but only 'that they cannot be otherwise than they are', so 'they who assert that everything is right do not express themselves correctly; they should say, that everything is best' (*ibid.*). In other words, it is not moral idealism but a theology of realism, a sort of ideal pragmatism or idealisation of adaptation. In the face of the vicissitudes of analysis this shared optimistic stoicism is appealing and it is not surprising that we as analysts might unknowingly accept the role of Dr Pangloss offered to us by some well-meaning patients. It is just such an analytic transference/counter-transference situation that I want to discuss in this paper. It is one in which the hardships of the depressive position *appear* to be suffered and acknowledged by the individual, but in truth they are tempered by the belief that he or she is more fortunate than others who are less able to come to terms with reality; analysis becomes the pursuit of moral excellence in the company of an approving parental figure and the notional 'depressive position' becomes a resting place rather than a staging post.

In contrast to the Panglossian approach, that of Betty Joseph has been to emphasise the need for constant questioning of appearance. This is crucial in learning how to work in such a way as to discover, not simply from the content, but also from the mode and development of the analysis itself, the 'specific constellations of object relations, anxieties, and defences' (Joseph 1989c: 126). As Betty Joseph put it in her paper on 'Defence mechanisms and phantasy in the psychoanalytical process':

> We can observe phantasies being attached to the analyst, as if forcing him into a particular role as a constant process going on in the analytic situation: so that anxieties arise, defences are mobilised, and the analyst is in the mind of the patient drawn into the process, continually being used as part of his defensive system.
>
> (Joseph 1989c: 126)

This chapter draws on two of her central ideas in particular: her view of the total transference situation as the most informative aspect of analysis, and her notion of the relationship between psychic equilibrium and psychic change. I want to discuss a particular group of patients in these terms; in some ways they resemble those referred to in Betty Joseph's own paper 'The patient who is difficult to reach' (1989a: 75–87), but are more able to participate in analysis than those described by Joseph. On a session-by-session basis it would not be true to say they are 'difficult to reach' but it is all too likely that the analyst would be in the position she describes, if after some time he reflected on the analysis as a whole. That is, to quote Betty Joseph:

> One finds oneself in a situation that looks exactly like an on-going analysis with understanding, apparent contact, appreciation, and even reported improvement . . . And yet . . . If one considers one's own counter-transference it may seem all a bit too easy, pleasant and unconflicted.
>
> (Joseph 1989a: 76)

The hallmark of the group of patients I want to consider, who differ in other ways, is in the counter-transference. It is one in which there develops a complacent, unconscious assumption in the analyst that one need not worry about these patients, in contrast to others who prey on the analyst's mind.

It is not, I want to emphasise, that there is no suffering, self-examination and self-reproach taking place in such analyses, but there is an unspoken belief that this is the proper order of things and that 'these things are sent to try us'. What I have found to signal real change in analysis in these cases is the eruption of indignation – not simply anger but a sense of outrage. It occurs when a previously existing unspoken, and unclaimed, sense of entitlement is felt to have been breached. At that moment the previously complaisant patient becomes, however briefly, like his or her invisible, difficult twin, unreasonable and demanding.

I have already suggested that in these patients analysis is usually regarded as a privileged state and that there is a sense of a moral quest which makes its hardships seem like part of an apprenticeship, with the analyst assumed to be a sort of master mason helping the patient to join the initiated. As quoted earlier, Betty Joseph said: 'the analyst is in the mind of the patient drawn into the process, continually being used as part of his defensive system' (Joseph 1989c: 126). As she taught us, this occurs not only in the mind of the patient, but also in practice in the analyst's unwitting counter-transference action and attitude. The question to be asked, therefore, in considering analytic sessions is not simply what of the unconscious is discoverable in the patient's words, but also *what is going on?* – in the cases I am describing, what is the role assigned to the analyst that is likely to be enacted by him or her?

If you will allow another literary allegory and see the patient, not as Candide now, but as Christian in Bunyan's *Pilgrim's Progress* (1684), the analyst would at first appear to be Christian's companion, Faithful, and then after poor Faithful's execution he becomes his second fellow-traveller, Hopeful. In Bunyan's story the character concerned was made Hopeful by 'the beholding' of the good relationship that had existed between Christian and Faithful: 'Thus one died to bear testimony to the truth, and another rises from his ashes' (*ibid.*: 109). Having become Hopeful, Christian's optimistic companion continued with him on his pilgrimage to their next adventure, escaping from Doubting Castle, where they were imprisoned by the Giant Despair. Any further recollections of the trial, execution and loss of Faithful were superseded by this adventure. However, how Faithful came to be executed cannot be without relevance if we take him to be a representative of the analyst. It happened in this way: on arriving at the town of Vanity Fair, when asked what they would buy, they replied: 'We buy the truth.' This created 'a hubbub', which led to their arrest (*ibid.*: 102). They were charged and found guilty of opposing the religion of Vanity Fair, and Faithful was buffeted, lanced, stoned and burnt to death. The Judge's name was Lord Hate-good. The prosecutor at his trial was Mr Envy, and the jury consisted of Mr Blind-man, Mr No-good, Mr Malice, Mr Love-lust, Mr Live-loose, Mr Heady, Mr High-mind, Mr Enmity, Mr Liar, Mr Cruelty, Mr Hate-light and Mr Implacable (*ibid.*: 108).

These are a prosecutor, judge, counsel and jury most analysts would recognise. I have felt myself, like Faithful, to be in the dock in such a court in a number of analytic sessions, but not with the patients to whom I am referring. In fact, and this I think is very relevant, they are the very antithesis of the patients who might induce such feelings in the analyst; they are not simply unlike them, but the very opposite of such characters. However, there is almost always someone significant in the lives of my complaisant patients with such characteristics, as a parent, sibling, spouse, lover, colleague or even as a child. Since people with such agreeable personalities often become analysts or psychotherapists, the dreaded antithetic twin is sometimes to be found among their own patients and, when they are in analysis themselves, to fill their own analytic sessions just as they haunt their minds. Before exploring the significance of this any further I need to give more clinical detail.

As previously stated, I have found in my own practice, and even more in supervision, a number of cases where there is a tendency towards excessive reasonableness in the patient and, in concert with this, a degree of complacency in the analyst. Although the patients' characters and analyses vary and their temperaments are similar in certain respects, their transferences and counter-transferences are, in a certain respect, the same. The patients' family histories vary in detail but contain a common factor: they are the healthiest members of their families. They have relatively equable temperaments and, in both life and analysis, they are easygoing. Although they often come for professional reasons, they see themselves as needing analysis and value it and their analysts, unlike more narcissistic patients. They think they need improving, the better to help everybody else.

In other words, I am not suggesting such patients are self-satisfied but, rather, that they are unrealistically free of discontent. They are ready to be self-critical because of their failures to remedy difficult relationships and they are very ready to agree, if it is suggested, that they are unconsciously hostile, rivalrous or unloving towards others. If one interprets that the difficult or nasty person one is dealing with is really an aspect of oneself denied and projected, one will agree with alacrity and with some relief. Analysis can provide such people with a great opportunity to blame themselves in a quiet way which suits them very well. I say in a quiet way, because the attribution of blame and the acknowledgement of guilt do not, in these cases, do more than ripple the calm surface of their analysis and their

85

relationship with their analysts. They are not insensitive; nor are they free of anxiety or depression, but they have a penchant for settling for relatively little and can make a feast of crumbs. Precisely what they are greedy for is at first hard to spot since it makes them ostensibly so undemanding. I think that they are greedy for virtue and covetous of innocence. I quoted Voltaire earlier because these patients remind me of Candide, who personified unmodifiable, optimistic innocence, and as their analyst one is invited to become Dr Pangloss, whose fidelity to the philosophy of Leibniz transcended experience.

They do not see themselves as needing much care and often fail to protect themselves from exploitation in their personal lives. In analysis, unlike most of their analytic siblings, they rarely blame their analysts for anything and accept whatever comes their way. In a way it is hard to convey the atmosphere of analysis in such cases because to describe the complaisance of the patient as I am doing now is to draw attention to it as a problem, whereas in practice it is precisely because there does not appear to be anything problematic that the analyst becomes complacent. It requires an effort by the analyst to do anything other than be pleased with apparent progress and gratefully accept calm seas after the choppy waters experienced in most of the other sessions of the day.

For this reason, except for educational reasons these patients are not often brought for supervision, unlike those regarded as 'difficult' cases, who are brought in large numbers. However, I have been fortunate in running a postgraduate seminar overseas for some years, where analytic cases have been brought routinely, and in other similar situations I have heard about the 'non-difficult' analyses. Not long ago, when I was acting as visiting supervisor in another country, an analyst brought me a case like this, which she selected simply because she wanted to bring a patient for whom she had not had any supervision. When, however, she prepared the case for presentation to me she started to worry for the first time about the analysis that had been taking place for a good many years. By the time she talked to me she began by saying:

> This is a patient whom I have never worried about before. The analysis seemed to be going along fine and we both seemed to be working quite well, but when I looked at it I realised that nothing much has changed and that, actually, though she doesn't complain, nothing has happened in her life that she hoped analysis would do for her. When she came initially, in part, it was to enable her to marry and have children. She has been in analysis for many years and neither of us have noticed the time passing, or that because of the biological clock this must have become quite urgent.

The patient was a psychotherapist and spent quite an amount of analytic time talking about her troubled and troublesome patients; she was very grateful, therefore, for her own analysis in helping her with her counter-transference. The analyst was easily able to link these work problems with her patient's family origins and appropriate aspects of the transference relationship. They worked comfortably together as analyst and patient, in marked contradistinction to the situation the patient was in with her difficult cases.

What I noticed as I listened to the case was that this patient, who came from a very troubled family, from which she had partly rescued herself, did not appear to have a life of her own outside her work and her analysis. In symmetry with this, I noticed that, although the analyst often interpreted the patient's reactions to breaks and weekends, and although the patient clearly missed the analyst in her absence, there was no real recrimination or anything that would make the analyst feel bad about it. There also was nothing in the patient's material that suggested that the analyst ever did anything during breaks other than be absent from sessions. This required a considerable use of the 'blind eye' by the patient, since she had, in a relatively small community, access to the social circle of her analyst, who was an attractive married woman a few years older than her patient and with a successful husband, lively children and expensive house. Naturally, envy was spoken of and acknowledged in this analysis, and the patient's Oedipus complex interpreted where it was clear enough in her dreams to be made explicit. I was impressed by the analyst's grasp of the analytic material and her use of analytic ideas. So what is it that I think was missing? One thing that was missing was sustained discontent; another was animosity, and completely absent was any malevolence. How was it, if envy and jealousy were interpreted, felt and acknowledged, that their presence did no more than ruffle the surface of the analytic relationship? I think the answer to this lay in the shared assumption that these were feelings to be expected in an analysis, like a price worth paying for a privilege.

I do not wish to pursue further the details of that analysis and want to make just one point, which I will return to later. What I think sustained the patient in a state of relative contentment and complaisance was the *belief* that her analyst *did not want her to change in any fundamental way.* Another element in this was the patient's unspoken assumption that she was, unlike others, a support to her analyst in her difficult vocation. Linked to this was a belief that the analyst's work was the centre of her life, and that her relationship with her patients, and this one in particular, transcended everything else. Thus jealousy was evaded and, without jealousy, envy had no foothold. In her turn, the analyst did not think her patient was fulfilling herself as she would wish; nor was she enamoured of her patient, but she did like her and appreciated her efforts, struggles and fortitude. Who would not?

What I think is interesting is that when the progress of the analysis was seriously questioned it became clear that the analyst thought it would be very cruel to want more of her patient or to allow any sense of dissatisfaction to colour her own counter-transference. To question the patient's obvious efforts to do her best under difficult circumstances immediately felt heartless to her analyst. In parallel with this, the analyst herself, once she questioned the success of her own work with the patient, was exposed to a quite savage process of self-recrimination. Following the first of the series of supervision sessions with the analyst, I also began to feel uncomfortable with the thought that I had upset the apple cart. There was some support for this apprehension of mine since the analyst's patient was, for the first time, unable to restrain herself from making intrusive telephone calls to her analyst over the analytic weekend and developed a hypochondriacal panic. When the patient's complaisance was disrupted, giving way to a panicky sense of persecution, the analyst's and/or her supervisor's complacency was interrupted by a sense of panicky guilt. It was as if the genie had been let out of the bottle as a frightening moral force with destructive potential. Thanks to the faith of the analyst in the necessity of exposing and exploring the current analytic situation and her patient's actual resilience and responsiveness, their shared fears of imminent catastrophe proved groundless. The struggle then was to prevent this itself from becoming further grounds for complacency.

In order to describe what I think was the inner situation that produced this episode I would like to return to the court scene I described from *Pilgrim's Progress* (Bunyan 1684). Seriously questioning the calm mutual regard and the virtues of untroublesomeness releases a destructive force which purports to be a moral force. It has the judicial powers of conscience, with the punitive methods of the Inquisition. Like Bunyan's judge and jury it resembles a destructive, envious super-ego and super-container of dissatisfaction. By its intervention faith in the analytic situation is quickly destroyed, and resort is taken to hope as a substitute for faith, optimism deputising for confidence. Faithful is executed and Hopeful takes his place. This harsh force of a quasi-judicial kind was never far away, but while the analytic pair could remain mutually hopeful it was believed that it could be kept at bay and never encountered. What was really needed for progress in the analysis was a long enough period imprisoned in Doubting Castle to explore it and not simply escape from it.

Like all the other patients of whom I am thinking in this paper, this woman was the healthiest and most equable member of a troubled family. I would like to include only those aspects held in common by otherwise different patients with different histories, partly for reasons of confidentiality and partly to make a general point. The patient I describe, therefore, is a composite picture of a patient in analysis, although any material I give is obviously specific. As I have already implied, such a patient is the untroublesome, relatively well child who has disturbed and disturbing siblings and parents, who have difficulties of their own. In analysis any picture of an untroubled past is soon dispelled and the forgotten anxieties experienced in childhood soon recalled and recounted. Psychosomatic problems, usually short-lived, have occurred in the course of analysis. Current emotional disturbance is most often manifested in hypochondriacal form, usually short-lived, but transiently very alarming and apt to lead to fear of imminent death. These fears are relatively easily surmounted. Because of the very unlikely nature of these hypochondriacal fears, and because of the readiness of the patient to see their unreality and to accept psychological explanation, the anxieties have little purchase on the analyst, who is therefore personally untouched by them. In childhood the patient kept to him- or herself such fears and other anxieties or readily accepted the automatic reassurance of a parent, who conveyed in doing so that 'we don't need to worry about you'. In analysis the patient takes advantage of the opportunity to expose such anxieties, both past and present, and feels considerable benefit from doing so. I do not want to minimise the benefit of this; nor would I for a moment suggest to the patient that it had no value. However, we should keep in mind Betty Joseph's maxim that we must also recognise that we are not only interpreting the transference, but living in it. While creating a situation in which the patient can explore a forgotten past of anxiety in the presence of a sympathetic listener, we are also in the process recreating a scene of an untroublesome child with an untroubled parent. It is what Freud (1913c) would have called a transference cure.

It is characteristic of such patients that they have brief intrusive hypochondriacal fears and similarly fleeting disturbing transference thoughts out of keeping with the ongoing mainstream current of belief that prevails in the transference. These thoughts are, to use Freud's word, '*unheimlich*' – translated by Strachey as 'uncanny', a word that does not really do justice to the German. *Unheimlich* means eerie, but it also means alien, and it is the antithesis of *heimisch*, meaning homely and familiar. Freud's explanation for the *unheimlich* experience is that one encounters something in the world that appears to reinstate a primitive belief which the individual had not eliminated but, in Freud's word, apparently *surmounted*. In his paper 'Das Unheimlich' ('The uncanny', Freud 1919), written before *The Ego and the Id* (Freud 1923a) and therefore before he had available to him the concept of an unconscious ego, he distinguishes between *repressed* infantile complexes, which he sees as belonging to *the Unconscious*, and *archaic beliefs*, which he sees as surmounted[1] but capable of re-emerging if given apparent support in the external world. He distinguishes between a state in which beliefs, though surmounted, remain latent, always ready to give rise to

89

unheimlich experiences, and a state in which they have been abolished. 'Conversely', he wrote, 'anyone who has completely and finally rid himself of animistic beliefs will be insensible to this type of the *Unheimlich*' (Freud 1919: 248).[2] I think this distinction is a most important one in analysis. I would make the distinction between beliefs that have merely been surmounted or apparently outgrown and those that have been worked through and relinquished. It is relinquishment that is necessary for psychic change, and this takes time, needs working through and entails mourning for a lost belief like mourning for a lost object. A belief that has been surmounted I regard as one simply overcome by another belief which itself remains dependent on the prevailing context. It is then like believing one thing when in company and in daylight and another when alone in the dark.

I think this is true of the patients of whom I am talking. They have surmounted certain beliefs but not relinquished or modified them; subsequently, they put in fleeting appearances as *unheimlich* thoughts – 'weird ideas', as one of my patients put it. Instead of sustained anxieties tethered in the transference, there are brief glimpses of terrifying ideas about the analyst or untethered images of a frightening or horrifying kind attached to nothing in particular. These transient incursions of archaic beliefs do not find a settled home in the transference and are rapidly dispelled by the reassuring familiarity of the analytic relationship.

I would like to illustrate this by describing some clinical material from a session some years ago which I used to illustrate what I called the willing suspension of belief in a paper on belief (Britton 1995b: 20–1). With hindsight, I take a more critical view of my work in that session and I hope to make a point about this. The patient was a lecturer in philosophy in a prestigious university who should, by this time, have been a senior lecturer. His family came from a foreign country where they had suffered persecution, and they had come to London as refugees. He had two sisters, one of whom was now homosexual and alienated from the family and one of whom was alcoholic; both women, unlike the patient, created problems for their parents. At the time of this session he had a girlfriend who worked in a City stockbroker's firm. They lived together but she would not commit herself to a mutually agreed long-term arrangement. He regarded her as emotionally dependent but difficult to satisfy and at times impossible to talk to.

He began by saying: 'When I came in I thought you looked fed up, not interested, hostile or cold.' He paused briefly and, as if beginning again, he said: 'It is very interesting, I used the toilet here for the first time. On my way here I felt I had to have a shit, but didn't want to be late so I didn't stop. But I didn't want to do it here. Anyway I came slightly early to do so. When I was in the car I thought "I have to" and I had a pain. I thought of a condition I was told I had years ago – don't know if you know it – *proctalgia fugax*, fleeting pain in the anus.'

By this time the patient had warmed to the subject, and talked of himself and his experiences in a steadily more expansive way. Clearly, he was now talking to someone he thought of as interested and friendly. However, the sense of something sudden, violent and sinister (like the pain of *proctalgia fugax*, a fleeting, stabbing, anal pain) remained in my mind as a disturbing image, but one that had vanished from his discourse, which was easy and relaxed.

I commented: 'You cannot direct your feelings towards me fully, and I think you dare not take your fleeting picture seriously, of me as hostile; so you have covered the picture with words.'

After a pause, he told me a story about himself and his girlfriend. It followed a pattern. Initially, his description of events gave a clear picture of her treating him badly and his withdrawing, but as the account went on their relative positions became obscure and, finally, he became objectively but unemotionally self-critical. He followed it with a story of an episode with colleagues at work which followed the same pattern. At first it seemed clear to him that he had been wronged; then, as he amplified it, what he really thought about it became obscure and the final version was one of theoretical self-criticism.

I remained silent, which he found uncomfortable, and he commented on it. He returned to talk of his girlfriend. With considerable feeling, he voiced his suspicion that when she received the substantial financial bonus due to her from her work she would keep it for herself, despite his investment of everything he had earnt, and more, in their life together. He continued to describe his great relief and warm feelings when he next saw her, because, despite their earlier sharp words, she was friendly.

I said: 'Here, also, you invest everything in me; that is, you credit me with more than you have in the way of a good opinion of me. When you idealise me like that, you feel favoured and welcome. This relieves you of your apprehensions about me and our relationship. When you lose the idea that I am good and you are well off, fortunate, and favoured, I think you are exposed to a sudden sharp discomfort, a fleeting painful doubt about me.'

The patient was thoughtful, and then said he was thinking of the story of the students who died in their flat because of the landlord's negligence. They were poisoned by the gas fire due to his disregard of its defects. [I have a gas fire in my room.]

I commented that when he puts himself in my hands that aspect of him that should protect his vulnerable self and take seriously his misgivings about his treatment prefers to dismiss danger in order to get on well with me on a basis of mutual esteem. So he allows himself to be, in effect, poisoned or buggered.

There was an intense silence, after which he said: 'I thought last week when I spoke to you about my colleague's anal fissure and you said that it was an example of a condition that gets worse before it gets better [I had linked this with analysis] . . . I understood what you meant about dilatation as treatment but I thought you said it with' – searching for a word – 'relish. I thought it showed your . . . um . . . can't think of the word . . . .'

'Sadism?' I suggested. 'You mean my sadism?'

'That's right,' he said, 'I thought you were sadistic.'

I described this session in the earlier paper, to make the point that until a patient discovers that he really believes an idea its correspondence, or lack of it, to external reality is irrelevant. In other words, until the patient's psychic reality is fully exposed its rebuttal or verification by reality testing is premature. The implication was that I thought that this had been accomplished in the session, that the patient knew by the end of it that he seriously entertained a persecutory belief that the analyst might be a dangerous, cruel figure, and that he had been attempting to evade this belief. However, I would now see it differently; I think the patient considered by the end of the session that he had entertained a wild idea that was interesting to both himself and his analyst, but that he would be crazy to believe it.

The way I see it now is that this patient momentarily believed that if he expelled things, like offensive words of real substance, in my direction it would precipitate a retaliatory sadistic anal attack from me in return. This belief, transiently conscious, was apparently surmounted by the rapid re-establishment of the belief that the analyst was a benign figure who was interested in the vagaries of his patient's thinking and who would be pleased to think he was getting in touch with the negative transference. This was so close to the reality of the situation that the patient's strong grasp of external reality could be recruited to reimpose this benign internal version of the analyst, and thereby to surmount the more archaic and fearful belief that momentarily surfaced, only to be dismissed as a 'weird idea'.

The technical problem arose because, however accurate the interpretation might have been in drawing attention to the transient emergence of an alarming belief about the analyst, the very process of communication followed by interpretation at that moment was itself enough to restore the status quo. The actual capacity of this patient to reflect on his own thoughts in the company of his analyst could be used to evade the sense of their subjective reality and hence of their emotional consequences. In Chapter 4 I described the achievement of 'triangular space' as a result of establishing a 'third position' so that individuals can think about themselves while being themselves. This is a position often lacking in borderline patients in analysis, who then remain marooned with their analyst in the sea of their own subjectivity. The patient I am describing did the opposite. In this session he used his ability to find a third position to provide himself with a place to escape to from the ineluctability of subjective belief. In other words, *he thought about himself in order to avoid being himself.*

The key, I think, lay in the phrase that I used, 'in the company of his analyst'. I think the recovery of equilibrium rested on the patient's basic assumption that the priority should be to re-establish a mutually thoughtful discourse in order to guarantee for both of us that all was for the best in the best of possible worlds. This, as both patient and analyst knew, was in marked contrast to what someone difficult, such as his girlfriend, would have done. She would have proceeded without question on the assumption that her ideas about the analyst's malign intentions were facts. We also both knew that, however professionally committed I might be, I would not actually anticipate an experience of that kind with pleasure. So at that moment if the patient exercised his capacity for reasonable thoughtfulness he had it in his power to spare me an unpleasant experience.

With hindsight, I think that, rather than pursue the interpretative line as I did, I could more profitably have commented on how keen he was to be a thoughtful person and how anxious he was to avoid being a difficult person, or a person with difficult ideas, like his girlfriend or some other, difficult patient of mine – just as in childhood when he did not want to be like his problematic sisters. If, unlike such difficult people, he could talk reasonably about these things it meant they need not be taken seriously any longer. In other words, we, unlike them, knew better than to believe such things.

This is what I think Freud's phrase 'surmounted (*überwunden*) belief' means. In this process a belief is not reality tested and finally relinquished, but temporarily overcome by the reassurance of the analytic situation itself. It is based on contrasting the world momentarily imagined and the one shared with the analyst. Like the eruption of a child's belief in monsters in the middle of the night, it is overcome by the reassuring presence of the parent for that night, but this lasts only until the next time. Some incarnation of the dreaded monster threatens to appear in the person of the analyst, but the process of the analysis itself becomes the means of banishing it. The analysis retains its *heimisch* (homely) qualities and the individual remains vulnerable to the intrusions of the *Unheimlich*, the horrifying *known-unknown* or *unknown-known*. The analyst unwittingly functions like the poet Rilke's mother, whose presence banished his childhood night terrors without modifying them, as he wrote in the third of *The Duino Elegies*. What Rilke discovered, painfully and slowly, over the next years was that his infantile relationship with his mother was the source of those very night-time terrors from which her presence shielded him, as I describe in Chapter 12.

To return to the clinical scene I was describing, I think we have a situation where the notion that '*we* can talk about these things' is sufficient to distinguish it from another imagined possibility, where this would not be the case. While we can talk about it, all is for the best.

Recently a colleague brought a case for supervision which illustrated this. The analyst was sensitive, thoughtful and good at her job, She had, like the other analyst I referred to earlier, brought the case for discussion, not because she felt she needed help with it, but for educational reasons. Indeed, she commented that what she would like was the opportunity to talk to me separately about another patient who was 'really difficult'. I am struck that, once again, the agreeable patient about to be considered was coupled in the mind of the analyst with someone who, in contrast, was felt to be really difficult. Nevertheless she introduced the presentation by saying that although everything seemed to be going all right she was concerned because there had been four years of analysis and nothing seemed to be happening. Nothing was changing in the analysis and nothing new was developing in the patient's life outside it. What I noticed particularly, listening to the sessions she described, was a characteristic, almost reflex response of the patient to any interpretations that opened up awareness of anxiety or potential conflict. This response was 'Yes, we talked about that'. I thought the implication was that anything that 'we' could 'talk about' was now included within a benign relationship, as if once something was part of an analytic discourse this was a guarantee that it could no longer give rise to anything really undesirable. 'Talking about' things was a means of joint disposal, and the unconscious assumption of the patient was that the underlying purpose of analysis was to dispose of all the disagreeable and alarming aspects of life by including them within the category of 'Yes, we know about that'. The *superficial* resemblance between this state of affairs and the notion of *containment* as a therapeutic function of analysis adds to the beguiling shared belief that things are taking their proper course and that development will follow.

It seems that only a view of what Betty Joseph (1989d) has referred to as *the total transference* will reveal this sort of situation, and this has to include the counter-transference activities and propensities of the analyst as well. I think it means constantly reviewing the prevailing state of analysis and its course, and not simply its session-by-session existence. Betty Joseph has demonstrated many times how the essence of the transference object relationship can be found in microcosm within the detailed interaction of an individual session. She has argued that in such moments of emergence it can be captured and may be open to real understanding. It involves repeatedly taking a hard look at the counter-transference activities and tendencies of the analyst in a particular case. This approach has been practised in the clinical workshop that she has presided over for many years. The belief in the fruitfulness of this approach rests on two convictions. One is that it is only in the minutiae of the analyst's functioning in a particular case that the unconscious aspects of the counter-transference of that case can be revealed, and the other conviction is the inevitability that some attitude or behaviour of the analyst will be influenced by his or her unconscious counter-transference, which can be revealed but not forestalled. This requires us to acknowledge that we operate within the prevailing transference/counter-transference, which we cannot transcend, but can possibly become aware of and understand, thereby achieving at least a degree of freedom. The next chapter describes an application of this approach which is based on a paper written jointly with John Steiner (Britton and Steiner 1994).

I would like to summarise what I have been saying about complacency in the analytic situation. With some of our patients we are apt to form a pair, unknowingly, like Dr Pangloss and Candide, unconsciously believing that although things are not right they are all for the best. Candide remains hopeful while Dr Pangloss knows best. I have suggested that this banishment of discontent from analysis is achieved by the patient thinking that even though the analyst wants him or her to improve, the analyst does not really want the patient to change. Change, it is assumed, would mean transformation into the patient's invisible, antithetic twin, who would be as unreasonable as the patient is reasonable. Likewise, the alternative to the cherished benign version of the analyst that is perpetuated is someone alien and potentially terrifying. External figures in the patient's past have made flesh these inner imagos and there are usually figures currently in the patient's life that have a similar antithetical twin role. Other patients, like imaginary siblings, are believed to be as disturbing to the analyst as the patient is undisturbing.

While the patient believes that he or she is the 'all right' patient jealousy in the transference is in abeyance, and hence so is envy. Hanna Segal recently commented (personal communication) that in some cases only the eruption of jealousy leads to the emergence of envy. I think that this is because a privileged relationship is believed to exist between analyst and patient that is thought to be profoundly enviable. There is, after all, no better defence against envy than being enviable. As a consequence of this the patients I have been describing, while cocooned in their privileged position, are often very afraid of evoking envy and tend to placate others by minimising their own accomplishments or even avoiding success.

The proximity of these unconscious beliefs to the actual situation in the analysis makes them particularly difficult to budge. Insight, once gained, can quickly generate the feeling that the patient is what the analyst wants, in contrast to other obviously less insightful people. The risk of chronicity is considerable. What seems to be required is the enhancement in both analyst

95

and patient of a sensitivity to the presence of complacency, and the development of some degree of allergy to smugness.

Notes

1 *Überwunden* – outgrown, overcome, conquered, vanquished.
2 *Die Aufhebung des Glaubens* – the abolition of beliefs.

8

The analyst's intuition: selected fact or overvalued idea?

The technique, however, is a very simple one. . . . It consists simply in not directing one's notice to anything in particular and in maintaining the same 'evenly suspended attention'.

(Freud 1912: 111)

This chapter is based on a paper written jointly with John Steiner (Britton and Steiner 1994). We wanted to describe the use by the analyst of the intuitively *selected fact* in the evolution of his or her interpretations and to draw attention to its hazardous similarity to the crystallisation of delusional certainty from an *overvalued idea*. Overvalued ideas are likely to arise from overdetermined unconscious beliefs. In that paper we discussed the problem of distinguishing between the two clinically, and stressed the importance of monitoring the subsequent development in sessions following interpretations in order to try to do so. We agreed to look together at clinical material from our own work for suitable examples where we thought the selected fact crystallised the current analytic situation and where we thought an overvalued idea impeded analytic understanding. The case material we chose I have used in this chapter. By not disclosing whose work it was in either of the cases we wanted to emphasise that at times in any analyst's work a selected fact is quite likely to be an overvalued idea. It also added some protection to confidentiality for the patients. For both these reasons I have written in this chapter as if I was the analyst in both cases.

Bion suggested that the organisation in the analyst's mind of thoughts about the patient resembles a process described by Poincaré in his 'Science and method' (Poincaré quoted in Bion 1967: 127). This process begins with some particular fact among an accumulation of facts arresting the attention of the scientist in such a way that all the others fall into a pattern or configuration by their relationship to this selected fact. Bion adopted the term

97

'selected fact' because he believed a similar process took place in the analyst's mind when, putting aside memory and desire, he achieved that state of 'evenly suspended attention' prescribed by Freud for analytic practice (Freud 1912: 111). Bion recommended this approach when reviewing the analytic method in his book *Second Thoughts* (Bion 1967: 127). There was in the analyst's thinking, he wrote:

> an 'evolution', namely the coming together, by a sudden precipitating intuition, of a mass of apparently unrelated incoherent phenomena which are thereby given coherence and meaning not previously possessed. . . . This experience resembles the phenomenon of the transformation of the paranoid–schizoid position to the depressive position. . . . From the material the patient produces, there emerges, like the pattern from a kaleidoscope, a configuration which seems to belong not only to the situation unfolding, but to a number of others not previously seen to be connected and which it has not been designed to connect.
>
> (Bion 1967: 127)

I will try to illustrate this with some clinical material from the analysis of a young woman from a Muslim country with a secular upbringing, who was a writer of some success and promise. The patient was married to a fellow Muslim who was also secular in outlook and they had one child. She had a younger brother who was a lawyer. Both her parents died in her early adult life. The material is chosen because, although it is from some years ago, the notes were made immediately after the session, and subsequent developments in the analysis and the patient's life give a reasonable degree of confidence that the selection of the interpretation in this session was appropriate when it was made.

At this point Mrs X had been in analysis for several years. Initially she was given to intellectualising, and identified with the analyst a good deal. This changed after some years of analysis, and there was a temporary period of quite considerable symptomatic and transference disturbance. There was a good recovery, with much greater insight but a tendency to negative therapeutic reaction. At the time of this clinical material she had taken positive new steps in her analysis and in her life, but the day before this reported session she had been 'backtracking', with the return of old beliefs, symptoms and discontent with her own work.

Mrs X began the session by complaining that I was a minute late and went on to describe herself as feeling cruelly evicted at the end of the previous session. After a short pause she told me a dream. She was on a mountain peak. Also on top was a giant mushroom. She was afraid of being pushed off, but she was also stuck there. Her husband said impatiently from somewhere beyond the peak: 'Come on! We have to move along to get there.' She then added: 'He must have been on a downward slope.'

Her immediate associations were of irritation with her father for always bringing large baskets of vegetables and fruit, and after a pause she spoke of the male patient whose session followed hers as more privileged because she suspected he was training as an analyst.

The item (selected fact) which completely took my attention was the notion that to 'move along' she would have to go down 'the slope'. I took this to mean that any progress meant for her going 'downhill' from her imagined position on 'a mountain peak' of present privilege. The rest of my thinking organised itself around this notion. The thoughts which had already accumulated in my mind from the time I collected her consisted of fragmentary ideas about her envy, my satisfaction at her relative recovery from a serious depression, my awareness of her jealousy of other patients and of her brother, and a theory I had of her identification with her rather grandiose father. To these as I listened to her in the session were added, in a rather automatic way, my translation of the symbolism in the dream and my awareness of her feelings of resentment. My own conscious counter-transference feeling was well represented in the dream by her husband's impatient 'Come on! We have to move along to get there'. Once my attention was taken by the notion that she believed that any forward progress meant her going downhill my random accumulating thoughts organised themselves around this idea and a configuration emerged in my mind.

This was that she believed giving up the nipple is not weaning – that is, moving on and developing – but eviction and displacement by a magic mushroom penis. Therefore if she had, or was, the penis she would have permanent possession of the breast. This meant simulating the penis or possession of one. This was concretely expressed in her mind in terms of 'being an analyst'. If she could give up this illusory place on the top she could make progress, but this, as she sees it, is on the downhill slope.

My actual interpretation was: 'You feel evicted and demoted by me because you cannot be like me.'

She responded to this by agreeing vehemently and adding: 'But that is how it is! and I am sure it will be like that forever.' It was only after this was well established within the session as her point of view that I completed my interpretation by adding that when she realised that taking in an interpretation did not make her an analyst, this was insight and forward movement but it felt to her like going down the slippery slope towards an inferior position.

She responded that she had the feeling once more of something irritating getting in her eye. I commented that she saw what I meant and it irritated her. 'I feel furious that you are who you are and I am who I am!' she said. After a brief silence, she said: 'I can feel that irritation beginning in my clitoris again and I was thinking about the cream.' [This genital sensation had formed part of a complex of symptoms, and she had adopted a tube of cream, prescribed for her by her doctor, as a fetish object, which she did not apply but carried everywhere to provide security against panic. The patient regarded this as foolish but it was compulsive for a time.]

I commented that she was intensely irritated to find she had a clitoris and not a penis, and that she thought that if she did my job she would feel as though she had a penis.

After a short silence she told me that she had taken on some new editorial, administrative responsibilities in relation to a journal for which she was a principal writer. These, she said, were very burdensome and inappropriate; she knew she should relinquish them but she felt that while she had them she was the one in charge and in control of everything.

Looking back at this I am struck by two things. One is that the selected fact not only oriented me but kept me close to the patient's thinking, when if I had more randomly followed the material I might have become caught up in making symbolic interpretations for the sake of demonstrating unconscious representation. This would have risked introducing predetermined overvalued ideas of my own attached to such emblematic part-objects as 'breast' or 'penis'. The second thing which strikes me is the patient's unconscious communicativeness and her readiness to take in and respond to interpretation, albeit with negative affect. It is even more clear to me now that the mode by which I selected the element in the dream for attention was by identification with the figure of the husband in the dream, who was, I think, meant to represent me and who also could be seen to speak for part of herself. This unconscious identification led to my psychic orientation, which I believe in this instance led to genuine understanding. I think this was itself a consequence of the patient being in a communicative mode at that time. This contrasts very much with earlier periods in her analysis when similar unconscious identifications by me would lead us into either an impasse or an unconscious collusion. These transference repetitions or collusions would be built around an overvalued idea representing itself as a selected fact.

A 'sudden precipitating intuition' (Bion 1967) in the analyst may be the harbinger of insight. However, its arrival can also resemble the emergence of delusional certainty. The difference between a creative use of a selected fact and the crystallisation of an overvalued idea may not be immediately evident. It would be arrogant of an analyst to suppose that he was immune from the unconscious processes that might lead to the emergence of an 'overvalued idea' masquerading as an intuitive insight. It is imperative, therefore, that work begins after giving the interpretation. Then it becomes crucially important in listening to the patient to take heed of his or her conscious and unconscious reactions to what the analyst has said.

Freud points to the difficulty of evaluating and validating an interpretation (or a construction) by emphasising that our formulations are no more
than hypotheses, which need to be tested in the material which follows
them. He writes:

> Only the further course of the analysis enables us to decide whether
> our constructions are correct or unserviceable. We do not pretend that
> an individual construction is anything more than a conjecture which
> awaits examination, confirmation or rejection. We claim no authority
> for it, we require no direct agreement from the patient, nor do we
> argue with him if at first he denies it. In short, we conduct ourselves on
> the model of a familiar figure in one of Nestroy's farces [*der Zerrissene*]
> – the manservant who has a single answer on his lips to every question
> or objection: 'It will all become clear in the course of future develop-
> ments.'
>
> (Freud 1937: 265)

The importance for the analyst of keeping an open mind about the
correctness or otherwise of his or her interpretation has long been
acknowledged, and narrow-minded analysts are easily and rightly criticised.
We are likely to find such offenders most easily among those who differ
from our own chosen approach to analysis. Balint, for example, describes his
stereotype of the Kleinian psychoanalyst as follows:

> The analyst using this technique consistently presents himself to his
> patient as a knowledgeable and unshakeably firm figure. In conse-
> quence the patient seems to be kept incessantly under the impression
> that the analyst not only understands everything, but also has at his
> command the infallible and only correct means for expressing every-
> thing: experiences, fantasies, affects, emotions, etc. After overcoming the
> immense hatred and ambivalence – in my opinion, aroused to a large
> extent by the consistent use of this technique – the patient learns the
> analyst's language, and pari passu introjects the analyst's idealised image.
>
> (Balint 1968: 107–8)

This is certainly at odds with Freud's approach. Many of us would not
agree that it was an accurate description of 'Kleinian' analysts. We would
like to think that it was a description of a misguided analyst of any species,
but perhaps we can all agree that this type of analysis would be extremely
persecuting and destructive of true development.

It may be very difficult to know how to understand the patient's reaction in terms of what it says about the interpretation. Agreement with the
analyst may be an expression of compliance, and disagreement may be a

protest about a correct but painful or provocative realisation. The subtle and sometimes prolonged work required to determine this, together with some understanding of why this response characterises this moment in this patient, is the essence of analysis as we try to practise it. A great deal depends on the spirit in which this is done. If the interpretation is offered by the analyst and is taken by the patient to be a hypothesis that the patient is being asked to consider, then an atmosphere of inquiry is able to develop. This is quite frequently not the case, and then an attempt must be made to understand the obstacles to achieving this. The failure may be due to factors in the patient or in the analyst, or (as often is the case) in the interaction of the two as an enactment of an unconscious pathological object relationship. This last possibility can itself become a fruitful area for reclamation from a hitherto unrecognised latent situation if the analyst can formulate their activity in words and communicate these to the patient; however, if it remains unacknowledged it can lead to an impasse.

Perhaps the most devastating and traumatic scenario arises when the patient feels that the analyst forces wrong interpretations on him in a manner which allows no doubt, as if the analyst is subjecting the patient to indoctrination or brainwashing. This may be linked to a delusional certainty on the part of the analyst, which may be connected to the autochthonous nature of the analyst's misuse of the selected fact to bolster his or her particular view of the world.

Shengold (1989) has described such events as 'soul murder', making connections with Schreber, who used this term with Winston, the hero of Orwell's novel *1984* (Freud 1911a: 14). It is particularly relevant to the experience of traumatically abused children, and it is often in such cases that such an analytic situation develops as an uncharacteristic counter-transference reaction in the analyst. In some patients, when such a sense of violation is followed by a refusal to listen, withdrawal in despair or turning away in anger may follow. It is even more difficult when it becomes the basis for a perversion, with a masochistic submission by the patient.

This scenario can, however, also arise when the analyst's original interpretation is experienced as 'soul murder' due to factors operating in the patient at that moment even though it is made in an enquiring mode by the analyst. This is probably when the patient is unknowingly operating in a 'mode of action' and believes the analyst is doing so. In such a situation the analyst first needs to clarify how the patient sees it and to communicate this before any further analytic work can be done to explore the reasons for the patient experiencing it in such a persecutory way. In other cases intense transference and counter-transference actions and reactions may be reclaimed for understanding only in the analyst's mind, his or her interpretation remaining unvoiced for the present. But this is essential, as at least it releases the analyst from active participation in an unconscious enactment, even though it does not release the analyst from the place he or she occupies in the patient's perception of the situation. A persecutory experience by the patient or analyst may not be the only scenario to which this need for reclamation applies; unconscious enactment may take other forms, for example erotic, idolatrous or oracular.

We have described two situations: one optimal, where the necessary conditions exist for the interpretation to be experienced as a hypothesis put forward by the analyst; the other where all interventions are experienced as actions. There is a third possibility, in which a perverse or worshipful use is made of interpretation. In some analyses an interpretation may be used as a religious doctrine, or as a fetish, or as an instrument for use in a sought-after sadomasochistic relationship. In this last category an interpretation encapsulating an overvalued idea of the analyst would be particularly welcome to a patient seeking misunderstanding as a masochistic satisfaction.

How is it possible, when the analyst thinks he or she understands something, to distinguish between the useful discovery of a formulation and an overvalued idea which the patient is then pressed to accept. An example of the analyst's use of an overvalued idea might help us to consider this.

The patient, Mr L, was a highly obsessional man who filled many of his sessions with detailed accounts of the way his wife blamed him and berated him for his various failures in life and in their marriage. One day he began describing how he was attacked for impulsively buying a suit. He was especially criticised for not taking his wife with him, which he explained was because it was the last day of a sale, so that he was unable to arrange a time which would accommodate her.

I interpreted that he seemed to have great difficulty waiting, so that acting impulsively helped him to avoid waiting.

He asked if I had said waking or waiting? I noted this misunderstanding and went on to suggest that his preoccupation with his wife's attacks and persecution gave him something to occupy his mind while he was waiting. I added that there was something anal in the way he controlled his objects during the waiting and I linked this with his preoccupation with money.

The patient responded by describing an incident a few days previously where he had waited for his wife upstairs at the theatre. He was sure she was late and doubted if she would come at all after her anger with him in the morning, but it turned out that she was actually waiting for him downstairs in the bar.

I had already felt uncomfortable about my interpretation. First, he had to ask was it waking or waiting, so it was probably not on his mind; second, it sounded theoretical and forced, especially my reference to anality without any actual anal material; and, finally, I knew that I was reading a book which discussed waiting in some detail and which had interested me.

Now I said: 'I think you are commenting on my interpretation. You seem to feel that we are in different places. My interpretation did not reach where you were and perhaps you felt it was something I was preoccupied with so that you are suspicious of it.'

The patient replied that he was not sure and he thought I was pointing to an important area. Certainly he had great trouble waiting, but also great problems in initiating action.

I was left quite unsure if we had made any useful contact or not and was rather unconvinced by his interest in the question of waiting, which might have represented his wish to placate or appease me, just as he habitually did his wife.

On the next day he began by saying that he wanted to return to the theme of waiting and began a somewhat overelaborate description of his way of gaining satisfaction from waiting. He said he was tempted to delay and avoid action as if lured by a temptress, something like a female equivalent of the Demon of Reason. He connected it with water and Venice, which he had been describing recently in connection with the theme of the attractions of death. There was something special about buildings rising out of the water and about the journey, which was like waiting to get to the buildings. Waiting was also like being in a warm bath, which he enjoyed. His wife criticised him for falling asleep in the bath, but after a long day he was tense and he finds that the tension gradually goes in the warm water.

After a pause he said: 'Have I latched on to the significance properly?' He then proceeded to suggest that the satisfaction of holding on to time was like holding on to money, and he supposed that both were very anal. Perhaps he was holding things back. There were problems in the office arising from the fact that he could write quick articles but the big ones in the areas he was really interested in were delayed as he went on collecting notes and ideas.

I suggested that the patient was still not sure if I was in the right place when I had raised the issue of waiting the previous day. Now it was difficult to tell, because he seemed to have latched on to my idea. He seemed to hold on to it like a lifeline (lifelines had been a recent theme), and it was unclear if it corresponded to anything which was going on in him or even truly interested him.

The patient said: 'Does it matter, if it is something I need to make sense of? There is a danger, though. It reminds me of the way I see a pattern in a random set of events. Once the pattern is visualised it is very difficult to stop seeing it even if it is not there. Analysis may be like that.'

I interpreted that he was tempted to latch on to a pattern like a lifeline, which helps him know where he is, and that he clings on to me by trying to latch on to something in my mind. It then does not appear to worry him that it may be a spurious pattern.

The patient went on to tell me about a major piece of work he was doing which involved the exposure and discrediting of important people. He had been told that the venture he had discovered had to be secret for a further four months and only then would he be given information about it through indirect sources. He began to work out a picture by piecing jigsaw pieces together. 'It is like Greek myth,' he said. 'There is a sort of Aladdin's cave with untold riches in it and a doorman who won't let me in. But I have found them out.' He was clearly triumphant and went on to speak of his anxiety if he exposed such important people. After getting the support of his boss he had decided to go ahead.

I interpreted that he felt encouraged by me to test out whether the pattern was spurious, and to risk investigating me and exposing me if he suspected that I was presenting him with interpretations which he thought might be suspect.

He replied by describing the dishonesty of his own methods of enquiry, in which he lulled witnesses by chatting about something they were interested in and only as an aside asked them for the information he needed.

I interpreted that perhaps in retrospect he felt that he agreed to speak about waiting, about Venice and about anal mechanisms because he thought that was what interested me, while perhaps what he really wanted to do was to be clearer about my way of working and, especially, whether it was spurious or not.

He said he was not sure how to think about such a question. Previously he had told me that he pointedly avoided reading about analysis or finding out if I had written books or articles. Now he admitted that he had seen an article in a French paper about wars breaking out again among Parisian analysts and he did wonder whether similar wars were going on in London. He assumed that I was Kleinian but he was not sure what that meant. He associated it with an interest in babies, which he thought was good, but he then said his real fear was of being put into a mental straitjacket. He described mathematics as a field which consists of tightly packed separate areas, so that if you get into one it is very difficult to get out.

The material seems to point to the fact that I had introduced an over-valued idea when I interpreted the patient's difficulty as waiting and that he used masochistic thinking to help him to wait. It may be that this theme was valid and important, but it seems to be the case that it was not where the patient was waiting in that session. Rather than insist that it was the analyst's job to reach him and help him, the patient was willing to leave his own mental place and join the analyst in his preoccupation. Thus he obliged me by providing further material about waiting and anal mechanisms, as if to corroborate my interpretation. His other associations, however, told a story of non-connection.

105

The defensive use of overvalued ideas

In a situation where meaning is not apparent and facts are accumulating, the relationship of one psychic particle to another is not determined until the analyst's attention is arrested by something, which thus becomes the selected fact, and there emerges a configuration as the other psychic particles cohere by their relationship to it. This newly formed configuration (the contained) is highly specific to *this* patient and *this* moment in *this* analysis. It finds a place in the analyst's mind provided by a pre-existing abstract form (the container) and fills it. The newly emergent configuration thereby becomes the incarnation of an abstract theory. This theory, like an empty form or 'state of expectation' (Bion 1962b: 91), was awaiting an exemplary situation to give it life and substance. These theories or expectant containers accumulate in the mind of the analyst and are derived from the analyst's general analytic theories, his or her own subjectively based theories about people, clinical experience of other patients and accumulating experience of the particular patient. Bion emphasised that the relationship is of pre-conception *to* realisation, as container *to* contained, and *not* the other way round (*ibid.*). In other words, it should be the case that the analyst's mind, primed with its theories, is waiting as a container for its imageless expectations to be fulfilled by the experience and material of the patient, rather than that a theory is looking for a patient! The movement from incoherent fragments, through selected fact into coherence and containment involves all three of the transformational sequences Bion described. From Ps to D; from uncontained to contained; and from pre-conception to conception.

In analysis both patient and analyst move through cycles of Ps and D as I described in Chapter 6: Ps(n)→D(n)→Ps(n+1). I think this is only possible where a sense of overall containment is already in existence which provides a limit to the sense of fragmentation and incomprehension so that it is not boundless, nullifying all meaning. Otherwise the experience is of 'nothingness', terrifying 'bottomlessness' or complete 'incoherence'. For many patients, for at least a good deal of the time, faith in the analyst and the setting provide this outer container. When, through lack of or loss of faith, this is not the case the situation is very fraught and often dramatic. Meaning is then sought, not to make sense of things, but to provide an alternative to the missing container – in the words of the second patient, as a lifeline. We suggest that this is one reason why ideas become overvalued in some personalities. They are used to buttress the fragile sense of stability in psychic space, and are therefore required to have the qualities of permanence and substance. In such circumstances interpretation may become a means of seeking security rather than inquiry, and its constancy may be more highly valued than its truth. In this scheme of things there is no waiting for the evolution of the selected fact. The overvalued idea is a *pre-selected fact* which is not emergent but mandatory in every psychic situation, compelling other psychic particles to orient themselves around it. The overvalued idea serves as a *permanent quasi-selected fact* that eliminates the anxiety of waiting for something to emerge.

Reviewed from this point of view, Mr L's 'latching on' to his analyst's pre-selected fact or overvalued idea to provide himself with a lifeline has further significance. 'Does it matter,' said Mr L, 'if it is something I *need* to make sense of?' He supplied his own answer: 'I see a pattern in a random set of events. Once the pattern is visualised it is very difficult to stop seeing it even if it is not there. Analysis might be like that.' If it were 'like that' analysis would be a joint enterprise in providing cognitive lifelines for fear of falling endlessly or drowning in uncertainty. Then waiting for the selected fact to turn up would be like the waiting of Beckett's characters in *Waiting for Godot*, the endless wait of the non-believer. Inability to wait appears, after all, to be at the heart of the session concerned, but to put in its first appearance in the analyst's counter-transference activity, where he mirrors the patient's method by providing himself with a pre-selected fact.

Two situations would seem likely to give rise to the intrusion of a pre-selected fact or overvalued idea into the analytic field, thus obscuring or preventing the natural evolution of the session. The first is when the patient with a pre-selected fact presents material or interprets the analyst's behaviour in conformity with an overvalued idea, thus constricting the analysis to the confines of his existing, mainly unconscious, beliefs. The second is when the analyst relieves his fear of losing his analytic identity in a situation of uncertainty or confusion by attaching himself to an overvalued idea, and then seeking confirmation in the patient for the beliefs which he unconsciously thinks are necessary for his own personal or professional equilibrium.

In the first of these instances the analyst's task is to discover the unconscious belief of the patient that is defining every situation in the analysis. In the second his task is to recognise his own overdetermined use of an idea and to try to understand his own behaviour. This may be unfinished business in his own analysis or it may be a specific counter-transference to his patient, in which case the unravelling of this is part of the patient's analysis and may reveal a re-enactment of an unconscious object relation in the transference.

As was discussed in Chapter 4, there are times when even though the analyst's interpretation is arrived at without unconscious prejudice and is put forward in an open-minded way the patient reacts as if his mind or soul is threatened with invasion. It is obviously important to distinguish this from the sensitivity some patients have to the risk of imposed belief, which leads them to react violently whenever an overdetermined idea of the analyst intrudes. It may not be possible to do this immediately or, in some patients, for some time.

The absent object is experienced in the paranoid–schizoid mode as a malignant presence, a '*no-thing*'. An interpretation reveals that what is referred to is not *the thing itself* but a representation or symbol of it. If the frustration and loss felt at the absence of the object itself can be tolerated, this enlarges the space available for thought by that amount. In Ps all 'thoughts' are experienced as space occupying 'no-things' and therefore interpretation is felt to be taking the place in the patient's mind that belongs to the missing object, the thing itself, which is regarded by the patient as his possession. There is therefore a sense of being robbed of a valued internal object by the analyst through the analyst's use of interpretation. We consider that in these very difficult situations in analysis it is necessary to explore very carefully the precise nature of the patient's negative experience of the analyst's interventions in order to sort out these differences.

With compliant patients like Mr L the difficulty is a different one. As with the patients described in Chapters 5 and 7, the problem is that the analyst will be encouraged to believe that his overvalued ideas are the selected fact, as consensual agreement is valued more highly than the truth.

9

Daydream, phantasy and fiction

History is the recital of facts represented as true. Fable, on the other hand, is the recital of facts represented as fiction.
(Voltaire, *Philosophical Dictionary*; in Tripp 1973: 218)

This chapter is devoted to formulating a different psychological explanation for the origins of serious fiction from those of escapist romance, and in it I suggest that this can be done by differentiation between unconscious phantasy and daydream, between psychic reality and psychic illusion. Freud spoke with two voices on literature: one when he was pursuing his general ideas on illusion and wish-fulfilment; and another when he had a theory derived from his clinical work that he wanted confirmed by his principal allies, the creative writers. In a chapter (Britton 1995a) that I wrote for a book on modern psychoanalytic views of Freud's 'Creative writers and daydreaming' (Freud 1908a) my criticism of Freud's paper was that it did not adequately differentiate between the *truth-seeking function* of some fiction and the *truth-evading function* of other fiction, that is, between serious creative writing and escapist literature: 'The difference between essentially truthful fiction and intentionally untruthful fiction can be accounted for once the concept of phantasy is enlarged beyond the wish fulfilling daydream' (Britton 1995a: 82–3).

The enlargement of the concept of unconscious phantasy was a result of the work of Melanie Klein, and was linked to her extension of the theory of sublimation and symbolism: 'Symbolism is the foundation of all phantasy, sublimation, and of every talent, since it is by way of symbolic equation that things, activities, and interests become the subject of libidinal phantasies' (Klein 1930: 220). She thought that what characterised the 'creative artist' was access to early infantile phantasy. '[if] symbol formation in infantile mental life is particularly rich', she claimed, 'it contributes to the development of every talent or even genius' (*ibid.*).

This enlargement of the term '*unconscious phantasy*' became contentious and was therefore a central part of the 'Controversial Discussions' which took place in the British Psycho-Analytical Society in 1941–5 to clarify the differences between Melanie Klein's views and those of Anna Freud. As Riccardo Steiner writes in the published account of the *Controversies*:

> [the] notion of unconscious phantasy (spelled with a 'ph' to differentiate it from the conscious 'fantasy') is probably the major theoretical theme of all the Scientific Discussions. When translating Freud from German into English during the twenties it had already been necessary to adopt a term, which would distinguish the unconscious character of 'phantasy', which Freud used relatively rarely, from its conscious aspects.
>
> (King and Steiner 1991: 242)

As a contribution to this debate Susan Isaacs produced a paper, 'The nature and function of phantasy', which is usually taken to be the Kleinian position statement on unconscious phantasy (Isaacs 1952: 67–121). In this she suggested that unconscious phantasy is the 'psychical expression . . . of instinctual needs' that Freud referred to in his comments on the id (Freud 1933a: 73). Unconscious phantasies, Isaacs maintained, are the mental representation of instinct, somatic and psychic experience, and underlie every mental process. This was a change in use of the term 'phantasy' from Freud's original *Phantasie* by extending it to include those psychic elements Freud referred to but which remained undefined and unnamed, lurking under such titles as 'psychical expression . . . of instinctual needs' (*ibid.*). Her justification for using the same term, *Phantasie*, as that which was applied by Freud and others to developmentally later more elaborated phenomena was that of genetic continuity.

I think an important aspect of this concept which got lost in the 'Controversial Discussions' and in Susan Isaacs paper is the distinction between infantile phantasies based on, or accompanying, actual experience (e.g. hunger pain as a biting object) and infantile phantasies conjured up to deny experience (a hallucinatory gratifying object). In part, this was because Klein had not yet introduced her theory of the paranoid-schizoid position and her concept of projective identification. Much was to follow which elucidated the ways in which unconscious phantasy is variously experienced and expressed, particularly by the work of Hanna Segal. As she wrote:

> The first hunger and the instinctual striving to satisfy that hunger are accompanied by the phantasy of an object capable of satisfying that hunger. . . . So long as the pleasure/pain principle is in ascendance,

phantasies are omnipotent and no differentiation between phantasy and reality-experience exists. The phantasised objects and the satisfaction derived from them are experienced as physical happenings.

(Segal 1964: 13)

This is also true, as she points out, of phantasies derived from negative experience:

a hungry, raging infant, screaming and kicking, phantasises that he is actually attacking the breast . . . and experiences his own screams which tear him and hurt him as the torn breast attacking him in his own inside. Therefore not only does he experience a want, but his hunger-pain and his own screams may be felt as a persecutory attack on his own inside.

(Segal 1964: 13)

Both these kinds of phantasy, of an ideal object as the source of goodness (based on somatic satisfaction) and of a bad object as the source of evil (based on somatic suffering), are in the mode of the paranoid-schizoid position. The hallucinatory wish-fulfilling object, with its function of the denial of loss by the omnipotent assertion of gain, is the forerunner of the *manic defence*.

In the mode of the depressive position, with the relinquishment of omnipotence and the notion of continuity the object can be felt to exist elsewhere in its absence. The suffering is felt to arise within the self as a consequence of something missing. When the absence of the object is recognised the place that the object originally occupied and left behind is experienced as space. If this space is felt to contain the promise of the return of the object it is felt to be benign, if idealised sacred. If, in contrast to this benign expectancy, it is believed that the space itself eliminates good objects – as an astronomical black hole eliminates matter – it is felt to be a malign space, possibly life-annihilating. The belief in benign space depends ultimately on the love for the object surviving its absence; thus a place is kept for the object's return. If manic omnipotent assertion is resorted to in order to sustain belief in the return, then some form of 'second coming' or millenarian hope becomes an article of religious faith. In contrast, *malignant space* arises when the idea of the object continuing to exist in its absence cannot be tolerated because it causes so much suffering. The object therefore is, in phantasy, annihilated. As a consequence of this, the space left by the object is presumed to be the cause of the object's disappearance and not simply to have been created by its absence. Hence a phantasy comes into existence of an *object-destructive space*.

Clinically, this gives rise to terror of space, external or internal, which leads to obsessive manipulation of space and time in order to eliminate the danger of gaps appearing in the external world, and compulsive space-filling mental activity to eradicate any gaps in psychic space. Some of this mental gap-filling is accomplished by auto-erotically based phantasy.

Klein did not regard auto-erotism as a preliminary stage of development but as co-existent with object-related activity, offering a compensatory alternative to or refuge from frustration or distressing sensations such as hunger. I think the phantasies associated with auto-erotic activity form the basis for hallucinatory gratification, and the line of phantasy development that stems from that primitive beginning reaches into the type of phantasies that Freud refers to as daydreams in his paper 'Creative writers and day-dreaming' (Freud 1908a). In *wishful psychosis* the deficit is denied by hallucinating the missing object, or by a delusion of *being it*.

Even when external reality is respected, auto-erotically-based phantasies may exist in parallel with a realistic attitude, as daydreams, in what Freud liked to describe as a *reservation*. He suggested in 'Formulations on the two principles of mental functioning' that 'with the introduction of the reality principle one species of thought-activity was split off'. He compares this psychic retreat with a Natural Park: 'a nation . . . will yet set aside certain areas for reservation in their original state . . . (E.g. Yellowstone Park)' (Freud 1911b: 222). I want to highlight this simile of a reservation, which he uses in other texts, because I think his choice of a spatial metaphor is significant and I have some ideas about the location of daydreams. I think that the psychic location in which daydreams take place, Freud's reservation, is a phantasised place, with physical characteristics resembling perceptual space attributed to it but clearly distinguished from perceptual space. In English this location is called *the imagination* when it is regarded as a place in the mind and not simply as a function. My theory on the origin of this phantasised psychic space is the subject of the next chapter.

In the earliest attempts to give an anatomical account of mental function imagination was represented as a *spatial compartment* of the brain, of equal proportion to the compartments of reason and memory. Later, in the *post-Enlightenment* period – when the newly emerging sciences rendered such anatomical naivety untenable, and the studies of brain and mind had begun to go their separate ways – Coleridge, with Wordsworth, made the most ambitious attempt to define the imagination. He subdivided what might be covered by the term under three headings: *primary imagination, secondary imagination* and the *fancy*. The first he held to be 'the living Power and prime Agent of all human Perception'; the second, 'an echo of the former, dissolving, diffusing, dissipating in order to recreate; struggling to idealise and to unify'; the third activity, for which he retained the old term 'the fancy', he regarded as an inferior activity doing nothing more than rear-ranging existing psychic materials in different time and space (Shawcross

1968, vol. II: 202). It is primary imagination that Mary Warnock has in mind when she concludes, after her impressive philosophical review of the concept of imagination from Locke through to the philosophers of the twentieth century, that 'we have come by a long and circuitous route to the place where Wordsworth led us. Imagination is our means of interpreting the world, and it is also our means of forming images in the mind' (Warnock 1976: 194). She added:

> We recognise a form as a form of something, as Wittgenstein said, by its relation with other things. It seems to me both plausible and convenient to give the name 'imagination' to what allows us to go beyond the barely sensory into the intellectual or thought imbued territory of perception.
>
> (Warnock 1976: 195)

Coleridge's *primary imagination* to my mind closely resembles Susan Isaac's concept of unconscious phantasy as the mental expression of all sensation and instinct. The *secondary imagination* is something taken to be creatively reconstructive and functions in the absence of the object; in Wordsworth's poetic accounts of secondary imagination it is usually consolatory, symbolic and sublimatory. Coleridge views the fancy as an inferior activity, much as Freud views *secondary revision* as a lesser function giving a superficial gloss to dreams in comparison with the other factors that constitute dream work (Freud 1900b: 490).

The more a work of fiction resembles obvious 'daydreaming', the more likely it is to be banal, emotionally undemanding, populist and to be ignored by serious critics. The more a work resonates with something unconscious and profoundly evocative, the more likely it is eventually to be recognised by the critically enlightened, even though its initial reception might be unfavourable. One could say that the more fictional writing resembles obvious daydreaming, the less weight it has, and the more it resembles real dreaming, the more seriously we take it. Freud's own comments on the profound effect of *King Lear* appear to provide some support for this idea. In 'The theme of the three caskets' Freud suggested that Shakespeare's 'regressive revision' of the traditional myth, which was the source of his *King Lear*, stripped away the distortions of wishful transformation and exposed us unconsciously to the powerful, disturbing, more archaic myth of three women in a man's life: 'the woman who bears him, the woman who is his mate and the woman who destroys him' (Freud 1913a: 301).

The part played by daydreams in the formation of real dreams is spelt out by Freud in *The Interpretation of Dreams*. Having described the first three factors, 'the tendency towards condensation, the necessity for evading censorship, and considerations of representability' (Freud 1900b: 490), he turned to the fourth factor, which he called secondary revision. He was more disparaging of this factor than of the other dream factors: 'This function behaves in the manner that the poet maliciously ascribes to philosophers; it fills up the gaps in the dream-structure with shreds and patches' (*ibid.*). He goes further, suggesting that it resembles daydreaming in its use of the raw material provided by the other dream factors to produce a narrative satisfying a naive desire for coherence and a plot to please its author:

> We might put it simply by saying that this fourth factor of ours seeks to mould the material offered to it into something like a day-dream. If, however, a day-dream of this kind has already been formed within the nexus of the dream-thoughts, this fourth factor in the dream-work will prefer to take possession of the ready-made day-dream and seek to introduce it into the content of the dream.
>
> (Freud 1900b: 492)

Just as Freud describes daydreams entering real dreams, so real dreams may penetrate daydreams and unconscious phantasies infiltrate conscious fantasies, thus giving an unexpected weight to fancifully constituted romantic or horrific fictions. The Frankenstein story ostensibly conjured up by Mary Shelley as her part in a literary game was based, according to her later account, on what Hindle calls a 'waking dream' (Hindle 1994: 6); it might as easily be described as a night terror (*pavor nocturnus*), a not uncommon neurotic symptom of childhood related to nightmare. Mary Shelley wrote in her Preface for the revised 1831 edition of the novel:

> I did not sleep, nor could I be said to think. My imaginations, unbidden, possessed and guided me, gifting the successive images that arose in my mind with a vividness far beyond the usual bounds of reverie. I saw – with shut eyes, but acute mental vision – I saw the pale student of unhallowed arts kneeling beside the thing he had put together.
>
> (Shelley 1831: 13–14)

She imagines the hope of Frankenstein that his creature, a terrible mockery of real Creation, would subside into dead matter, but after sleep the artist 'opens his eyes; behold the horrid thing stands at his bedside. . . . I opened mine in terror' (*ibid.*: 13). She then writes that the hideous phantom still haunts her; she cannot get rid of it. She continues:

> I must try to think of something else. I recurred to my ghost story. . . . O! if I could only contrive one which would frighten my reader as I myself had been frightened that night!

Swift as light and as cheering was the idea that broke in upon me. 'I have found it! what terrified me will terrify others'.

(Shelley 1831: 13–)

She continued 'On the morrow I announced that I had *thought of a story*' (*ibid.*: 14). So night terror becomes ghost story, which in due course becomes the great science-fiction, philosophical novel *Frankenstein (or, The Modern Prometheus)*. Her first thought appeared to be simply to rid herself of terror by projective identification, by evoking terror in others. The second thought is the creative one of making her night terror itself into a work of art, at which point she is both relieved and stimulated.

The ensuing story, though startlingly original, is like a real dream, obviously overdetermined. It has evident connections with her own birth, which caused her mother's death, and with her own baby's death at the age of ten days, as well as with the disturbing presence of her stepsister Claire Clairmont, pregnant by Byron, and her fear of being a victim of the omnipotent Utopianism of her husband, Shelley, as, in a sense, she had been of that of her father Godwin. Even the day's residue as progenitor is provided for us in her Preface when she tells of the conversations of the previous day between Shelley and Byron on Erasmus Darwin's experiments and the possibilities of revitalisation with galvanism. But I would suggest that its continuing power as a modern myth derives from the profound, primitive, unconscious phantasies derived from the dream life of Mary Shelley which inhabit the story.

Having described a real dream, or night terror, being transformed into daydream and then into a work of fiction, I would like to return to the reverse situation, where daydream is used as fiction but may carry into the fiction unconscious phantasy. One of the best examples of the use of daydreams as source material for later literature must be that of Emily Brontë, who used them in particular for her poetry. Emily and Anne Brontë started the Gondal game as children and continued to play it, together or alone, until their deaths. It was set in an imaginary island in the North Pacific called Gondal, with very detailed dramatic events and characters with strong Byronic overtones. They wrote an extensive prose story of Gondal that is no longer extant; what remains are the poems based on this background, its characters and their situations. Emily was a great poet and some of the Gondal poetry is very fine, but it is likely that its prose sources had strong resemblance to the daydreams of adolescent girls. Derek Stanford, who feels strongly about this, suggests that 'what is good in Gondal is incidental and irrelevant to it . . . the lyrical beauty of expression, the fervour and profundity of thought in these poems is out of all proportion to the ramshackle structure and childish melodramatic plots' (Spark and Stanford 1966: 125). He further suggests – and this has considerable

115

relevance for our theme – that 'the Gondal structure of characters and incidents represented a conscious creation on the part of Emily and Anne; and
that this conscious framework acted as a magnet, a call boy, to Emily's
unconscious mind' (*ibid.*: 129).

I think we can see an example of this in a Gondal poem of thirty-eight
stanzas called *The Prisoner*. The first three stanzas are well written and
evocative, setting the scene; they remind one of the opening part of
Wuthering Heights. From stanza four to stanza seventeen the verse is close to
the plot of unjust imprisonment, in a dank dungeon, of a beautiful, tragic,
heroine discovered close to death by a childhood friend and potential
admirer, Lord Julian. These verses are melodramatic, thinly disguised
masochistic, erotic daydreams. The seventh stanza gives an example of their
quality:

> The captive raised her face; it was as soft and mild
> As sculptured marble saint or slumbering, unweaned child;
> It was so soft and mild, it was so sweet and fair,
> Pain could not trace a line nor grief a shadow there!
> (Brontë 1992: 14)

We can echo Charles Morgan: 'no genius was needed for the composition of that!' (Spark and Stanford 1966: 129). However, there follows a
change in quality so sudden, violent and considerable that Charles Morgan
thought that the connection between the earlier and later sections might be
an editorial error, which was not the case (*ibid.*: 132). The 'poem . . . , from
being a dreary exercise in a then outmoded style of Gothic gloom, buds
out into one of the greatest statements of mystical experience in English
verse' (*ibid.*: 129). From the middle of stanza seventeen to stanza twenty-
three the poetry reaches considerable heights as the heroine speaks of her
wish for death and touches a universal desire to be free of life. In stanza
twenty-one she raises the spirit of negation with a sequence of inversions –
unseen/revealed, sense gone/essence feels, on wing/in harbour,
stoops/bound – evoking a sense of freedom from the restraints of logic,
time and place that are to be found at the reality frontier of the ego:

> Then dawns the Invisible, the Unseen its truth reveals;
> My outward sense is gone, my inward essence feels –
> Its wings are almost free, its home, its harbour found;
> Measuring the gulf it stoops and dares the final bound!
> (Brontë 1992: 15)

In the subsequent stanza she describes her longing to be free of the
restraints of the physical senses:

116

Oh, dreadful is the check – intense the agony
When the ear begins to hear and the eye begins to see;
When the pulse begins to throb, the brain to think again,
The soul to feel the flesh and the flesh to feel the chain!

(Brontë 1992: 15)

In these verses it is Emily who speaks, from a different place in her internal world from the make-believe world of Gondal. The verse implies that a more profound truth is expressed: that she feels imprisoned, not in a cell, but in her own mind and her own body:

When the pulse begins to throb, the brain to think again,
The soul to feel the flesh and the flesh to feel the chain!

(Brontë 1992: 15)

We are led to hear this as 'the flesh *is* the chain', and to feel that life itself is the unwelcome morning intruder and death the deliverer. As in other places in her writing, a *death-wish* finds a poetic voice.

In order to speculate further on this poem I would like to anticipate the notion developed in the next chapter. This is the idea that the imagination as a place in the mind where unwitnessed events take place is in origin the phantasised primal scene. In the next chapter this mental space is called *the 'other room'*. Gondal, for example, is an imaginary world located in the mental space first developed by the phantasy of a never to be entered 'other room' in which parental existence continues during parental absence. Emily therefore has a Gondal daydream which is based on and elaborates a real unconscious phantasy of the primal scene. The version we have just been looking at is sadomasochistic, with mother as chained victim of a tyrannical father. Into this scenario, by projective identification, Emily inserts in the place of her mother a romanticised version of herself as heroine and victim, producing an erotic-masochistic Gondal daydream which forms the conscious basis for the poem. I am inclined to think that the unconscious sadomasochistic primal scene is itself an exciting defensive transformation of a depressive phantasy of a dying mother and an abandoned infant. Having by projective identification put herself in mother's place, she calls up her phantasy of death as the seductive rescuer. What he rescues her from was in origin her own infantile distress, incarceration and separation from her mother, now projected into the phantasised primal scene and erotised in the process. By this means the scene is transformed into one where intercourse with death forms the basis of an erotic scene. When this more profound material finds its way into the poem it speaks to us differently, resonating with our own unconscious phantasies.

Having pursued a lengthy diversion in order to explore daydream and unconscious phantasy, I would like to return to my contention that, on literature, Freud speaks with two voices: one when he is pursuing his general ideas on illusion and another when he has a theory derived from his clinical practice that he wants confirmed by his allies, the major figures of literature.

Freud was to change his ideas fundamentally on the relation of the inside to the outside world in the years after *The Ego and the Id* (1923a). He even relented on his evaluation of religion:

> I perceived ever more clearly that the events of human history, the interactions between human nature, cultural development and the precipitates of primeval experiences (the most prominent example of which is religion) are no more than a reflection of the dynamic conflicts between the ego, the id and the super-ego, which psycho-analysis studies in the individual – are the very same processes repeated upon a wider stage. In the *Future of an Illusion* [Freud 1927a] I expressed an essentially negative valuation of religion. Later, I found a formula which did better justice to it: while granting that its power lies in the truth which it contains, I showed that truth was not a material but a historical truth.
>
> (Freud 1935: 72)

Though *he* neglected to do so, *we* can apply this to literature and borrow his revised formula. The power of fiction lies in the truth it contains, which is not historical or material but psychic truth; fiction can express the truth just as facts can be used against it. This is not material truth based on corre-spondence with external reality, but psychic truth based on its correspondence with psychic reality. Clinically, just as we meet denial in relation to external events, so we meet denial in relation to internal events. In writing we find at times falsification of the external world, but it is prob-able that falsification of the internal world is even more common. It is not something that need remain theoretical and abstract, certainly not for an analyst; daily we hear serious fiction and escapist fiction in our practice. Some of the phantasies of our patients express psychic reality and some create psychic unreality. Our question, when hearing these phantasies, is not whether they correspond to external reality, but whether they are attempting to reach for unconscious beliefs or to evade them. We do not meet *super-realism* as a not uncommon defence against the internal world; it is achieved by adhering to the outside world and constructing a *pseudo-psychic* life to fit it. *Absolute idealism*, practised not as a philosophy, but as an everyday defence against external reality, we also meet not uncommonly. Winnicott (1960b) dichotomised the *true self* and *false self* in patients who divided themselves between a facile adjustment to external objects and an authentic but *inner* and entirely subjective life. Rosenfeld (1971), in contrast, described patients whose hostility to significant object relationships *outside* the self manifested itself as a *destructive narcissism* which insisted that attention should be paid and value attached only to solipsistic ideas. In Chapter 13 I explore these alternative configurations in the writings of Milton and Blake.

In art and literature, I think, the analogue of the false self is social realism, representation devoid of emotional significance. The analogue of destructive narcissism in the arts is that version of the Aesthetic movement that insists that art is autotelic, in the sense that it neither comes from life nor affects it, and that it is only about art itself – that a poem is only about poetry, a painting only about painting.

Unconscious phantasy through symbolism seeks sublimation in daily life. Religion was, prior to the wholesale secularism of our own century, part of daily life and offered symbolic expression of unconscious phantasy; theology was the means of studying in its own terms the psychological facts it expressed. No doubt theologians were sometimes reaching for the truth and sometimes trying to evade it with their formulations. Since the decline of religion, art has assumed a more significant role as the provider of a shared area, outside the self, for the symbolic representation of those forever unseen unconscious phantasies that are the bedrock of psychic reality – the psychic counterparts to Kant's noumena, the unknowable *things in themselves*. In my opinion, literature and the arts, at their best, are attempting to realise what is most profoundly internal in the external.

There is a place for escapism in literature as in life, just as there is a place for dreamless sleep. Freud's reservation for the preservation of wishful thinking, or Winnicott's resting place of illusion can be provided by books, films, the theatre and television, but these resting places are not staging posts on the way to fulfilment in life or satisfaction in literature. They are species of what John Steiner (1993) has called psychic retreats, which if taken to be permanent areas of refuge become pathological organisations. If used excessively, escapist fiction in such forms as soap opera becomes just such a refuge, with the element of addiction that characterises such psychic retreats.

Freud's (1911b) 'reservation', Winnicott's 'resting place of illusion' (Rodman 1987: 123) and John Steiner's (1993) 'psychic retreats' all have spatial connotations, as does our everyday use in English of the phrase 'in the imagination'. Earlier in this chapter I said that I wanted to pursue a speculation on the phantasised location of this psychic space called the imagination when it is regarded as a place in the mind and not simply as a function. This is the subject of Chapter 10, 'The other room and poetic space'.

119

---------------- 10 ----------------

The other room and poetic space

> And as imagination bodies forth
> The form of things unknown, the poet's pen
> Turns them to shapes, and gives to airy nothing
> A local habitation and a name.
>
> (Shakespeare 1969: 125)

According to Scott Ellidge:

> The psychology of Milton's time was . . . neat and simple. The brain, seat of mental *faculties* . . . consisted of three cells. To the first cell, that of the fancy (literally *phantasia* or 'imagination'), the spirits communicated the messages from the five senses. The fancy passed these images on to the second cell, that of reason, which acted upon the image (creating perhaps what we might call an idea) before passing it on to the third cell, that of the faculty of memory.
>
> (Scott Ellidge 1975: 463–4)

At night only reason slept. There are two things which strike me particularly about the seventeenth-century brain–mind model: one is the size of the faculty of imagination in relation to reason and memory; and the other is that a physical space, a compartment in the brain, is given to it.

When we imagine things taking place we do so in a space, therefore we have also to imagine the space they take place in. Gaston Bachelard, in *The Poetics of Space*, envisaged this as a room 'inhabited thanks to the image, just as one inhabits an image which is "in the imagination" . . . a room which the author bears within himself, and which he has made live with a life that does not exist in life' (Bachelard 1964: 228–9). This passage surprised and encouraged me when I first read it because I had already equated *the imagi-*

120

nation, conceived of as a place in the mind, with something I had begun to call *the 'other room'* on the basis of my clinical work. The room described by Bachelard, which 'the author bears within himself' (*ibid.*), seemed to me to be the same room. I had adopted the phrase 'the other room' as a result of the imagery represented in the dreams and discourse of a particular patient. Once I noticed it, I found it in various forms in the material of a number of patients. I was to meet it again clinically under the title 'another place', signifying a space that could be imagined or imaginatively created by a work of art but never physically entered. If this imaginative space, as in the visual arts or the theatre, is made to appear coincident with actual physical space it lends to that space of actuality the properties of the 'other room' in which phantasised events take place – but only while the participating observer allows the artist to enter his own 'other room' of imagination and refurnish it. It requires on the part of the audience that willing suspension of disbelief described by Coleridge (Shawcross 1968, vol. II: 6).

When we place our phantasies about events in this psychic 'other room' we know we are *imagining* something. It is the space for fiction. When we misguidedly locate phantasies that properly belong in the 'other room' of our imagination in the actuality of perceptual space instead, we are having visions. This is a privilege normally reserved for our night dreams. In waking life such visions are hallucinations or are regarded as privileged supernatural visitations sanctioned by religious belief. If when we witness actual events that generate phantasies we fail to locate the phantasies aroused by events in the imagination and thus believe that we witnessed, not only events, but also our phantasies, then we are deluded. If we are prepared to accept that the proper place for these phantasies is the 'other room' we can use our imaginations.

In his writings on 'transitional phenomena' Winnicott described a mental space as arising by the mutual consent of the two persons of the dyadic relationship of mother–infant; he conceived it as a sort of no-man's land between subject and object, a neutral zone for illusion (Winnicott 1951: 229–42). Where I differ from this is in seeing it as arising from within triadic *triangular space*. I said in Chapter 4 that I think triangular space origi- nates when a position comes into existence from which one can be an observer of a relationship between two others. What I am suggesting in this chapter is that the 'other room' of the imagination comes into existence when this relationship is invisible. It is, in other words, the location of the unwitnessed *primal scene*. I think the quintessential primal scene is not observed but imagined, that it is the activity we believe takes place in our absence between our primary object and the other member of what we have come to call the Oedipal triangle. The invisible primal scene is popu- lated only by our imagination; it is the space for fiction.

As I said, this room which 'the author bears within himself' I thought of as the 'other room' because I took the phrase from a patient. He used it as a recurrent expression to describe any room other than the consulting room in which the analysis took place. It was in this 'other room' that events took place which he could never know about, he said. I became convinced from his material that the prototype for this 'other room' was the parental bedroom, a place which has acquired mythic qualities in the world of psychoanalysis.

In psychoanalytic discourse the parental bedroom has been the location of the primal scene since Freud's description of it in the 'Wolf Man' case (Freud 1918). There he not only took great trouble to establish it in the actual history of his patient, but also suggested that it was an *Urphantasie*, a primal phantasy or innate idea. This moved him on to ground shared with Jung, and he takes a lot of trouble to differentiate his ideas from those of Jung. In particular, Freud thought that Jung had discarded the reality of infantile sexuality, the importance of early sexual experience and the intensity of the erotic imagination of the child. Nevertheless, at the moment of suggesting the existence of an innate phantasy of parental intercourse Freud was moving on to common ground. A number of Jungian analysts think that this move has gone further in the work of Melanie Klein and Bion.

Klein placed the primal scene centre stage; indeed she suggested, following Otto Rank (1915), that the theatrical stage had its origins in the imaginary location of the parental sexual act (Klein 1924). In her analysis of Erna, a 6-year-old girl, she found 'that theatre and performances of all kinds symbolised coitus between her parents' (*ibid*.: 39). Klein added a footnote: 'In my paper, "Early Analysis", I have considered in greater detail the universal symbolic significance of the theatre, performances, productions, etc., representing intercourse between the parents. I may also refer to Rank, "Das Schauspiel im Hamlet" [1915]' (*ibid*.). In her account it is clear she thinks the primal scene is an innate psychic template waiting for events to furnish it with content. Bion's (1967) notion of innate pre-conceptions makes it even clearer that Jung's (1959) theory of *Archetypes* anticipated these developments. What the Klein/Bion conceptual development does that, perhaps, Jung's theory does not is to include infantile sexuality, phantasy and actual experience in the incarnation of innate forms, which are therefore not just fulfilled by experience but given shape by it. There is an archetype of Jung's, 'the divine syzygies, the male–female pairs of deities' (*ibid*.: 59), which I think of as the primal romantic couple, that is, the idealised Oedipal parents who exist only in the 'other room', the imagined, unwitnessed part of their lives. In my version of this I had thought of it as a phantasised ideal, super-sexual parental couple – the figures of myth, the stuff of opera, the stars of the Screen and the objects of endless media voyeurism. It is this couple that is represented by Milton as the prelapsarian, primal couple Adam and Eve. We, as the non-participating observers, are represented by Satan in this account of the primal scene; already dislodged from Heaven we are compelled to imagine Paradise. At that moment Eden is the 'other room'; Satan, however, complains that this 'room of bliss' has been stolen from him and if he cannot regain it he can at least have its occupants evicted (Milton 1975: 95–6).

In Paradise Lost, Book IV, Satan first surveys Eden as a cormorant, perched on 'the tree of life . . . devising death' (Milton 1975: 90). But it is in his next series of disguises, first as a lion and then as a tiger, that he witnesses his first primal scene; the coupling of our ancestral parents, Adam and Eve:

> . . . aside the devil turned
> For envy, yet with jealous leer malign
> eyed them askance, and to himself thus plained.
> Sight hateful, sight tormenting! Thus these two
> Imparadised in one another's arms
> The happier Eden, shall enjoy their fill
> Of bliss on bliss, while I to hell am thrust,
> Where neither joy nor love, but fierce desire,
> Among our other torments not the least,
> Still unfulfilled with pain of longing pines.
>
> (Milton 1975: 99)

His curse on the couple still haunts us:

> . . . Live while ye may,
> Yet happy pair; enjoy, till I return,
> Short pleasures, for long woes are to succeed.
>
> (Milton 1975: 100)

Therefore we fear the evil eye when we believe we are once more 'imparadised'.

When we claim to be one of the 'happy pair' we rid ourselves by projection of that aspect of ourselves which is forever 'unfulfilled with pain of longing', and with it we project our potential for envy and jealousy. Having done so, we fear the envy of others, become anxious with success and prone to placation by sacrifice or renunciation. Clinically, this is familiar and frequent in analysis in various intensities, and in various forms of negative therapeutic reaction we pay a sacrificial price for our good fortune. You will have noticed that I described this as happening when we claim to be one of *the* happy pair, that is, not just one of *a* happy pair but one of *the* happy pair, one of the primal couple. We can never be the participants in our own phantasised primal scene; nor can we ever occupy a place in that 'other room' where our objects meet in our absence. If we claim to have a place in our own imagined primal scene – to be one or the other, or both, members of the primal couple – we do so by projective identification, thus creating an illusion designed to protect us from the jealousy and envy intrinsic to the Oedipus situation. By becoming one of a parental couple we do not become one of our own parents; nor by sharing a nuptial bed do we become participants in what is forever the primal scene of our internal parents. Similarly, by becoming analysts we do not finally become the analyst of our own transference phantasies. If, as is not uncommon, this illusion is buttressed by actual success, then I think the *real* achievement is felt to be stolen property or false goods, and therefore the occasion of depressive guilt, manic assertiveness or persecutory anxiety.

Clinically, this seems to me prone to occur where the primal scene has remained idealised, where the parental relationship, rather than the infantile relationship itself, has been seen by the child as the ultimate source of happiness or triumphant success. In some cases this results in an idealisation of marriage and everything thought to be 'adult' in life; in others it gives rise to what might be called complacent coupling; in yet others it leads to a sense of permanent grievance that the individual has not simply suffered a deprivation in life but been deprived of a birthright.

Sometimes the idealised parental sexuality is claimed for the self by projective identification with one or other of the primal couple. This last use of the primal scene, I think, gives rise to hysteria, with its histrionic sexuality and erotisation of most of life's transactions. I take the view that hysteria first described in analysis as arising from phantasised incestuous sexuality is based on projective identification with one or other member of the primal couple – in other words, the so-called classical Oedipus complex, in which incestuous sex with one parent and murder of the other are given effect by the usurpation, by phantasised projective identification, of one or other parent's place in the primal scene. This gives substance to what is otherwise only a conscious or unconscious daydream; in other words, it is believed and therefore has real psychic consequences, such as guilt. It also imbues the afflicted individual's sexual life with a dramatised quality arising from the fact that the individual is unconsciously playing a leading part in a theatrical performance scripted by him- or herself, based on his or her own phantasies of the primal scene. I would like to illustrate what I mean by describing a dream from the analysis of a patient who suffered from hysterical symptoms.

The patient was a young American professional writer of considerable talent but who was suffering from writing block and suicidal thoughts; she was also prey to hysterical and psychosomatic symptoms. In contrast to her intellectually serious, rather tormented fiction, which was usually about marriage, she was given to daydreaming in a blatantly unsophisticated way

124

about romantic encounters. In analysis she formed an erotic transference of delusional intensity, precisely as described in Freud's paper 'Observations on transference-love' (Freud 1915). The following dream was reported after a little time in analysis. The manifest dream contained a number of details which, by the patient's associations, linked the man in the dream both to her analyst and to her father; the girl-woman on the bed looked like an actress with the same name as the patient's mother.

The room in the dream was vaguely historical in appearance. An older man was doing something sexual on a bed to someone who was somehow both a woman and a girl; the patient felt the girl-woman to be herself, but at the same time she was watching the scene secretly from within a sort of closet. As the watcher she was feeling afraid; as the girl-woman on the bed she was aware of feeling very excited sexually.

My point in describing this is to suggest that in her dream the patient was watching a phantasised version of the primal scene in which she had inserted herself into the identity of her mother, producing the girl-woman. The sequence I am suggesting is as follows: the young woman had an unconscious phantasy of herself watching the primal scene between her parents; this was transformed by a phantasy of her taking her mother's place by projective identification. The dream was enacted, in phantasy, by the patient, who believed herself to be involved in a secret sexual transaction disguised as an analysis, the outcome of which she thought would be marriage with the analyst. In the context of our discussion it is of interest that the relinquishment of this Oedipal illusion in the course of analysis exposed the patient to intense jealousy, envy and various aspects of a negative transference not previously present; it also enabled her, after a period of mourning, to pursue her own work and sexual life freely and productively.

Psychoanalysis provides us with an opportunity to explore these ideas about psychic spaces because they are manifest directly in practice and not as theoretical abstractions. In hysteria, I have suggested, individuals try to solve the problem of the 'other place' by living in it through projective identification, thus vacating their own room and the one shared as a patient with the analyst. In this way, the consulting room becomes in phantasy the parental bedroom. The risks of enactment that arise from the powerful phantasies provoked by that transformation in the transference and counter-transference are testified to in the history of psychoanalysis and remain a constant threatening complication of the process.

There are two other clinical situations that I think the concept of the 'other room' throws some light on. In one the 'other room' remains a distant unexplored place ignored and free of phantasies. The result is that the individual is described as 'lacking in imagination'. In the second, in contrast, the dividing psychic wall of distinction between 'this room' and the 'other room', the perceived and the imagined, has collapsed. At these times such patients take the room they share with the analyst to be the 'other room', and whatever phantasies they might have about events taking place in the 'other room' they presume are taking place in the consulting room. In other words, they take their imagination to be actualised in the consulting room, to use Joseph Sandler's (1976a, 1976b) concept of perceptual identity. Just as triangular space collapses into a dyadic mode of two psychic dimensions, leaving no room for reflective thought, as I described in Chapter 4, so no mental space exists for non-consequential phantasy about events in absentia. In such circumstances here and there, like now and then, collapse into one time-space. Everything the primary object does is done in a dyadic mode, whether it is done in the presence or the absence of the self; there is no conception of an independent relationship with a third object and therefore everything that the object does is done for or against the self. At these times the analyst's absence is taken to be an assault on the patient and not an event in the analyst's life. The problems for the analyst of finding him- or herself moving through the patient's psychic space when moving within his or her room have been discussed in earlier chapters. I want to contrast this with the other clinical extremity of 'lack of imagination' in order to delineate the customary place of the imagination in analysis.

I will call one such patient Mr D. He described himself as lacking in imagination, and that is how he was described by others. What this meant in common parlance was that he did not use his imagination when thinking about other people or alternative possibilities. In analysis this was manifest in relation to the analyst. He made no claim whatever to know, on the strength of his imagination, what the analyst was thinking or doing, either in his presence or in his absence. Far from it; he claimed instead that he never imagined anything about it. It soon became evident, however, that his mind was not wholly occupied with objective reality as he spent an unusual amount of his time daydreaming. These daydreams were not clearly identified by the patient as imaginary, as he took them to be possible adventures, usually of an erotic kind, but they were clearly differentiated from any serious intentions in that direction and were free from anxiety. Mr D vaguely believed that only moral restraint on his part was preventing these pipedreams becoming projects. In this he clearly took no account of the reality of the other person or of any external circumstance. There was no fear of fulfilment and no fear of disappointment; there were no emotional consequences, as he did not believe in them. Nor did he altogether disbelieve in them; belief was willingly suspended. In this area of his mental life the state of mind I characterised in Chapter 5 as the 'as-if' mode was operating. However, unlike the 'as-if' personality, his personal relations and dealings with the external world were sharp and realistic.

In the terms I am using, Mr D, within his daydreams, placed himself in the 'other room'. Thus he never imagined what people did elsewhere in his absence; he used his imagination to live in a daydream. Unlike the hysteric, his phantasised occupation of the primal scene was uncontaminated by reality, either psychic or external. His conscious fantasies were inconsequential because he never believed in them.

One of his most important screen memories was that his mother told him when he was a child he would never be the man his father was; whatever he was like when he grew up he could never be such a wonderful man. Mr D took her at her word and preserved this version of an unassailable, incomparable father in his mind as his mother's husband. This unfortunately did not resemble the father he grew to know from his own dealings with him; he saw him instead as a neurotically inhibited man who regarded himself as a failure. The 'father he could never be', however, persisted as an image of what he was not and became the template for men he admired. In the analysis it formed the basis of an idealised transference. This unfortunately left him with a low opinion of himself and his prospects. The father who dominated his internal life in this idealised way was the father of the 'other room', whom he, in his heart of hearts, really believed was a fiction of his mother's. The figures he admired in his adult life he thought of as successful in impressing others but probably defective in their private lives or within themselves. Therefore when by projective identification he became in phantasy this Oedipal father he became not only a character of fiction but a fictional character, not an imagined hero of the primal scene but a figure of his mother's daydream. Thus it gave him space for fiction, but the only fiction it produced was relatively unelaborated wish-fulfilment.

Such daydreams are the source of the sort of fiction I have described as escapist and which Freud saw as existing as a reservation for the preservation of wishes. Though capable of deep feeling and a fine aesthetic sensibility, my patient saw anything romantic as unreal. His view of everyday life, in contrast, was all too real and earnest. In this he could not differ more from William Blake, who saw Beulah as the route to divine reality and this material world as illusion. As I will describe in Chapter 14, Blake described Beulah as 'a realm of mild moony lustre, and soft sexual delusions' and 'a place where Contraries are equally True' (Blake 1927: 518). Mr D placed a very high value on realism, and the equally high value he placed on any sensuously based phantasy led to its internal segregation in daydreaming. He was clear that the price he had to pay for the retention of his daydreams was their separation from life and the withholding from them of belief. It meant that he was unusually free from self-deception and wish-fulfilling beliefs about the external world, but it left the everyday transactions of his life denuded of coloration and his curiosity impaired about events beyond the compass of his factual knowledge.

11

Wordsworth: the loss of presence and the presence of loss

> . . . let him never come back to us;
> There would be doubt, hesitation, and pain,
> Forced praise on our part – the glimmer of twilight,
> Never glad confident morning again.
> (Browning 1845: 60)

The man castigated by Browning in the poem for being the inspirational leader lost to young radical poets was William Wordsworth. Browning wrote this when he was 32. As an older man, perhaps having undergone similar changes, he partially retracted it. 'I did in my hasty youth', he wrote in a letter of 1875, 'presume to use the great and venerable personality of Wordsworth as a sort of painter's model' (Browning 1845: 61). In 1845, when he wrote the poem, he felt affronted by Wordsworth's change of political and poetic persona from revolutionary eighteenth-century innovator to established Victorian Poet Laureate, the more so because of a sense of being betrayed by the best:

> We that had loved him so, followed him, honoured him,
> Lived in his mild and magnificent eye,
> Learned his great language, caught his clear accents,
> Made him our pattern to live and to die!
> (Browning 1845: 60–1)

However, denunciation or not, Browning's lines ' . . . the glimmer of twilight,/Never glad confident morning again' echo the lines of Wordsworth's famous 'Ode', in which he describes the loss of the 'visionary gleam':

There was a time when meadow, grove, and stream,
The earth, and every common sight,
To me did seem
Apparelled in celestial light,
The glory and the freshness of a dream.
It is not now as it has been of yore;–
Turn whereso'er I may,
By night or day,
The things which I have seen I now can see no more.

(Wordsworth 1984: 297)

The first four stanzas of this poem Wordsworth wrote on 27 March 1802, a few days before his thirty-second birthday, and he took them the next day to Coleridge. It provoked an even more despairing poetic response from Coleridge, in the form of a poem that began as an unpublished 'Letter' to Sarah Hutchinson, his very recently lost love, and ended as 'Dejection: an ode', which was published in the *Morning Post*. As Richard Holmes describes, 'The first version is a passionate declaration of love and renunciation, of almost hysterical intensity; the final version is a cool, beautifully shaped, philosophical Ode on the loss of hope and creative power' (Holmes 1989: 318). Wordsworth also was involved in a crucial moment in his love life in the spring of 1802, and the two poet's crises involving the Hutchinson sisters and Dorothy Wordsworth were clearly interactive if not interrelated. A month before writing *The Ode* Wordsworth had become engaged to Mary Hutchinson. He was planning before marrying to meet Annette Vallon, after ten years' separation, and their illegitimate child Caroline, whom he would see for the first time. The meeting was to be in France, a country he had been excluded from since his days there of passion and revolution ten years before. His marriage would not end only that emotional connection; it also challenged the poetic trinity of Coleridge, Dorothy and himself. No doubt these external events, with their immediate emotional implications, played a part in the verses, which are so expressive of a lost perceptual past. There is ample evidence, however, that more basic internal processes were at issue. Both poets focus on a feared loss of imagination or spontaneity and both had expressed this earlier in their different ways. A year earlier Coleridge had declared: 'The Poet is dead in me' (quoted in Gill 1989: 200). Wordsworth had anticipated this in his 'Lines written a few miles above Tintern Abbey' in 1798, when he was 28 and regarded himself as mature. In that poem he contrasts the sober, sad reflection of maturity with his youth, when he had direct access to joy:

. . . For I have learned
To look on nature, not as in the hour

129

Of thoughtless youth, but hearing oftentimes
The still, sad music of humanity.
(Wordsworth 1984: 132)

Accompanying the 'still sad music' is the feeling of a 'presence' that is 'interfused' with 'setting suns', 'round oceans', blue skies, 'the mind of man' and 'all objects of thought'. This 'feeling of a presence' and the capacity for thought are the 'abundant recompense' Wordsworth believed he gained for the loss of bliss, in which nothing intervened between passionate expectation and physical presence. His verse is often at its best when evoking a sense of loss:

Though nothing can bring back the hour
Of splendour in the grass, of glory in the flower;
We will grieve not, rather find
Strength in what remains behind.
(Wordsworth 1984: 302)

It is when the *presence of loss* disappears from his verse that something of the quality implied by Browning is really lost. It seems to me that in 1804, when he completed the remaining stanzas of *The Ode*, he was speaking with two voices on the subject of the loss of a direct visionary presence. When he sings with one voice, as in the ode quoted above and in some of the lines of the 1805 *Prelude*, the presence of loss is unmistakable and the feeling profound; in other places there is another voice in which it seems denied or, as in the 'Ode to duty', repudiated and there is sense of assertion rather than realisation. In Book 6, lines 61 to 63, of the 1805 *Prelude*, written on his forty-fourth birthday, he denies the loss later referred to by Browning:

Four years and thirty, told this very week,
Have I now been a sojourner on earth,
And yet the morning gladness is not gone.
(Wordsworth 1979: 188)

Wordsworth's notion of a *presence* which in his youth provided him with a direct physical experience of bliss and later, after its disappearance, interfused all things, is like the incarnation of Christ, followed after his disappearance by Pentecost and the 'inspiration' of the Holy Ghost. Wordsworth's own theory about the origin of this presence is to be found in the first version of his poetic self-analysis, now known as the two-book or 1799 *Prelude*. William Wordsworth was 29 when he wrote it. We are separated from that relatively unknown radical young poet by Wordsworth the eminent Victorian. This is a particular difficulty with Wordsworth because, unlike Keats, Shelley or Byron, he lived to be an old man and, though he remained a considerable writer, I believe that he did not survive as the great poet he once was beyond his thirty-fifth year. He wrote very good verse later but it is generally thought that all his great poetry was written by 1806, including *The Prelude*, though this was not published until after his death. In this respect he is a striking example of one possible outcome for the creative artist, which Elliot Jaques described in his paper on 'Death and the mid-life crisis' (1968).

Jaques coined this term when he noted 'a marked tendency towards crisis in the creative work of great men in their middle and late thirties' (Jaques 1968: 226). This crisis may have different outcomes in the work of the artists who survived beyond 35. On the negative side, output might come to a stop, as in the case of Rossini, or become less original; on the positive side, it is for some, such as J. S. Bach or Beethoven, the point where the nature of their work deepens. Elliott Jaques suggested that, 'With the awareness of the onset of the last half of life, unconscious depressive anxieties are aroused, and the repetition and continuation of the working through of the infantile depressive position are required' (*ibid.*: 242). He vividly describes familiar defences against the renewed depressive position and the risk of character deterioration if this is not successful. Associated with the working through of the depressive position integration would be the task and the problem in the artistic work itself. Coleridge, both in the deterioration of his character and the cessation of his poetry, would appear to exemplify it. This would correspond with his long-term problems of integration and his inability to complete his work, as in the case of *Christabel*. Wordsworth, however, I would see as affected in a different way, and he therefore affords us with an example of someone whose creativity was diminished by a mid-life crisis, not at the frontier of the depressive position, but in the *post-depressive position*. I think his mid-life difficulty was in confronting change and uncertainty when his poetic world fragmented once more, and once too often, with a defensive, regressive move into a psychic retreat of coherent belief and moral certainty. In the terms I used in Chapter 6, Coleridge lost his way between $Ps(n) \rightarrow D(n)$, that is, in the pre-depressive position, whereas Wordsworth's mid-life crisis appears to have been between $D(n) \rightarrow Ps(n+1)$, in the post-depressive position.

The Ode and a good proportion of *The Prelude* could be described as poetic accounts of the depressive position as Wordsworth gives us a description of the internal struggle to relinquish the unselfconscious bliss of a youth with an idealised future in favour of the imperfect but realised present of maturity. But in another poem written at much the same time, in 1804, he gives us a sad premonition of the eventual outcome of his mid-life crisis. He begins this on a note of triumphal obedience, 'Stern Daughter of the Voice of God! O Duty'. Later in the poem, in a spirit of anguish, he declaims as to why it is that now he must only have recourse to such a source for guidance:

> Me this unchartered freedom tires;
> I feel the weight of chance desires:
> My hopes no more must change their name,
> I long for a repose which ever is the same.
>
> (Wordsworth 1984: 296)

What a contrast to the passage from the 1799 *Prelude*, where he asserts that the survival of poetic power and of human insight depends on the constant struggle of the 'first creative sensibility' to resist what he called the 'regular action of the world' (Wordsworth 1979: 24).

It was in 1804 that he assembled his second version of *The Prelude* in thirteen books, and he was such a secondary reviser that before his death in 1850 he had completed another version in fourteen books. It was this latter version that his wife published after his death, and it was only in this final version that *The Prelude* was known to the public until the 1920s, when the 1805 version became available. The two-book *Prelude* of 1799 did not appear in print until 1974. Thanks to the wealth of Wordsworth scholarship of our own times, we now have contact with the poet of 29 who produced this incredibly original, self-based notion of psychic development.

The 1805 thirteen-book *Prelude* contains some of the finest poetry in our language in its unexpurgated and untrimmed form, unlike the 1850 version. However, I think that the full impact of his originality is greatest in the earliest two-book 1799 version, where it is closest to its origins in the flood of recollection, association and interpretation that took place in Wordsworth during his exile in the cold winter of 1798/9 in Germany and in the immediacy of his return to his beloved North of England in the summer and autumn of 1799. It is in this first version that his anticipation of some of the psychoanalytic discoveries of our own century is most evident.

His purpose was to explore mental development, particularly the origins of creative sensibility; what was unique was that he set about doing so in the form of a psychic autobiography. Wordsworth was being strongly urged by his twin soul Coleridge to write, as the first true poet-philosopher, the definitive work on 'man, nature and society'. Nothing less would do for Coleridge, who, having found his friend to be a sublime poet, had convinced himself, perhaps more by projective identification than observation, that he was also the great philosopher of his age.

Wordsworth begins the first part of his two-part poem by describing himself as a 4-year-old 'naked savage . . . /making one long bathing of a summer's day', prompting us to think of Rousseau in the process. He continues with episodes from what might be called the 'latency period'. In these he describes some moments he considers of great import, which crystallise the past and carry forward latent significance to the future. He called them *spots of time* and they resemble what, a century later, Freud described as *screen memories* (Freud 1899). Like screen memories, the spots of time condense experience, and, thanks again to modern scholarship, we can see how Wordsworth has unconsciously conflated different episodes and different times in reproducing these crucial memories. To a psychoanalytic eye the three incidents he describes are alive with Oedipal themes. In the third of them he waits for the horses coming from his father's house at a point overlooking the meeting place of two tracks; his journey home is then followed by his father's death, which he describes as a punishment for his own presumptuous desire. This has such Theban echoes it has always prompted for me the following questions: did Wordsworth identify himself with Oedipus as consciously as Freud did? Was he familiar with *Oedipus Rex*? What I have learnt from Duncan Wu is that Wordsworth was examined as a student on Sophocles' *Oedipus at Colonus* at St John's College, Cambridge, and 'had considerable merit' (Wu 1993: 129). It seems very likely that he knew the other Theban plays.

If on the strength of this I call Part I of the 1799 *Prelude* proto-Freudian I would like, for other reasons, to call Part II proto-Kleinian. In this second part, before he can tackle the transcendental experiences of his adolescence that he wants to account for, he finds it necessary to produce his theory of infantile psychic development. Like Melanie Klein, Wordsworth sought an explanation of the numinous in infantile experience:

> . . . when the soul
> Remembering how she felt but what she felt
> Remembering not – retains an obscure sense
> Of possible sublimity.
>
> (Wordsworth 1979: 23)

Wordsworth's scheme of his psychic development is in three phases. The first is infancy, described as 'beyond the twilight of rememberable time' (Wordsworth 1979: 20). Then comes childhood, a time when he thought he absorbed Nature's forms adventitiously as they formed a crucial but disregarded background to his boyhood activities. Finally comes adolescence, when between his fourteenth and seventeenth years his previously unselfconscious love of nature erupted into passion and Mother Nature became the primary love object of his life, 'with an increasing weight ; he was o'erpowered/By Nature, and his Spirit was on fire/With restless thoughts . . . /The mind within him burnt' (Wordsworth 1985: 26–7).

He describes a number of transcendental states, which I suggest are of two distinct types. In the first everything is in the present, exalted, thoughtless and fused with nature, which is taken to be the primal object and not simply *symbolic* of it. In the second type of transcendental state there is a poignant sense of a past that cannot be recollected but only felt. Melanie Klein referred to such experiences as occurring sometimes in the course of analysis and called them '*memories in feelings*' (Klein 1957: 180).

The first kind of exalted state Wordsworth describes is nature worship, whereas the second kind leads from a love of nature to a love of man. I believe the first of these mental states is part of a manic defence, very common in adolescence, against a world 'dead to the eye', whereas the second is evocative and consolatory. The first denies the loss of the ideal object in an orgy of symbolic transfiguration; the second remedies it with a sublimatory symbolism produced in the depressive position, that is, with 'thoughts that spring out of human suffering' (Wordsworth 1984: 302).

Before pursuing this further I want to return to the 1799 version of *The Prelude* to examine the account of infancy which Wordsworth felt he had to provide before grappling with the experiences of adolescence and young adult life it sought to explain. Within the poem he interrupts his biographical narrative to share an aside with his absent intellectual associate Coleridge. He shares with his friend a reassuring comment on the folly of those who make cognitive distinctions in the world of the mind and treat these distinctions as perceptions. He writes of the foolishness of attributing all mental activity to identifiable specific moments of sensory experience. It is not hard to see this as a critique of Locke. The two poets felt that the empirical school of philosophy, with its assembly of a filing cabinet of sensory experiences as a picture of the mind, annihilated man's sense of himself. In Wordsworth's own words, 'we murder to dissect' (Wordsworth 1984: 131). 'Hard task', however, he continues in *The Prelude*, 'to analyse a soul' if 'not only habits and desires, but each most obvious and particular thought hath no beginning' (Wordsworth 1979: 20). Here he is confiding that his previous standby in his account of psychological development, namely David Hartley (Wu 1993: 72), with his theory of *associationism*, is proving inadequate for his purposes. In fact no eighteenth-century philosophical theory is adequate for his purposes and he makes a conjectural leap into the theories of the middle of the twentieth century, where such psychoanalytic writers as Klein (1952b, 1952c), Balint (1952) and Winnicott (1945) sought explanations for adult psychological developments in early infancy.

In a relatively short passage of forty-four lines Wordsworth gives an account of infantile experience in subjective terms, though it is written in the third person. In it he describes the infant's attachment to the mother, the infant's extension of this to the external world, and the founding of an internal world. This set of ideas provided him with a means of reconciling his intuitive philosophical idealism with his equally strong natural materialism. The infant of his poem is 'creator and receiver both', allowing the author to acknowledge both his mind's imaginative creations and his perceptual debt to the external world.

> . . . Blessed the infant babe –
> For with my best conjectures I would trace
> The progress of our being – blest the babe
> Nursed in his mother's arms, the babe who sleeps
> Upon his mother's breast, who, when his soul
> Claims manifest kindred with an earthly soul,
> Doth gather passion from his mother's eye.
> Such feelings pass into his torpid life
> Like an awakening breeze, and hence his mind,
> Even in the first trial of its power,
> Is prompt and watchful, eager to combine
> In one appearance all the elements
> And parts of the same object, else detached
> And loath to coalesce. Thus day by day,
> Subjected to the discipline of love,
> His organs and recipient faculties
> Are quickened, are more vigorous; his mind spreads,
> Tenacious of the forms which it receives.
> In one beloved presence – nay and more,
> In that most apprehensive habitude
> And those sensations which have been derived
> From this beloved presence – there exists
> A virtue which irradiates and exalts
> All objects through all intercourse of sense.
> No outcast he, bewildered and depressed;
> Along his infant veins are interfused
> The gravitational and the filial bond
> Of Nature that connect him with the world.
> Emphatically such a being lives,
> An inmate of this *active* universe.
> From Nature largely he receives, nor so
> Is satisfied, but largely gives again;
> For feeling has to him imparted strength,
> And – powerful in all sentiments of grief,
> Of exultation, fear and joy – his mind,
> Even as an agent of the one great mind,
> Creates, creator and receiver both,

Working but in alliance with the works
Which it beholds. Such, verily, is the first
Poetic spirit of our human life –
By uniform control of after years
In most abated and suppressed, in some
Through every change of growth or of decay
Pre-eminent till death.

(Wordsworth 1979: 20–1)

I shall try to summarise the 'infant babe' passage's main propositions in my own words, with their background of psychoanalytic meaning:

1 Adult and childhood mental phenomena have their origin in infantile experience.
('For with my best conjectures I would trace/the progress of our being')

2 The infant, from birth, seeks an object relationship as the fulfilment of an inborn expectation. The infant is fortunate if when it does so it finds itself the object of the mother's passion.
('blest the babe . . . who, when his soul/Claims manifest kindred with an earthly soul,/Doth gather passion from His mother's eye')

3 The infant takes in the mother's feelings for him or her in such a way that they become a source of strength within the infant's own mind and kindle the infant's enthusiasm for the world outside him- or herself.
('Such feelings pass into his torpid life/Like an awakening breeze')

4 This presence of feelings reconciles the infant to the integration of his or her experience in different modalities and to the integration of his or her part-object relationship to the mother so that the infant recognises her as a whole person. Wordsworth explicitly affirms that otherwise there is a natural resistance to this process of integration.
('Parts of the same object, else detached/And loath to coalesce')

5 The infant, given this favourable emotional environment, incorporates more objects and has a tenacious hold on them, thus enriching his or her inner world.
('his mind spreads,/Tenacious of the forms which it receives')

6 The qualities of the beloved mother suffuse all objects and all the links to them through all sensory modalities.
('From this beloved presence – there exists/A virtue which irradiates and exalts/All objects through all intercourse of sense')

7 As a consequence the infant has a bond with the natural world and a sense of living inside a living world of which he or she is a part and which is a part of him or her.

('along his infant veins are interfused/The gravitation and the filial bond/Of Nature that connect him with the world')

8 Thus the infant takes in from nature and gives out to it. Having developed the capacity to entertain freely feelings of grief, exultation, fear and joy, the infant is equipped to animate the outside world with significance and to benefit from his or her subsequent experience of it. He can, in Melanie Klein's words, project, introject, project again and re-introject, thus creating an external world of significance and an internal world of substance: 'Creates, creator and receiver both.' The infant self shapes the external world with his projections and re-introjects the world thus created, together with its own qualities. The mother's qualities are then reinvested by symbolisation in the objects of the external world. Such is the nature of symbolisation that it not only represents her but also contains her 'beloved presence'.

9 Wordsworth firmly suggests that this process is the source of the 'poetic spirit'.

('Such, verily, is the first/Poetic spirit of our human life')

In these passages in which he seeks to trace the origin and nature of his poetic gift he seems to be saying the same thing that Klein did as a consequence of her experiences in analysing children and adults. She thought that what characterised the 'creative artist' was access to early infantile phantasy; if 'symbol formation in infantile mental life is particularly rich', she claimed, 'it contributes to the development of every talent or even genius' (Klein 1930: 220). She extended the concept of symbolism in psychoanalysis and made it more centrally significant: 'symbolism is the foundation of all sublimation and of every talent, since it is by way of symbolic equation that things, activities, and interests become the subject of libidinal phantasies' (*ibid.*: 220). She went further and without knowing it echoed Wordsworth's 'infant babe' passage: 'not only does symbolism come to be the foundation of all phantasy and sublimation but, more than that, it is the basis of the subject's relation to the outside world and to reality in general' (*ibid.*: 221).

Hanna Segal (1957) threw more light on the crucial distinction between the psychotic and non-psychotic relation to symbolic objects. She described the vicissitudes of symbolic development in psychotic modes of thought .These modes not only characterise actual psychotic states but also can be found in obsessionality, perversions, addictions, in the psychopathology of our everyday life and, of course, in art. What she demonstrated was that in these modes of thought where we would expect to find symbols we found instead what she termed '*symbolic equations*' (*ibid.*: 168). The symbolic equation, unlike the true symbol, is taken to be the original object transformed. In a mental state, therefore, in which symbolic

137

equations proliferate, symbolic thoughts are treated not as thoughts but as things. Thus Segal's symbolic equation is different from the symbol proper in that it is psychic made matter not matter imbued with psychic significance. It gives rise to idolatry rather than idealism. 'In the symbolic equation, the symbol substitute is felt to *be* the original object . . . [it] is used to deny the absence of the ideal object'. In contrast:

> the symbol proper . . . is felt to *represent* the object. . . . It arises when depressive feelings predominate over the paranoid–schizoid ones, when separation from the object, ambivalence, guilt and loss can be experienced and tolerated. The symbol is used not to deny but to overcome loss.
>
> (Segal 1957: 168)

The symbolic equation arises from an arrested development of the symbolic process at the point of the relinquishment of the original object. The object is falsely preserved by a sustained projection of the self into the place vacated by the absent object and which denies its disappearance.

In such thinking there is no world outside the mind: existence of self and object world are conterminous: 'The world ends when I end: I only end when the world ends. Either I am immortal in the eternal world or the world will end when I cease to believe in it.'

I can illustrate what I mean by reference to the patient whom I previously referred to as Miss A. She lived in a world furnished with symbolic equations as a consequence of her omnipotent phantasies. She believed her thoughts were things and that they had to be disposed of by such methods as flushing the lavatory. She believed her bad thoughts got into the objects around her, which therefore had to be destroyed or avoided. Her greatest fear was that if she did not see her mother she would go blind, and that if she did not feel her mother's touch she would no longer be able to feel anything. Such was the absoluteness of the identification between her perceiving, desiring self and the object of her perception or desire that to lose one was equated with losing the other; therefore not to see the loved object was literally not to see. This was the converse of a belief that she sustained the objective world in existence solely by the activity of her mind. The relationship between seeing and blindness she symbolically extended from her mother to the moon, just as later in analysis she was to transfer it to me. She thought, 'If I do not see the moon I will go blind', and as a consequence she filled her life with moon tables and weather forecasts to forestall the disaster of inadvertently exposing herself to 'not seeing' the moon when she expected to.

She knew nothing of philosophy but was imprisoned in a subjective, monistic world exactly like that envisaged by such philosophers as

Schelling, in his 'Transcendental idealism', or Hegel, in his 'Absolute, objective idealism' (Flew 1979: 292 and 128–32). In Schelling's system 'there are not two kinds of stuff in the world – mind stuff and matter-stuff: there is only one' (Warnock 1976: 66); for Hegel, all that exists is a form of one mind (Flew 1979). For my patient this was not a matter of philosophical speculation but constituted the facts of her daily life; unlike Schelling and Hegel, she could not leave the study for a street in which she could assume that life and its objects had been carrying on without her attention. She lived in a world that required her constant activity to continue its existence; such were her beliefs and, like all real beliefs, they were not theories but convictions.

A phrase of Wordsworth's, 'this abyss of idealism', aptly described my patient's psychic reality. He employed this phrase, not in a poem, but to describe an experience of his own in his childhood, a state in which he felt that nothing existed outside his own mind, a state of de-realisation and panic which he described as occurring episodically in his school days. This is recorded in the I.F. notes, that is, a record of Wordsworth's associations with his former poems communicated by him to Isabella Fenwick and subsequently written out by Wordsworth's daughter Dorothea and her husband Edward Quillinan. He gave this particular description of these episodes of de-realisation in childhood in association with his 'Ode on the intimations of immortality'. He is quoted as saying 'Many times while going to school I have grasped at a wall or tree to recall myself from this abyss of idealism to the reality' (I.F. Notes 1843: 123). He linked it with another belief of his childhood, namely that he would never physically die, whatever might become of others. It is not difficult to locate this as the period of his life that followed his mother's death when he was 8 years old.

Wordsworth describes recalling himself to reality by grasping at walls or trees as if his sense of touch, unlike his visual sense, was not under the solipsistic domination of his mind. He speaks as though he had a means of contact with rocks and stones and trees which was more basic and real than that provided by what he elsewhere called his tyrannical sense of sight. Tyrannical, because it could be used not only to take in what was there, but also to impose on the external world an omnipotent phantasy.

His reliance on the physical sense of touch reminds me of the passage in part two of the 1799 *Prelude* which immediately follows the 'infant babe' sequence and so powerfully describes the pre-verbal, tactile relationship with his mother:

> . . . that first time
> In which, a babe, by intercourse of touch
> I held mute dialogues with my mother's heart.
> (Wordsworth 1979: 21)

A complaint of Coleridge that there was something too palpable about Wordsworth points to a difference between the two in the degree of their philosophical idealism. An idealistic full-blooded Platonism came much more naturally to Coleridge. One could say that Wordsworth had, in addition to his powerful projective tendency, a capacity to be in touch with something external that was not himself and yet was indispensable to himself. In contrast to my patient who feared blindness in the absence of her object, Wordsworth, in *Tintern Abbey*, describes precisely the opposite:

> Though absent long
> These forms of beauty have not been to me
> As is a landscape to a blind man's eye
> But oft in lonely rooms, and mid the din
> Of towns and cities I have owed to them
> In hours of weariness sensations sweet.
>
> (Wordsworth 1984: 132)

Here Wordsworth anticipates Klein's theory of *internal objects*, that is, the installation of the *qualities* of the external object into an *inner world*, where they are represented by personification as *objects*. If one of those qualities is continuity, it provides us with an inner sense of security. If we acknowledge the object's independent existence, which includes the property of '*going on being*' then we can rely on something which transcends the limitations of our own immediate intentional capacities or just deserts. As an internal object this provides a basis for hope. Indeed, I think 'hope' is based on an unconscious phantasy of an internal object which has that vital quality of the good mother of infancy of returning unsummoned and unmerited – of an object that transcends expectation, belief and justice. In Wordsworth's own words:

> The morning shines
> Nor heedeth man's perverseness; Spring returns –
> I saw the Spring return, when I was dead
> to deeper hope.
>
> (Wordsworth 1979: 416)

The essence of this transaction with the object is the recognition of its separate and distinct identity. Thus there is an interface between self and object, between what is internal and what is external. At this interface between psychic and material reality is the symbol, and it therefore contains the tensions which appear inherent in that frontier situation. The tendency to eliminate the difference between what is mental and what is material is ubiquitous, and the temptation to deny either ideality or reality and to opt for one or the other is perennial, as in philosophical idealism or social realism. It is part of our reluctance to accept that what is ideal cannot be real and that what is real cannot be ideal.

Wordsworth wrestled with these issues at the deepest level, and for him the deepest level of his thought is always to be found in his poetry. In his account of his adolescence and its aftermath he was to describe the flux between the real and the ideal, but before he reached that point he suffered a loss that profoundly affected his relationship with the world and fuelled his relationship with nature: the death of his mother. Unlike the death of his father, it is not spelt out in *The Prelude*, but we find it expressed in a veiled but powerful way in the poem a few lines after the 'infant babe' passage:

> For now a trouble came into my mind
> From obscure causes. I was left alone
> Seeking this visible world, nor knowing why.
> The props of my affection were removed,
> And yet the building stood, as if sustained
> By its own spirit. All that I beheld
> was dear to me, and from this cause it came
> That now to Nature's finer influxes
> My mind lay open.
>
> (Wordsworth 1979: 22)

We could say that, unlike the infant babe blessed at his mother's breast, this infantile Wordsworth does feel himself to be 'an outcast bewildered and depressed'. He goes on to suggest that he turned as a consequence to nature, and when he became adolescent it 'haunted him like a passion' and became his primary love object.

As I said, I think that in his account of his adolescent relationship with nature he describes two distinct kinds of mental state, both of which could be called 'transcendental'. The first was exalted and thoughtless; the second thoughtful, sad and obscure. In the first, with bliss ineffable all is feeling and feeling is all. He describes this absolute identification in both a projective mode and an introjective mode. In the projective mode he feels 'spread over all that moves and all that seemeth still'; in an introjective mode what he sees outside himself appeared like something inside, like 'a dream' or a 'prospect in my mind'. In both directions he achieved this total identification by abolishing awareness of his own intervening sensory apparatus. 'The agency of sight' and 'the fleshy ear' were forgotten or, like thinking itself, were effectively abolished: 'Thought was not; in enjoyment it expired'. He wrote:

141

> . . . his spirit drank
> The spectacle. Sensation, soul and form,
> All melted into him; they swallowed up
> His animal being. In them did he live,
> And by them did he live – they were his life.
> (Wordsworth 1985: 23)

All was incorporation or envelopment. When at the height of his pantheism he describes these transcendent objects of his exalted state as manifestations of God, he makes it explicit that this was not a god who could be thought of as a person; in this mood it was only a god felt as manifestation. Everything was manifest and manifestation was all. There was no separation between thought and thing. The landscape was not simply symbolic and evocative of something, but it was the 'thing itself'; it was a symbolic equation, not a symbol. The natural was the supernatural. The external object was the internal object incarnate.

In *Tintern Abbey* he uses this thoughtless state as a contrast with what he regards as its more mature successor. In his first thoughtless state he felt:

> . . . more like a man
> Flying from something that he dreads, than one
> Who sought the thing he loved.
> (Wordsworth 1984: 133)

If the lost object is not experienced as something missing, as *the presence of loss*, it is felt to be *the presence of something* – something dreaded, something from which to fly. In the paranoid-schizoid mode the absent object is felt, not to be lost, but to be present as a bad or fearful thing; thus the alternative to bliss is nightmare. Coleridge, in Wordsworth's company, wrote of just such a thing:

> . . . like one that on a lonely road
> Doth walk in fear and dread,
> And having once turn'd round, walks on
> And turns no more his head:
> Because he knows, a frightful fiend
> Doth close behind him tread.
> (Coleridge 1985: 60)

In the move from the paranoid-schizoid position to the depressive position this frightful fiend changes its character from fiend to dead object, now dreaded because of its deadliness, which is feared as nullifying. This figure was conjured up by Coleridge in *The Rime of the Ancient Mariner* as the female 'Night-mare Life in Death':

Her lips were red, her looks were free
Her locks were yellow as gold:
Her skin was as white as leprosy,
The Night-mare Life in Death was she,
Who thicks man's blood with cold.

(Coleridge 1985: 52)

I suggested earlier that Wordsworth feared perceiving some lifeless object or seeing some live object in a dead way, particularly visually: 'dead in my eyes as is a theatre/Fresh emptied of spectators' (Wordsworth 1979: 182), or 'as is a landscape to a blind man's eye' (Wordsworth 1984: 132), or like a 'soulless image on the eye which usurped a living thought' (Wordsworth 1979: 212). I am now suggesting that this *thoughtless* state, in which the external world was treated as the incarnation of a psychic ideal, was a defensive denial of something dreaded, the *dead object*. It is, I think, best symbolised in his poem 'The Ruined Cottage'. Margaret, the tragic figure of this poem, dies slowly, first in mind and then in body, following the departure of her husband and her growing despair over his failure to return from the war. Her cottage decays with her and its dereliction is skilfully used to convey her inner state:

Meanwhile her poor hut
Sunk to decay: for he was gone, whose hand
At the first nipping of October frost
Closed up each chink.

(Wordsworth 1984: 43)

Her eventual death leaves a deadly space in the world of the poem and in the mind of the poet:

. . . she is dead
And nettles rot and adders sun themselves
Where we have sate together while she nursed
Her infant at her breast.

(Wordsworth 1984: 34)

This prompts me to think of Wordsworth's mother's death and of his own feelings at having abandoned Annette Vallon and their child, of the confusion between feeling abandoned himself and guilty for abandoning her, the sort of confusion that is the essence of the depressive position. It is against such an aching place in the mind – 'Where we have sate together' – with its stinging feelings and poisonous thoughts that the manic defence is erected. In the exalted state, when he is 'spread over all that moves and all

143

that seemeth still', the distinction between animate and inanimate is gone. Animism claims that all is alive and eliminates the risk of anything being perceived as lifeless. Manic reparation demands that the world must be reborn or transcended, if not by revolutionary action, then by revolutionary imagination. When this is based on denial of the psychic reality of a world 'dead to the eye', imagination becomes that 'false secondary power' deplored by Wordsworth, as it produces:

> . . . a work
> Of false imagination, placed beyond
> The limits of experience and of truth.
> (Wordsworth 1979: 404)

True imagination, celebrated and sought after by both Wordsworth and Coleridge, is the individual's transcendence of his or her experience of loss through symbolic reparation. This therefore necessarily includes an element of loss colouring the pleasures of renewal which arise from the discovery of a new symbolic version. In essence, I believe this to be the second transcendental state, which I have described as 'thoughtful'. It combines an obscure sense of possible sublimity with the 'still sad music of humanity'. Wordsworth finds a voice for the depressive position that speaks for and to all of us 'when the rain beats on our roofs at midnight'. The philosopher John Stuart Mill, in his *Autobiography* (Mill 1924), described how the only thing that relieved his own depression was the poetry of Wordsworth. I suggested earlier in this chapter that it was problems in relinquishing the achieved depressive position and sustaining the post-depressive position that were eventually to stifle his creativity. Emotionally precocious, he seems to have addressed his mid-life crisis in his verse from the age of 28:

> Me this unchartered freedom tires;
> I feel the weight of chance desires:
> My hopes no more must change their name,
> I long for a repose which ever is the same.
> (Wordsworth 1984: 296)

The sequence begun in infancy and which needs to be recycled throughout life I described in Chapter 6 as $Ps(n) \rightarrow D(n) \rightarrow Ps(n+1)$ . . . $\rightarrow D(n+1)$. I have therefore added to Elliott Jaques's (1968) concept that for some it is not the revisiting of the pre-depressive position that is the mid-life crisis, as he suggests, but the post-depressive position of relinquishing coherent belief for new uncertainties. I suggested that Coleridge provided a good example of Jaques's description of creative collapse at the point of renewal of the infantile depressive position, whereas Wordsworth's case

144

illustrated the block occurring in a post-depressive position, Ps(n+1). For the creative artist this willingness to relinquish and move on from D(n) is a necessary condition of continuous creativity. The enormous achievement of Wordsworth represented by the articulation of his arrival at his own personal D(n) in his thirties must have made this settled place all the harder to leave. In 1802, after staying in Calais for a month in order to talk with Annette Vallon before finally planning his marriage to Mary Hutchinson, he wrote a number of heartfelt sonnets celebrating his return. These included the celebrated sonnet 'Earth has not anything to shew more fair', composed on Westminster Bridge. They also included one that ended with the following lines:

> The immortal Mind craves objects that endure:
> These cleave to it: from these it cannot roam,
> Nor they from it: their fellowship is secure.
>
> (Wordsworth 1984: 287)

Wordsworth subsided into a conventional religious belief that he could share with his wife, friends and neighbours. The restless radicalism of his youth gave way to settled convictions and moral imperatives. The romantic lover became the Victorian father. *The loss of the presence* had occurred earlier; *the presence of loss* was brilliantly articulated for a time in his poetry, but then it too was lost in a comfortable-mindedness that must have seemed irresistible to one who suffered so much and had so many unwelcome changes.

12

Existential anxiety: Rilke's *Duino Elegies*

If my human mind cannot acknowledge that all that is, is right; yet since what is, must be, I will sit amidst the ruins and smile. Truly we were not born to enjoy, but to submit, and to hope.

(Shelley 1826: 399)

Rainer Maria Rilke was born in 1875, nineteen years later than Freud; both were German-speaking citizens of the Austro-Hungarian Empire, but Rilke, unlike Freud, was Roman Catholic. I discussed in the Chapter 11 Wordsworth's theory of the relationship of infantile experience to poetic sensibility. Rilke, like Wordsworth, sought understanding of himself and his poetry in his childhood origins, but his subjective account of his early experience and its psychic sequelae is very different. Wordsworth described himself as 'the blessed babe', because at the breast he gathered passion from his mother's eye; Rilke came to view himself as 'the unblessed babe' who felt annihilated by his mother's unseeing eyes.

We can contrast Wordsworth's well-known epiphany on the bond between childhood and adult life with Rilke's reflection on a similar theme:

My heart leaps up when I behold
A Rainbow in the sky:
So was it when my life began;
So be it now I am a Man.

(Wordsworth 1994: 122)

146

Rilke wrote, not of a rainbow, but of the exposed remnant of a demolished house:

> And from these walls, once blue, green, and yellow, . . . the air of these lives issued. . . . The sweet smell of neglected infants lingered there, the smell of frightened schoolchildren, and the stuffiness from the beds of pubescent boys. . . . You would think I had stood looking at it for a long time; but I swear I began to run as soon as I recognised this wall. For that's what is horrible – that I did recognise it. I recognise everything here, and that's why it passes right into me: it is at home inside me.
>
> (Rilke 1910: 47–8)

One thing both poets did have in common is something they shared with Freud, a belief that what they discover within themselves is of general significance; that in fundamentals all men are the same, transcending culture and period; and that internal reality is as significant as the external world and has its own validity.

Where does the poet find his powers, we might ask, and what are his sources? I think Rilke tries to answer this in *The Duino Elegies* and the *Sonnets to Orpheus*, just as Wordsworth, using himself as subject, sought to answer this in *The Prelude*, particularly in his passage on the 'infant babe'. Through the symbol we renew our relationship with the lost primary object from which we seek satisfaction; we are, as Wordsworth put it, 'creator and receiver both'. Hanna Segal, taking this further, showed that the artist can through his creation repair his internal objects which are damaged, lost or annihilated in phantasy (Segal 1952). I think the *Elegies* provide a strong example of an attempt at validation of self and reparation of internal objects through art. It was this that gave to Rilke his conviction that he had to complete them in order to continue living.

Wordsworth, like Freud, was convinced of the primacy of the 'pleasure principle'. Therefore, just as Freud raised the question of why, given the pleasure principle, painful and fearful subjects are in our dreams, so Wordsworth asked why they are in our poetry. In his Preface to the lyrical ballads he gives this answer:

> However painful may be the objects with which the Anatomist's knowledge is connected, he feels that his knowledge is pleasure . . . what then does the Poet? He considers man and the objects that surround him as acting and re-acting upon each other, so as to produce an infinite complexity of pain and pleasure.
>
> (Wordsworth 1850: 291)

The satisfaction imparted to the poet is of gaining or regaining knowledge and of encompassing even unpleasant facts. A similar twentieth-century answer to the question of why tragedy satisfies audiences came from Louis MacNeice: 'The defeat of the hero in the play is their defeat because he is their hero but the whole is their triumph because it is their play' (MacNeice 1941: 107). This brings to my mind Bion's (1967) theory that we offer ourselves as containers for experience, that we transform raw sensation into thoughts and that we think in order to deal with thoughts. This has particular resonance with Rilke's conclusions in *The Duino Elegies*:

> these phenomena and things should be understood and transformed in a most fervent sense. The *Elegies* show us at this work, at the work of these continual conversions of the beloved visible and tangible into the invisible vibrations and excitation of our own nature.
>
> (Rilke 1969: 374; letter of 13 November 1925)

The ten poems known as *The Duino Elegies* take their name from the castle in Austria in which he was staying when he began them in January 1912; it took him ten years to complete them. In contrast, his *Sonnets to Orpheus*, which followed immediately, were written very quickly and completed within a month. Together the *Elegies* and the *Sonnets* constitute Rilke's own way of trying to address the same agenda as Wordsworth did in *The Prelude*, to give an account of 'man, nature and society' through self-examination. Both poets approach it through memory and imagination, using that latter word, as did Coleridge, to mean what Klein later meant by phantasy.

Rilke wrote that 'poems are not, as people think, simply emotions . . . they are experiences' (Rilke 1910: 20). To write poems, he made clear:

> You must have memories. . . . And yet it is not enough to have memories. You must be able to forget them when they are many, and you must have the immense patience to wait until they return. For the memories themselves are not important. Only when they have changed into our very blood, into glance and gesture, and are nameless, no longer to be distinguished from ourselves – only then can it happen that in some very rare hour the first word of a poem arises.
>
> (Rilke 1910: 20)

Both Wordsworth and Rilke accept the necessity of that return to their origins to find themselves, but their rediscoveries are vastly different, as we see when Rilke describes the return of his childhood:

> And now this illness again, which has always affected me so strangely. . . . This illness doesn't have any particular characteristics; it

takes on the characteristics of the people it attacks . . . it pulls out their deepest danger, which seemed passed, and places it before them again. . . . All the lost fears are here again . . . I prayed to rediscover my childhood, and it has come back, and I feel that it is just as difficult as it used to be, and that growing older has served no purpose at all.

(Rilke 1910: 62–4)

We can see Wordsworth as illustrating some aspects of Klein's depressive position and mourning. In contrast, we see Rilke offering us what sound like illustrations of her paper on the paranoid-schizoid position (Klein 1946) or Herbert Rosenfeld's clinical descriptions of psychotic states of mind (Rosenfeld 1965). The extract I quoted above is from Rilke's novel *The Notebooks of Malte Laurids Brigge*, which he originally entitled *The Journal of My Other Self*; the passage continues:

here and there on my blanket, lost feelings out of my childhood lie and are like new. The fear that a small woollen thread sticking out of the blanket may be hard, hard and sharp as a steel needle; the fear that this little button on my night-shirt may be bigger than my head, bigger and heavier; the fear that the bread crumb which just dropped off my bed may turn into glass, and shatter when it hits the floor, and the sickening worry that when it does, everything will be broken, for ever . . . ; the fear that some number may begin to grow in my brain until there is no more room for it inside me; the fear that I may be lying on grey granite; the fear that I may start screaming, and people will come running to my door and finally force it open, the fear that I might betray myself and tell everything I dread, and the fear that I might not be able to say anything, because everything is unsayable.

(Rilke 1910: 63–4)

In describing Rilke as the poet *of* the paranoid-schizoid position I am not describing the writer as *in* the mode of the paranoid-schizoid position. Indeed, in order to be able to write as he did he had to be functioning in the mode of the depressive position. I would go further and suggest that the act of composing was the *means* of moving from the paranoid-schizoid to the depressive position in relation to writing, whether or not he was in that position in relation to other aspects of life.

The two poets give very different accounts of infancy, but I think they are stories of different infants rather than that they require different theories of infancy. Wordsworth's account of the 'infant babe', as I described in Chapter 11, is the story of an infant at the breast fortunate enough to 'gather passion from his mother's eye', an infant who thereby has awakened in him 'like a breeze' the strength to invest the outside world with beauty and goodness, which in turn he reintrojects. Rilke, on the other hand, wrote of his mother 'From her to me no warm breeze ever blew' (Rilke 1981: 65). Wordsworth's account corresponds to *one* of Klein's descriptions of infancy, one where things are favourable: 'The "good breast" that feeds and initiates the love relation to the mother is the representative of the life instinct and is felt also as the first manifestation of creativeness' (Klein 1957: 201). The story Rilke tells corresponds to Klein's description of the infantile situation where things are *not* favourable. In this situation she describes the lack of a good object as resulting 'in a very deep split between an idealised and an extremely bad one' (*ibid*.: 192). 'I also found', she said, 'that idealisation derives from the innate feeling that an extremely good breast exists, a feeling which leads to the longing for a good object and for the capacity to love it' (*ibid*.). In the original typescript of 'Envy and Gratitude' she wrote the following footnote, which was not included in the published paper. The footnote has a particular relevance for Rilke's poem:

> Babies who constantly need attention and cannot be happy on their own for any length of time are, as I suggested, insecure because their good object is not sufficiently established. This can be observed in any child who clings excessively to his mother. He most of all wants his anxiety and ultimately his destructive impulses which endanger his internal and external world allayed by the mother's presence.[1]

Rilke wrote in the third elegy of just such a situation, where the mother's presence was needed to keep inner terrors at bay:

> Mother, you made him small, it was you who started him;
> in your sight he was new, over his new eyes you arched
> the friendly world and warded off the world that was alien.
> Ah, where are the years when you shielded him just by placing
> your slender form between him and the surging abyss?
> How much you hid from him then. The room that filled with suspicion
> at night: you made it harmless; and out of the refuge of your heart
> you mixed a more human space in with his night space.
>   (Rilke 1987: 163)

This passage is from the third of *The Duino Elegies*, which he began in January 1912 and completed eighteen months later. It was begun at a moment when he was contemplating entering analysis with a psychiatrist, Baron Emil von Gebsattel. The *Elegies* appeared to be an alternative to analysis. His wife was in analysis with Gebsattel. Rilke commented: 'with her it is a different matter, her work has never helped her, while mine, in a certain sense, was from the beginning a kind of self treatment' (Rilke 1969: 45). Somewhere between 20 and 24 January 1912 he decided not to begin analysis and wrote to Lou Andreas Salomé: 'I know now that analysis would have sense for me only if I were really serious about . . . not writing any more' (*ibid.*: 49).

That is not really the end of the story of Rilke and analysis, but I want to return to the picture of childhood in the third elegy. In this poem, unlike the mother of Wordsworth's 'infant babe', the mother is not the source of all the goodness in the world, but only a soothing presence shielding him from terrors beyond the pale and horrors within. By splitting she was kept as a good but limited external presence, divorced from the alien terrors of outer space and unconnected with the seductive demons of the inner world.

> he seemed protected . . . But inside: who could ward off,
> who could divert, the floods of origin inside him?
> . . . dreaming . . .
> . . . he was caught up
> and entangled in the spreading tendrils of inner event
> already twined into patterns, into strangling undergrowth, prowling
> bestial shapes. How he submitted. Loved.
> Loved his interior world, his interior wilderness,
> that primal forest inside him, . . .
> . . . Left it, went through
> his own roots and out, into more ancient blood, to ravines
> where Horror lay, still glutted with his fathers. And every
> Terror knew him, winked at him like an accomplice.
> Yes, Atrocity smiled . . . Seldom
> had you smiled so tenderly, mother. How could he help
> loving what smiled at him. Even before he knew you,
> he had loved it, for already while you carried him inside you, it
> was dissolved in the water that makes the embryo weightless.
> (Rilke 1987: 165)

Rilke, in his own terms, discovers his dependence on external love to mask and deny the awful truth of his internal world. Later, therefore, he feels compelled to renounce the love he thinks compels him to live in a world in which he cannot be himself. He epitomises Winnicott's description of the *true and false self* (Winnicott 1960b), and Rilke's exploration of this schism between the subjective self and the self's relationship with the object world adds considerably to our understanding of this particular pathological organisation (Steiner 1987), which is discussed further in Chapters 13 and 14.

Rilke's first account of the beginning of a pilgrimage to find himself is in his novel *The Notebooks of Malte Laurids Brigge* (Rilke 1910), which concludes with his version of the story of the Prodigal Son, which he thinks is 'the legend of a man who did not want to be loved' (*ibid.*: 251).

Before pursuing this further, and the breakdown both in his writing and of his mental health which followed the completion of this novel, I think more facts about his life are needed.

Rilke's father was an army officer who became a railway clerk, and his mother was a devoutly religious woman. The year before he was born his mother had lost a baby girl and she named him René Maria, dressed him in feminine clothes and in their games called him 'meine kleines Fräulein' (little miss). His schooling must have abruptly changed things, particularly since he went to a harsh military academy at his father's instigation. After his school days he drifted through philosophy, history, literature and art in Prague, Munich and Berlin. He changed his first name to Rainer after meeting Lou Andreas-Salomé when he was 22 and she 36. In his letters to his mother, however, he continued to sign himself René. He and Lou Andreas Salomé became lovers and made two trips to her native country Russia, in 1899 and 1900. She was crucial to Rilke's poetic development, and she is also of particular interest to us because she became a pupil of Freud and a psychoanalyst in the latter part of her life. Her past did not lack for intellectual interest either as she began her career, in Freud's phrase, as the great 'comprehending woman' of intellectual men at an early age; first with Paul Rée, a Jewish positivist-philosopher, and then with Nietzsche, when she was 21. Though Rilke and she parted as lovers and he married Clara Westhoff in 1901, Lou remained to the end of his life the one person who he believed would always understand him. He died of leukaemia in 1926. His first important work, *The Book of the Hours*, had the dedication 'laid in the hands of Lou' (Rilke 1989: xvii), and his phantasised autobiographical novel began its life as a series of letters written to her. In the emotional crisis which followed its completion he turned to her again in a letter:

> I deeply need to know what impression this book made on you . . . no one but you, dear Lou, can distinguish and indicate whether and how much he resembles me. Whether he . . . goes under in it, in a sense to spare me the going under.
>
> (Rilke 1969: 32)

He goes on to say that what is left of his everyday self is completely arid:

> the other fellow, the one who went under, has somehow used me up . . . he appropriated everything with the intensity of his despair;

scarcely does a thing seem new to me before I discover the break in it, the rough place where he tore himself off.

(Rilke 1969: 33)

The beginning of his search for himself is recounted in the novel in the allegory of the Prodigal Son. The Prodigal Son leaves because he has to escape from love because love falsifies him, or, to be more precise, a loving attachment leads him to falsify himself by becoming what all the others want to believe that he is.

My God, how much there was to leave behind and forget. . . . The dogs, in whom the expectation had been growing all day long, . . . drove you . . . into the one they recognised. And the house did the rest. Once you walked into its full smell, most matters were already decided. A few details might still be changed; but on the whole you were already the person they thought you were . . . whom they had long ago fashioned . . . out of his small past and their desires.

(Rilke 1910: 252–3)

So Rilke as Prodigal Son purges himself painfully of love until 'He didn't love anything, unless it could be said that he loved existing' (*ibid.*: 256). He returns and is taken aback by the love which greets him and terrifies him. He reconciles himself to it by realising that it had nothing to do with him; it was obvious how little they could have him in mind: 'How could they know who he was? He was now terribly difficult to love' (*ibid.*: 260).

This was the point in his writing and in his life that led him to turn once again to Lou Andreas-Salomé and simultaneously to begin *The Duino Elegies*. There are ten of them, written intermittently over a decade, with protracted intervals of stasis, frequent despair and great difficulty. And yet, on reading and rereading them, when I understood the last of them I realised that what he says in the final elegy is implicit in the first and yet this implicit meaning can only be properly understood in the light of the final elegy. He says something to this effect himself in his letters. The *Elegies* were written as a quest, but it was a quest with a difference, and in this respect it was very like an analysis. It was a search for something already present but not yet discovered, like a journey of exploration to a country already lived in.

Just as the first three elegies are a prospectus for the next ten years of his emotional life, so his novel *The Notebooks*, which he completed in 1910, serves as a prospectus for the whole of the *Elegies*. In it he wrote:

he decided to retrieve the most important of the experiences which he had been unable to accomplish before, those that had merely been waited through. Above all, he thought of his childhood, and the more calmly he recalled it, the more unfinished it seemed; all its memories had the vagueness of premonitions and the fact that they were past made them almost arise as future. To take all this past upon himself once more, and this time really, was the reason why, from the midst of his estrangement he returned home.

(Rilke 1910: 258–9)

The Duino Elegies were written in spasms, in groups which do not correspond to their eventual numbers in the final arrangement of the *Elegies*. The first group, written in the winter of 1912/13, consisted of what we know as the first, second, third and sixth elegies. The fourth was written in bleak isolation in 1915. Seven years later, in 1922, the seventh, eighth, ninth and tenth were completed in a very short space of time. The last to be written, which is numbered the fifth, was a celebration of the completion of the intense, difficult tenth elegy.

I think the actual time of composition of the *Elegies* is important in understanding them because of Rilke's way of working. They are all spontaneous effusions written after intense periods of what he called *Ausfühlen*, his own invented word meaning 'feeling through', analogous to 'working through'. It is possible to follow this process thanks to his copious letters, which are a commentary on his work as well as on his life. I want to select themes from the *Elegies*, taking them in the order they were written since they represent an interesting psychic development which, I believe, resembles the possible progress in analysis of a similarly disturbed, unhappy person.

Rilke begins by making clear that there is no fulfilment of deepest expectation in this world and that the recurring belief that something might prove to be 'it' only generates a desire for the unattainable. The ideal object of desire and fulfilment precedes life; it does not have its origins in experience and is never to be found in experience: 'I have been living away from myself as though always standing at a telescope, ascribing to each woman who came a bliss that was certainly never to be found in any of them' (Rilke 1969: 96). He cannot imagine lovers who can do more than deceive each other into believing that they have found 'it'. He cannot therefore incorporate into his thinking a prototypical ideal primal couple; he cannot conceive of a couple which represents a real union of two valid, separately existing beings, *except* in the negative form of *that which can never be*. His postscript elegy is fifth but was actually written in celebration of the completion of his task; it shows him in high spirits, because he had resolved so much in the tenth elegy. It describes a real, much admired, three-generation family of acrobats, who complete their aerial gravity-defying endeavours by the painful procedure of landing with their feet on the ground. Rilke's final verbal flourish was to add as an ironic contrast to this picture of skilful realism a fanciful daydream of imaginary lovers in an imaginary world mastering such manoeuvres, finally coming down to earth successfully, and then being thrown the 'final, forever saved up, coins of happiness' by 'the innumerable soundless dead' (Rilke 1989: 181), that is, by those who had died waiting for any couple successfully to achieve a non-catastrophic ascent and descent.

That, however, was Rilke in 1922; in 1912 there were no high spirits. In the second elegy he writes of love as incompatible with maintaining an identity because when we love we disappear into the elusive object, which is itself insubstantial.

> But we when moved by deep feeling, evaporate; we
> breathe ourselves out and away . . . Though someone may tell us:
> 'Yes, you've entered my bloodstream, the room the whole springtime
> is filled with you' . . . what does it matter? he can't contain us,
> we vanish inside him and around him . . .
> what is ours floats into the air, like steam from a dish
> of hot food.
>
> (Rilke 1987: 157)

The sixth elegy, written just after the third, he called the 'Hero Elegy'. In it Rilke claims a position as the hero of his own saga. But it is very different from the way Freud and Wordsworth cast themselves as heroes in their own myths. For Freud, 'A man who has been the indisputable favourite of his mother keeps for life the feeling of a conqueror' (Jones 1957, vol. I: 6). When he was ill at ease or full of doubts Wordsworth reminded himself: 'Why should I grieve? – I was a chosen son' (Wordsworth 1979: 96). Rilke, in contrast, can only protest that at least he chose himself by triumphing over all the other spermatozoa that might have taken over his mother's womb.

> Wasn't he a hero inside you, mother? didn't
> his imperious choosing already begin there, in you?
> Thousands seethed in your womb wanting to be him,
> but look: he grasped and excluded – chose and prevailed.
> (Rilke 1987: 183–4)

Significantly, the hero Rilke has in mind in this elegy is Samson, and the counterpart to the destruction by the blinded Samson of the house of the Philistines is our hero's birth, when he burst from his mother's body 'into the narrower world', where again he 'chose and prevailed' (Rilke 1987: 184). He implies in this passage, as in his earlier novel, that his assertion of his own identity is fatal for his objects. If *he* is not shaped by their desires, *they* are in danger from his omnipotence. His self-assertion becomes their destruction. He takes Samson to be himself as the hero, and blindness the chosen method of subjugating himself. In other words, he is blinded by his parental captors and tempted to pull down their house, destroying them and himself in the process.

After this outburst of poetry there is a long silence in the *Elegies*, followed by the isolated production of the bitterest of them all, written in November 1915, now numbered fourth and known as the 'Marionette Elegy'. This emerged in a period of despair: 'For I no longer doubt that I am sick, and my sickness has gained a lot of ground and is also lodged in that which heretofore I called my work so that for the present there is no refuge there' (Rilke 1969: 114). This is from a letter to Lou of 9 June 1914; in it he accuses himself of destructiveness, for which in the past he has always blamed others, and he makes clear that he can no longer entertain a sense of persecution. Two weeks later he wrote another letter, which contains a poem, posted with the ink hardly dry, called *Turning Point*, and it represents just that; this 'turning', he wrote, 'must come if I am to live' (Rilke 1969: 115). The necessary turning is from taking pleasure in an omnipotent control achieved by gazing at things, to learning to love that which he has taken in and transformed:

> Long he had won it by looking.
> Stars would fall on their knees
> under his strenuous up-glance . . .
>
> Towers he would gaze at so
> that they were startled:
> building them up again, suddenly, sweeping them up!
>
> (Rilke 1981: 47)

In this poem he finds himself guilty because he realises the world wants to be loved, not just gazed at. Now he tells himself:

> Work of seeing is done,
> now practise heart-work
> on those images captive within you; for you
> overpowered them only: but now do not know them.
> Look, inward man, look at your inward maiden,
> her, the labouriously won
> from a thousand natures, at her the
> being till now only
> won, never yet loved.
>
> (Rilke 1981: 49)

In this poem he acknowledges that he must learn to love those internal objects established by the possessive yet unloving use of his eyes. He must do 'Herz-Werk', a neologism with elements of both hard work and love. To understand this term it helps to remind ourselves of his notion that there were memories of childhood that had not been experienced but only 'waited through', and which now had to be retrieved and lived through, but 'this time really' (Rilke 1910: 258–9). Judging from what he wrote in 1915 the 'heart-work' was painful and bitter, involving the discovery of considerable hate and grievance in his search for viable love. He wrote to his friend and patron Princess Marie in 1913: 'I am no lover at all, it only takes hold of me from outside, perhaps because I do not love my mother' (Rilke 1969: 116).

In October 1915, in the mid-point crisis of the *Elegies*, a month before composing the bleak fourth elegy, the 'Marionette Elegy', he wrote an untitled – and never published – poem about his mother. When I came across this it further encouraged an idea I had formed that Rilke had felt profoundly unrecognised by his mother, that he thought he had never come to life in her mind – in Bion's words, that *maternal containment* had failed for Rilke. In compensation for the failure of maternal introjection I think he developed a hypertrophied use of self-projection into his love objects which led him to feel that he disappeared into people the moment he desired them: 'we vanish inside him and around him . . . what is ours floats into the air, like steam from a dish of hot food' (Rilke 1987: 157).

In this untitled and unpublished poem he describes how 'meine Mutter reißt mich ein', which is translated as 'my mother tears me down'. The full sense of *reißt* is best conveyed by realising that this word is used in German for the demolition of buildings.

> Oh, misery, my mother tears me down.
> Stone upon stone I'd laid, towards a self
> and stood like a small house, with day's expanse around it,
> Now comes my mother, comes and tears me down.
>
> She tears me down by coming and by looking.
> That someone builds she does not see.
> Right through my wall of stones she walks for me.
> Oh, misery, my mother tears me down.
>
> Birds overhead more lightly fill my space.
> Strange dogs can sense it . . .
> Only my mother does not know
> My oh how slowly incremented face.
>
> (Rilke 1981: 65)

The fourth elegy, which followed shortly after this poem, is the most despairing. It has a defiant, bitter, stoic assertion in it and rejection of a compromising half-life. Better a puppet show than a sham, half-filled human drama; he claims he'll put up with 'the stuffed skin, the wire, the face that is nothing but appearance':

> . . . Here I'm waiting.
> Even if the lights go out; even if someone
> tells me 'That's all'; even if emptiness
> floats toward me in a grey draft from the stage ;
> even if not one of my silent ancestors
> stays seated with me, not one woman, not
> the boy with the immovable brown eye –
> I'll sit here anyway. One can always watch.
>
> (Rilke 1987: 169)

More recently Beckett, in his writing, has shown this same loyalty to a seemingly empty world by valuing the truth of its representation; 'perhaps they have carried me to the threshold of my story', wrote Beckett in *The Unnameable*:

> before the door that opens on my own story, that would surprise me, if it opens, it will be I, it will be the silence, where I am, I don't know, I'll never know, in the silence you don't know, you must go on, I can't go on, I'll go on.
>
> (Beckett 1979: 382)

Then comes Rilke's point: that by acknowledging the presence of nullity in life we transform and integrate it, thus finding a place for winter among the seasons of life. He asks the parents of his childhood: 'am I not right/to feel that I *must* stay seated, must/wait before the puppet stage' (Rilke 1987: 171). He asks his father, who he thought was unable to like him:

> Am I not right? You, to whom life tasted
> so bitter after you took a sip of mine,
> the first, gritty infusion of my will.
>
> (Rilke 1987: 171)

He continues with his insistent question; 'am I not right?' he asks the 'dear women' who cared for him but in whose features there were blanks that changed 'into cosmic space' where they no longer were – Rilke's concept of 'absence' as meaning 'without identity'. Then he asks again:

... am I not right
to feel that I *must* stay seated, must
wait before the puppet stage, or rather,
gaze at it so intensely that at last,
to balance my gaze, an angel has to come and
make the stuffed skins startle into life.

(Rilke 1987: 171)

Much has been written about Rilke's angels in the *Elegies*, but perhaps it is best to see what he says himself:

The angel of the *Elegies* is that creature in whom the transformation of the visible into the invisible, which we are accomplishing, appears already consummated . . . that being who vouches for the recognition in the invisible of a higher order of reality. – Hence 'terrible' to us because we, its lovers and transformers, do still cling to the visible.

(Rilke 1969: 375)

I think of this as a poetic personification of Plato's Forms or a precursor of Bion's pre-conceptions. In his letters Rilke is explicit about his use of theological figures for psychological entities and says much the same as Freud, who said that if God is a projection of the unconscious, then metaphysics becomes metapsychology (Freud 1904: 259). Rilke also sees fear of death as a projection and he seems to anticipate Melanie Klein's theory that the fear of external annihilation arises from the projection of the death instinct. He wrote:

And so you see, it was the same with death. . . . it too was pushed out; death, which is probably so near us that we cannot at all determine the distance between it and the life-centre within us without it becoming something external, daily held further from us, lurking somewhere in the void in order to attack . . .

God and death were now outside, were the other, oneself was now our everyday life which at the cost of this elimination seemed to become human, friendly, possible . . . Now this might still have made a kind of sense had we been able to keep God and death at a distance as mere ideas in the realm of the mind; but nature knew nothing of this removal.

(Rilke 1969: 148–9)

This, then, makes sense of the strange lines in the 'Marionette Elegy':

Angel and puppet: a real play, finally

159

Then what we separate by our very presence
can come together. And only then, the whole
cycle of transformations will arise,
out of our own life-seasons

(Rilke 1987: 171)

In other words, we achieve everyday comfortable but unreal selves by denial and projection. Out of our psychic aspiration we conceive of angels as pure spirits unencumbered by bodies and human limitations. Out of our wish for an existence free of psychic life and its ineradicable accompaniments of pain and longing we conceive of ourselves as puppets. Thus by allowing our denuded daily selves to exist in our physical bodies in a state of complacent, compromise-formed half-life we prevent the meeting of our desire for mental life and our longing to be free of it. We prevent the angel and the puppet from coming together. In this elegy Rilke claims that even the most disturbed, effulgent, body-denying psychic life or the puppetry of a mindless life is preferable to the halfway house of a domesticated, half-minded, self-dramatised existence which pretends to be real and complete.

If no one else, the dying must notice how unreal, how full of pretence
is all that we accomplish here, where nothing
is allowed to be itself.

(Rilke 1987: 171)

So he has resolved that he must look within, even if it means he finds emptiness or deadliness, because to identify emptiness and non-existence and to find a home for them is a way of transforming and including them. This I take to be what he had in mind in his own retrospective account of the composition of the *Elegies*:

Two inmost experiences were decisive for their production: the resolve that grew up more and more in my spirit to hold life open toward death, and, on the other side the spiritual need to situate the transformations of love in this wider whole differently than was possible in the narrower orbit of life (which simply shut out death as the other).

(Rilke 1969: 330)

This again was a new prospectus, but it was years before he could fulfil it. The final clutch of the *Elegies* did not emerge until February 1922, in a burst of productivity that also engendered the *Sonnets to Orpheus*. He had isolated himself in a tower in Muzot, Switzerland, even forgoing the company of dogs for fear that attachment would dilute the purity of his isolation and the 'winter experience' he needed to complete the remainder of the elegies.

160

Finally, in a celebratory letter to Lou he described 'laying aside' his pen after completing the tenth elegy: 'Now I know myself again. It really had been like a mutilation of my heart that the Elegies were not here' (Rilke 1969: 292).

These last elegies – seven, eight, nine and ten – are distinct, but they run together. Rilke reiterates the idea that it is our function to transform the visible external world into the invisible internal world, but he does so now optimistically since he sees this as creative and reparative. He adds considerably to this by declaring that 'everything here apparently needs us, in this fleeting world' (Rilke 1987: 199), in order to register it, to experience it, and now a new idea to name it

> . . . Perhaps we are here in order to say: house,
> bridge, fountain, gate, pitcher, fruit-tree, window –
> at most column, tower . . . but to say them you must understand,
> to say them more intensely than the Things themselves
> ever dreamed of existing.
>
> (Rilke 1987: 199–200)

We should give new life to things by naming them so that they have life beyond their own material transient existence. He makes it clear that experiences and feelings are among the things that need a name. Angels, he begins to see, can deal with glorious emotion but not with things. There is another area of experience of which, he decides, angels know nothing, and to which he now gives great value, and that is grief:

> . . . How we squander our hours of pain.
> How we gaze beyond them into the bitter duration
> to see if they have an end. Though they are really
> our winter-enduring foliage, our dark evergreen,
> one season in our inner year – not only a season
> in time – but a place and settlement, foundation and soil and home.
>
> (Rilke 1987: 205)

This is to be the conclusion and resolution in the tenth elegy. In an amazing allegory the 'Laments' take the place of the angel as authoritative and final guide. The Laments are female figures whose forefathers had mines in 'the mountains of primal grief'. At the foot of the mountains of primal grief is the fountainhead of joy.

> . . . sometimes even
> among men you can find a polished nugget of primal grief
> or a chunk of petrified rage from the slag of an ancient volcano.
>
> (Rilke 1987: 207)

This is his own version, I think, of the depressive position, and what he has reached is an ability to value his grief because in it he values what is lost and what he has never had. The latter is crucial since what he seems to have lacked is someone to do for him precisely what he concludes he needs to do for the world: to name things, to register what exists, to transform experience from visible to invisible form, to mourn what has gone and to distinguish what is living from what is dead. I have suggested that this is what his mother had been unable to do for him, perhaps in particular to bury her dead little girl and bring to life her little boy. The moment Rilke reached this point in the *Elegies* he wrote, almost automatically and at great speed, the *Sonnets to Orpheus*. They are, he wrote, 'of the same birth as the Elegies' and sprang up 'in connection with a girl who had died young' (Rilke 1969: 373); this, he said, moved them closer to that realm we share with the dead and those to come: 'We of the here and now . . . are incessantly flowing over and over to those who preceded us, to our origins and to those who seemingly come after us' (*ibid*.).

This prompts the thought that having completed the *Elegies* Rilke could at last bury the sister who died before he was born and with whom he had always been confused. This was not only because his mother had failed to mourn her but also because the phantasised identity with the dead baby sister had provided him with a location for a part of himself that wanted death, that wanted to live in the perpetual womb of the unborn.

Rilke's message in the sonnets is twofold: that we should be glad Euridyce is in the underworld giving us a relationship with the dead and a season, winter, in which to renew it; and that Orpheus, the voice that transforms even the experience of death into song, is alive whenever there is poetry. Rilke anticipates this theme in the first elegy when he evokes the legend that the painful crying at the death of Linus was the birth of music:

> Is the legend meaningless that tells how, in the lament for Linus,
> the daring first notes of song pierced through the barren numbness
> . . . The Void felt for the first time.
> (Rilke 1987: 155)

In the sonnets Rilke celebrates his new found voice and the position it gives him as Orpheus. So by articulating for the dead, and for the unrealised, he has a legitimate place and can at last contain his own deficits by naming them.

Wordsworth's 'infant babe' was a fortunate personality whose expectation of finding a loving and understanding object was realised in his first encounters with his mother, who was then its incarnation and embodiment, giving him a belief that the world would always contain such objects. For other infants such as Rilke the pre-conception of a loving and understanding object has met with only a negative realisation and can therefore be preserved only in the idea of an ever to be unmet object, a pure spirit, Rilke's omniscient but disembodied angel.

I think that in such personalities there is great value in truthfully recognising *what is not* and in the acceptance of *nullity*. Rilke himself wrote in the *Sonnets to Orpheus* (II, 13): 'Sei – und wisse zugleich des Nicht-Seins Bedingung' (Rilke 1987: 244). Roughly translated this means 'Be – and know what it is like not to be'. The experience of an inner void – so dreaded by some individuals who are prey to it, like Rilke – is derived from contacting a potential space within the self that was never occupied, an innate hope never realised, an imageless expectation never given shape. By conceiving of such emptiness, of *Nicht-Sein Bedingung*, as an experience of non-fulfilment, a sense of being and knowing is re-established. If one uses Bion's terminology, a 'realisation in O' (i.e. of being) is co-existent with a 'realisation in K' (i.e. of awareness) of non-being.

Rilke said that he began to write in French after the *Elegies* because there was nothing in his own language that adequately captured the meaning of the French word '*absence*'. How much he valued the idea of space being kept empty for something that would never materialise is best conveyed in the *Sonnets to Orpheus* (II, 4) by the unicorn, the philosopher's paradigm of that which is known though it has never been seen.

> Oh this is the animal that never was.
> It had not been. But for them it appeared
> in all its purity. They left space enough
> And in the space hollowed out by their love
> it stood up all at once and didn't need
> existence. They nourished it, not with grain
> but with the mere possibility of being.
>
> (Rilke 1987: 241)

I would like to add as a postscript to this chapter a fascinating passage by Freud. A German colleague told me when I was discussing my ideas about the *Elegies* that Rilke was the anonymous poet Freud referred to in his essay 'On transience' (Gekle 1986). I will quote a few sentences from this paper, which Freud wrote in 1915, shortly after completing 'Mourning and melancholia'. 'On transience' refers to a walking holiday in the Dolomites in August 1913, a few months after Rilke had written the first group of the *Elegies* and before the *Turning Point* referred to above. I presume the 'taciturn friend' was Lou Andreas Salomé, and her friend, the 'already famous poet', Rilke.

Not long ago I went on a summer walk through a smiling countryside in the company of a taciturn friend and of a young but already famous poet. The poet admired the beauty of the scene around us but felt no joy in it. He was disturbed by the thought that all this beauty was fated to extinction, that it would vanish when winter came, like all human beauty. . . . I could not see my way to dispute the transience of all things. . . . But I did dispute the pessimistic poet's view that the transience of what is beautiful involves any loss in its worth. . . . As regards the beauty of nature, each time it is destroyed by winter it comes again next year, so that in relation to the length of our lives it can be regarded as eternal. . . . What spoilt their enjoyment . . . must have been a revolt in their minds against mourning. . . . I believe that those who think thus, and seem ready to make a permanent renunciation because what was precious has proved not to be lasting, are simply in a state of mourning for what is lost. Mourning as we know, however painful it may be, comes to a spontaneous end. When it has renounced everything that has been lost, then it has consumed itself, and our libido is once more free.

(Freud 1916a: 303–7)

This appeared to be the case for Rilke. His mourning for objects lost and hopes unrealised, 'things silently gone out of mind and things violently destroyed', appeared to be achieved through the composition of the *Elegies*. Hanna Segal suggests that, 'for the artist, the work of art is his most complete and satisfactory way of allaying the guilt and despair arising out of the depressive position and of restoring his destroyed objects' (Segal 1952: 198). She also comments that 'in a great work of art the degree of the denial of the death instinct is less than in any other human activity' (*ibid.*: 204). Rilke's *Elegies* certainly illustrate this and it seems that until the death instinct was fully expressed in his poetry he remained in its grip. The renunciation or relinquishment of the dead object seems to require this full acknowledgement of the desire to be at one with the dead: 'the resolve that grew up more and more in my spirit to hold life open toward death' (Rilke 1969: 330). As Freud said of mourning, 'When it has renounced everything that has been lost, then it has consumed itself, and our libido is once more free' (Freud 1916a: 307).

Such appears to have been the case for Rilke. After he had finally completed the *Elegies*, nine years after his walk with Freud, he had an enormous surge of poetic energy. In addition to the sonnets and a number of other poems in German, he wrote some 400 poems in French in the four years that remained before his death, of leukaemia, in December 1926.

In conclusion I will quote Rilke's retrospective remarks on his own lines from the beginning of *The Duino Elegies*: 'For beauty is nothing/but the beginning of terror, which we still are just able to endure' (Rilke 1987: 151). His comment on this passage was contained in a letter of April 1923:

> Whoever does not, sometime or other, give his full consent . . . to the dreadfulness of life, can never take possession of the unutterable abundance and power of our existence: can only walk on its edge, and one day, when the judgement is given, will have been neither alive nor dead.
>
> (Rilke 1987: 317)

Note

1 The typescript is in the Melanie Klein Archive, held by the Melanie Klein Trust.

Milton's destructive narcissist or Blake's true self?

The mind is its own place, and in itself
Can make a heaven of hell, a hell of heaven.
(Milton 1975: 16)

If we take Freud's suggestion that we treat metaphysics as metapsychology even further and apply it to metatheology, William Blake would recommend himself as the voice of subjectivism, which today finds expression in self-psychology and the advocacy of the authentic, and in which the pathological risk is seen to be false compliance with a powerful object. Milton, on the other hand, speaks for those who would seek salvation from relations with the 'good object' and see destructive narcissism as the impediment to that union. The primacy of *love* – that is, the belief that God is love personified – unites Blake and Milton; where the divine is to be found is what divides them. They also differ as to the source of truth; for Milton it comes from God in his heaven, for Blake it comes from within the divine self. Blake saw the worship of something entirely separate from the self as folly and the source of evil; Milton saw the worship of the self as the source of sin. For Blake, Nobodaddy, the law-giving sky-God, did not exist but was the creation of human illusion and the real source of sin (Keynes 1959: 171). In Milton's account it was Satan, the personification of self-regard, envy and pride, who came between God and mankind (Milton 1975). In terms more familiar in psychoanalysis, Blake saw human problems as arising from disregard of our ideal *true selves* (the divine image) in favour of seeking a dependent relationship with a *false ideal object* (the God of the Church), while Milton saw the human downfall as arising from the opposition of our *narcissism* (Satan) to our worship of our *ideal object* (God).

Blake is in sympathy with the character Satan in Milton's *Paradise Lost*, and he argues that all Satan has done by defying God is to escape from humiliating servitude. The angel Abdiel, on the other hand, speaking for Milton in *Paradise Lost*, says to Satan that there is no servitude in doing what God (the father of morality) or nature (the mother of reality) bids and says to him that he is in self-servitude, to himself 'enthralled'. In other words Milton's diagnosis of Satan's crew as a pathological organisation is that of *destructive narcissism*, whereas for Blake that which is subjective is authentic and that which contradicts it on grounds of natural morality or objective reality is false.

Milton's imagination produces hell, whereas for Blake 'imagination' as the divine source creates heaven. Blake's 'imagination' rescues him by substituting a visionary world, the return to Paradise, for his experience of this material world. Hell for Blake is only the imagination of the Antagonist, the 'other', who imposes his alien psychic reality on that of the self. In *The Marriage of Heaven and Hell* (Blake 1927) Blake reverses Milton's *Paradise Lost*, producing the 'Proverbs of Hell', and claims that it is only the perceptions of God's officials, the good angels, that create the familiar picture of hell. Its inhabitants, the devils, perceive it as a pleasant land:

> As I was walking among the fires of hell, delighted with the enjoyments of Genius; which to Angels look like torment and insanity, I collected some of their Proverbs; thinking that as the sayings used in a nation, mark its character, so the Proverbs of Hell, shew the nature of Infernal wisdom.

> (Blake 1927: 6)

Blake claims that Milton, his literary hero, was really, unknown to himself, on the same side when writing *Paradise Lost*: 'Note. The reason Milton wrote in fetters when he wrote of Angels & God, and at liberty when of Devils and Hell, is because he was a true Poet and of the Devil's party without knowing it' (*ibid.*).

In Blake's theological version of the apocalypse, last judgement and final revelation the triumph is that of the 'Divine Imagination' (of the self) over the imagination of the 'Antagonist' (Satan). Satan's crime in Blake's eyes is not committing sin but inventing it. Danger comes, therefore, in Blake's psychic cosmology from other men's minds and anything other than personal belief or morality. The solution is that each should love the creations of his own mind and not seek to reconcile them with that of others. It was when, some years ago, I was looking at a picture by Blake entitled *The Good and Evil Angels*, based on an engraving in *The Marriage of*

Heaven and Hell, that the idea occurred to me that the two clinical models, the *destructive narcissistic organisation* and the *true/false-self structure*, were symmetrical inversions of each other, that what was construed as 'good' or 'bad', 'true' or 'false' depended on where the essential self was located. A description of the picture and Blake's comments on it will make clear what I mean.

At first sight it appears that a good angel, white and fair, is protectively clasping an infant (representing mankind) to keep it from a bad angel, of dark coloration, who is pictured rising from the flames, where he is chained, to reach for the child. This would appear to illustrate the essence of Milton's account of the Fall in *Paradise Lost*, with Satan trying to get his clutches on infant Adam, who is in the protective arms of a good angel, Raphael or Michael. This looks like a perfect allegorical illustration for Rosenfeld's (1987) clinical description of the attempts of the destructive narcissistic organisation to steal the infant self from the care of the analyst, as transference parent. Blake's own explanation of his picture, however, is exactly the reverse. He says that the ostensibly 'good' white angel is a representation of diabolical, organised religion stealing infant mankind from himself, and that the 'Devil' who is attempting to liberate him represents 'energy' (Blake 1927: 4).

These two alternative theological configurations resemble the two contrasting metapsychological models, both of which have been very influential in psychoanalysis since the 1960s. The first, Herbert Rosenfeld's concept of a destructive narcissistic organisation resembles 'Satan and his crew', as described by Milton. The second metapsychological model, that of Winnicott's concept of the true self masked and betrayed by a false self based on compliance with the external world, resembles Blake's description of the spectre occluding the self.

To take first Rosenfeld's clinical formulation of destructive narcissism:

> In some narcissistic patients the destructive narcissistic parts of the self are linked to a psychotic structure or organisation which is split off from the rest of the personality . . . the whole structure is committed to narcissistic self-sufficiency and is strictly directed against any object relatedness . . . When narcissistic patients of this type begin to make some progress and to form some dependent relationship to the analysis, severe negative therapeutic reactions occur as the narcissistic psychotic part of the self exerts its power and superiority over the analyst, standing for reality, by trying to lure the dependent self into a psychotic omnipotent dream state which results in the patient losing his sense of reality and his capacity for thinking.
>
> (Rosenfeld 1987: 112)

In Milton's *Paradise Lost* we find Satan, as I see him, personifying destructive narcissism, excluded from God's heaven, determined to see his exile as a triumphant entry into his own diabolical narcissistic kingdom:

> . . . Farewell happy fields . . .
> Infernal world . . .
> Receive thy new possessor; one who brings
> A mind not to be changed by place or time.
> The mind is its own place, and in itself
> Can make a heaven of hell, a hell of heaven . . .
> Here we may reign secure, and in my choice
> To reign is worth ambition though in hell:
> Better to reign in hell, than serve in heaven.
>
> (Milton 1975: 16)

I would now like to pair in a similar way Winnicott's description of the 'true/false self' with Blake's 'eternal self' and its 'spectral shell'. Winnicott wrote of 'the False Self, which can now be seen to be a defence, a defence against that which is unthinkable, the exploitation of the True Self, which would result in its annihilation (Winnicott 1960b: 146–7). Blake develops the notion of a spectral self obscuring and betraying the divine self:

> Negation is the spectre, the Reasoning Power in Man,
> This is a False Body: an Incrustation over Immortal
> Spirit: a Selfhood, which must be put off & annihilated away
> (Keynes 1959: 533)

As I will make clear later in this chapter, I regard both of these metapsychological descriptions as valid clinical accounts of particular personality organisations that manifest themselves characteristically in analysis. Later in the chapter I will attempt to describe these further. However, both descriptive structures have been taken to be models of more general application at times, and if either of them is taken to be normative they become the basis of theoretical disputes among analysts, just as they might have been amongst theologians. If primary narcissism is taken to be the starting point of the individual's development the 'true/false self' model will more easily be adopted and the hazards will be perceived as an assault on subjective authenticity. If, on the other hand, a primary object relationship is seen as the developmental origin, the model of destructive narcissism will be more readily adopted and the potential impediment to development will be seen as the individual's narcissism.

Blake's belief system was based on the notion of a divine eternal self masked by a compliant false self that slavishly accepted the objective world.

It is a literary account of what I call *epistemic narcissism*. I define an epistemic narcissist as someone who believes *only* in his or her own ideas, a counterpart in the realm of knowledge to the libidinal narcissist in the realm of love. The next chapter is devoted to further exploration of Blake's belief system, and in this chapter I will discuss Milton's picture of man oppressed and traduced by Satanic self-idolatry. Before discussing further either destructive or epistemic narcissism, however, I need to give a brief account of the concept of narcissism and how it has developed in psychoanalysis.

Freud took the term 'narcissism' from Paul Nacke, who in 1899 used it to denote the attitude of a person who regards his own body in the same way as the body of a sexual object is ordinarily regarded (Freud 1914: 67). Freud went on to suggest that it might claim a place in the regular course of human sexual development and to describe psychological states which could be called narcissistic, in that the love object was the self rather than another person (*ibid.*). The name is derived from the Greek myth of the beautiful young man Narcissus, who fell in love with his own reflected image in a pool and, unable to leave it, remained there until death transformed him into a flower. In Ovid's account this is a punishment for his rejection of all those who loved him, in particular the nymph Echo, who, after her rejection by Narcissus, pined away her substance and was reduced to being just a voice which could only repeat the words of others. In *Paradise Lost* it is Eve who is entranced by her reflection in a pool before meeting Adam. When she does meet him she is momentarily drawn to return to her own image in the pool in preference to the new and different object, the man. Milton thus locates narcissism in our female progenitor, whose vanity was later exploited by the serpent, leading to our downfall.

Having adopted the term 'narcissism', Freud put it to clinical use. His purpose was to explain those states of mind in which emotional investment in anybody or anything outside the self appeared to have been withdrawn. 'We see', he wrote, 'broadly speaking, an antithesis between ego–libido and object–libido. The more one is employed, the more the other becomes depleted' (Freud 1914: 76). He saw, at one extreme, absolute narcissism, manifested as 'paraphrenia', and, at the other extreme, absolute libidinal investment of an object, manifested by 'being in love'. In the state of being in love, which he regarded as the psychopathology of everyday life, an individual seems to give up his or her own personality in favour of the love object. In contrast, the paraphrenic abandons all psychic investment in the world outside him- or herself. This results in a phantasy of the end of the external world. Freud suggested that the delusions found in paraphrenia are secondary to this 'end-of-the-world catastrophe' as part of an attempt at recovery designed to lead the individual back to an involvement with objects in the world outside him- or herself (*ibid.*: 74). In these terms, the

Narcissus of the myth is paraphrenic and Echo has a severe case of self-depletion due to love.

Freud thought that the clinical state of narcissism found in psychoanalytic practice was secondary to a rejection of object relations by the individual. However, he went on to hypothesise that there was an original infantile state of mind that pre-existed object relations. He called this hypothetical state *primary narcissism*, which he also referred to as infantile megalomania. Primary narcissism has been, and remains, an area of controversy in psychoanalytic theory. Those analysts such as Melanie Klein, Fairbairn and Balint who believed that some sort of external object relation exists from birth disputed the existence of a phase of primary narcissism preceding object relations, regarding narcissism as co-existent with object relating and in opposition to or as a defence against it.

I mention primary narcissism particularly because, in his own terms, Blake very clearly believed in it and saw a return to it as salvation. In these terms, Blake's developmental series was primary narcissism (innocence), followed by object relations (experience) and concluding in a resumption of primary narcissism (redemption). I find Ferenczi's speculative psychoanalytic descriptions of primary narcissism almost identical to Blake's poetic accounts of our origins. Ferenczi wrote:

> By means of a kind of empathy into the infantile mind, I arrived at the following hypothesis. To a child kept innocent from any pain, the whole of existence must appear to be a unity – monistic, so to speak. Discrimination between 'good' and 'bad' things, ego and environment, inner and outer world, would only come later; at this stage alien and hostile would be identical.
>
> (Ferenczi 1926: 371)

In Blake's account the divine self finds itself compelled to live in the alien environment of *experience* until it is liberated from the perceptual world by the visionary imagination.

I see both destructive narcissism and the true/false-self personality structures as pathological organisations. The first, that of destructive narcissism, is easily seen in the patient I described in Chapter 2, Miss A, who was compelled by threats from within herself to empty out her thoughts. Within her mind she believed she had an enemy who yet was part of her self, who threatened or cajoled her and at times effectively took her hostage. Her psychic world was governed by a divinely good mother and a satanic, evil father. Clearly the destructive narcissistic organisation was based on her phantasies of her father and also on that aspect of herself that identified with him. Her good object relationship was with her mother historically, externally and internally, and this was, in the main, reproduced

171

in the transference. Goodness was personified by her mother, but in comparison to the diabolical power of the devil it was feeble and required mother's physical presence. As a consequence of the massive projective identification of all her own envious and hostile impulses into her father, his internal representation was always present in her mind. The structure of her analysis was therefore of a desperate appeal to the analyst for knowledge and salvation from the tyranny of her own thoughts. Obedience to the good object, represented by the analyst, was the solution she sought, but obedience to the bad internal object was also her problem.

The second of these two pathological organisations, the true/false self, was described by Donald Winnicott in a number of places; my comments are largely based on his papers of 1949, 1954, 1960b and 1971. Linking my own clinical experience with reading these papers, I have the impression that two rather different types of patient have been subsumed under this heading. One variety has the qualities I described under Helene Deutsch's term the 'as-if' personality (Chapter 5) and the other has the features of the 'thin-skinned' narcissistic or borderline personality described in Chapter 4. It is those in this latter group who would say with Blake: 'I must Create a System, or be enslav'd by another Man's' (Keynes 1959: 629).

In religious terms, the 'as-if' personality would not be the wholehearted believer and advocate of the authority of the spiritual self of Blake's school, but a conformist seeking a comfortable church where he or she could suspend both belief and disbelief. The analytic experience with patients in the borderline group is very different; 'chaos always threatened', wrote Winnicott (1954: 280). In this description Winnicott emphasised how necessary he found it to adapt to the patient and what an enormous impact the patient's belief system had on his own thinking: 'I cannot help being different from what I was before this analysis started' (*ibid.*). I think this is a general phenomenon, and this group of patients have, in my opinion, had an influence on psychoanalytic theory and practice incommensurate with their numbers. It appears to be part of the syndrome itself, which is not surprising when one considers that a key element in such patients is the conviction that in order to make way for their psychic reality the analyst must eliminate his own.

In Chapter 4 I suggested that the belief that 'I must Create a System, or be enslav'd by another Man's' (Keynes 1959: 629) is due to the fact that a fear of malignant misunderstanding by any other independent mind makes absolute agreement necessary and this can only be achieved through tyranny, obedience or magic. From the outset I have argued that this originates from a failure of containment with subsequent problems in negotiating the depressive position and the Oedipus situation. Destructive narcissism, true/false self and the 'as-if' personality all have that in common. What differentiates them from each other as organisations is the nature of their defensive belief systems and their location of power and intention, that which would have been called 'the will'. Coleridge saw Milton's *Paradise Lost* as part of the controversy of its day on the nature of evil and the place of human will in the moral universe. Milton, he thought, took a line that was neither for predestination nor for a theory of complete freedom: 'he declared for the enslavement of the will out of an act of the will itself' (Coleridge 1818: 497). The will, he continued, is 'man's most precious possession as free will . . . But in its utmost obstruction and conse-quent state of reprobation, the will becomes Satanic pride and rebellious self-idolatry' (*ibid.*). This would well do for a definition of destructive narcissism, and Coleridge thought Milton's Satan was its personification. He then described its operation very much as we find it clinically, 'by the fearful resolve to find in itself alone the one absolute motive of action, under which all other motives from within and from without must be either subordinated or crushed' (*ibid.*. In psychoanalysis we could say that the ego's functions, loosely called the will, have been by internal projective identification located in the narcissistic organisation, where, perversely, they are used against the ego. However, if we take Milton's *Paradise Lost* as a description of the internal world the only other possibility is to locate the will in a cruel, ruthless God. In other words, the only alternative to the internal Satanism of destructive narcissism would be the internal self-flagellation of *melancholia*.

Milton, through his description of Satan, suggests that the answer to the problem of evil is that it arises from pride and envy. I want to explore the relationship between pride and envy and will use Milton's Satan to do so. Satan's quarrel with God begins when his pride in his privileged position as a favourite son leads him to take offence at the position given to Jesus.

> Satan . . .
> . . . he of the first,
> In favour and pre-eminence, yet fraught
> With envy against the Son of God, that day
> Honoured by his great Father, and proclaimed
> Messiah king anointed, could not bear
> Through pride that sight, and thought himself
> impaired.
>
> (Milton 1975: 131)

Pride is what is hurt when events conspire to expose us to our limitations and to prove that our expectations of ourselves and our belief in the posi-tion we occupy in the estimation or affection of others are falsely based. Our pride is injured, or, in current jargon, we have suffered a narcissistic wound.

I think that pride appears at a moment when envy is aroused and interposes itself between the situation that arouses envy and the feeling of envy it might give rise to. Instead of the poignant feeling of futile, unjustified hostility that characterises an experience of envious feeling there is a sense of injured pride. While pride is wounded and its accompanying sense of grievance is sustained, envious feeling is kept at bay. Wounded pride produces hurt, outrage, recrimination, self-righteousness and an impulse for revenge. If hurt pride is what follows displacement or deprivation by an object, it implies that a belief exists that the object is a possession in a sense that it is an attribute of the self. Hence outrage follows with its quota of indignation rather than simple rage, with its accompanying sense of helplessness. While a belief exists that the object is a possession of the self and the desired object relationship is a personal attribute, envy does not arise. Even when events conspire to deprive the individual of this privileged place and position in relation to the object, though pride is hurt and a sense of injustice felt, envy is not experienced. I think this is one of the reasons why suffering is embraced, and this maintains pride and prevents the relinquishment of the belief in entitlement:

> To reign is worth ambition though in hell:
> Better to reign in hell, than serve in heaven.
> (Milton 1975: 16)

The fear that envy will be unbearable – and, hence, avoidance of it at all costs – is not simply a matter of its absolute quantity as an element in the personality but of its quantity relative to the individual's capacity to contain it. Like anxiety or aggression, it can provoke a fear of being overwhelmed. Envy, like anxiety, has to be accepted as a natural part of life. A necessary condition for this is the presence of an internal object unsparing in the accuracy of its observations but also understanding and compassionate in its judgements. Milton's God possessed the first of these qualities but singularly lacked the second. Like a perceptive but tyrannical parent, He senses his child's reluctance to acknowledge His superiority and brutally requires submission. Satan, his belief in his supremely important position challenged, feels wounded, but his pride is stimulated rather than annihilated. He is like a plant severely pruned in the spring which effloresces in a summer of triumphant defiance and revenge. His envious feelings are kept at bay by his pride and relish in his misfortune; his revenge is to deny God the father parental satisfaction by subversion of his younger siblings, the newly born Adam and Eve. Satan's envy is nevertheless provoked directly, not by God's omnipotence, but by His declaration that 'This day I have begot whom I declare/My only Son, and on this holy hill/Him have anointed, whom ye now behold/At my right hand' (Milton 1975: 129). We are told by Milton, via the Angel Raphael, that Satan was 'fraught with envy against the Son of God' and 'could not bear through pride that sight, and thought himself impaired' (*ibid.*). Once this notion of injustice is established, pride appears to replace envy and prompt his defiance. This enables him to escape from the force of a new reality provocative of envy by choosing instead to endure defeat and injured pride, not through truth, but at the hands of God's superior power.

We are given another situation where Satan's envy is painfully provoked by his having to witness the human couple's intercourse:

> . . . aside the devil turned
> For envy, yet with jealous leer malign
> eyed them askance, and to himself thus plained.
> Sight hateful, sight tormenting! Thus these two
> Imparadised in one another's arms
> The happier Eden, shall enjoy their fill
> Of bliss on bliss, while I to hell am thrust,
> Where neither joy nor love, but fierce desire,
> Among our other torments not the least,
> Still unfulfilled with pain of longing pines.
>
> (Milton 1975: 99)

It is this that renews Satan's intention to plot their downfall as a means of avenging himself on God, but now with the added incentive of robbing the primal couple of their bliss:

> Live while ye may,
> Yet happy pair; enjoy, till I return,
> Short pleasures, for long woes are to succeed.
> So saying, his proud step he scornful turned.
>
> (Milton 1975: 100)

In these few lines Satan is also restored in his pride by scornfully imagining the unsuspecting couple's downfall, and once this is re-established he is free from the torments of envious and jealous feeling. This again is linked to a belief that the place now occupied by the couple, their 'room of bliss', really belongs to him and his 'devilish crew':

> O hell! what do mine eyes with grief behold,
> Into our room of bliss thus high advanced
> Creatures of other mould, earth-born perhaps,
> Not spirits.
>
> (Milton 1975: 95)

175

The 'room of bliss' – that imaginary space, or space for imagination, that is forever the 'other room' because its existence depends on our absence from it, where phantasised events take place between the primal couple – is claimed by Satan to be the place in heaven from which he has been expelled. Another psychic version of the 'other room' is hell, and by making a hell of any and every place Satan preserves his belief in his claim on the 'room of bliss'.

Thus pride is restored as injured pride, and envy as an experience evaded, with its painful realisation of the separateness of others and their private ownership of their own desirable qualities, and the bottomless antipathy to life this engenders.

> O thou that with surpassing glory crowned,
> Look'st from thy sole dominion like the God
> Of this new world; at whose sight all the stars
> Hide their diminished heads; to thee I call,
> But with no friendly voice, and add thy name
> O, sun, to tell thee how I hate thy beams
>
> (Milton 1975: 86)

In Book IV of *Paradise Lost* Milton surprisingly presents us with Satan in what in 'Kleinian' language would be called the depressive position. He who had seemed to be a part-object, a personification of pride and envy, the exemplar of evil, the bad object of the paranoid-schizoid position in person, becomes a whole person experiencing conflict, remorse and dread.

Satan arrives at the beginning of Book IV planning revenge on God by tempting the primal couple to betray their Creator. His future as the dragon of the Apocalypse is invoked to remind the reader of his future contest with God for the soul of mankind and of his ferocious destructive-ness. At the moment of his arrival, fuelled by his rage, he is hell-bent on revenge and insulated by his indignation from doubt, dread or pity. He is not simply in a rage; he is outraged. His hurt pride reassures him, by telling him that he is wronged, usurped and unnaturally deprived, that his pre-existing belief in the supremacy of his position need not be questioned. While he continues to believe this he is protected not only from reproach but also from envy. However, at the moment of giving birth to his vengeful project, his boiling feelings:

> . . . like a devilish engine back recoils
> Upon himself; horror and doubt distract
> His troubled thoughts, and from the bottom stir
> The hell within him, for within him hell
> He brings, and round about him, nor from hell

One step no more than from himself can fly
By change of place: now conscience wakes despair
That slumbered, wakes the bitter memory
Of what he was, what is, and what must be
Worse; of worse deeds worse sufferings must ensue.

(Milton 1975: 85)

Satan recoils upon himself; in our language, he ceases to project and finds that hell is within himself and is not his unjustly imposed prison. Milton also, like his character Satan, has 'back recoiled' upon himself, in the sense that he has looked inwards into his own human nature to find an explanation for Satan's continuing destructiveness. He does so in the vicissitudes and complexities of a depressive position compounded by despair and unbearable envy. He makes Satan human, and in this short passage makes clear why this particular human cannot remain in the depressive position and is left with a choice between melancholia or the role of the destructive narcissist.

Satan cannot bear the thought that if he repents and is forgiven he will once again feel provoked by envy into a rebellious attack. He cannot imagine that he will be able to contain his feelings and integrate them with his acknowledged admiration and gratitude. In a psychological sense, Milton produces an answer to the problem of evil in this passage. It is a consequence of a failure to contain inevitable hostility in such a way that it might be mitigated, and of the choice, instead, to split love from hate more and more, producing eventually a pure culture of hatred of anything good. Whereas ordinary human badness and aggression are inevitable, evil comes about only as a consequence of *serial splitting*. Spitefulness is commonplace, but pure malice is the product of distillation. In this passage we see this process in Satan.

Milton gives us a splendid opportunity to benefit from his insight into the relationship of pride to envy and the interaction of both with the depressive position and the Oedipus situation. In Book IV of *Paradise Lost* I think we can see the genesis of destructive narcissism in the failure to work through the depressive position and the subsequent regression to a particular paranoid defensive organisation which in Chapter 6 I have described as $D(n) \rightarrow Ps(path)$.

---------------------------------14---------------------------------

William Blake and epistemic narcissism

And am I wrong to worship where
Faith cannot doubt nor Hope despair
Since my own soul can grant my prayer?
                                   (Emily Brontë 1992: 23)

I think William Blake was a great writer. He was also a great believer. He is
often described as a visionary poet, a term also applied to others, such as
Wordsworth, who are regarded as members of the English Romantic
movement. In Blake's case, however, the term has a particular meaning
because from childhood to the end of his life he had visions, in the sense
that Joan of Arc or Bernadette of Lourdes had visions; he insisted on their
perceptual reality and the validity of their content. He had a one-person
religion, or perhaps two-person, as Catherine Blake, his wife, played Echo
to his Narcissus in a thoroughgoing way.

In this chapter I suggest that what Blake saw as a religious system necessary to redeem mankind from its calamitous fall from eternity I would see
as a psycho-pathological organisation meant to remedy a psychological
catastrophe. In some of his writings, for example *The Everlasting Gospel* or *A
Vision of the Last Judgement*, he articulates his system as a religious creed. In
his prophetic books he describes, in the form of a series of epics
concerning his own mythological characters, a mental catastrophe and a
psychic remedy. He insisted that these epics were not allegories, but visions.
And he believed that mankind's fall and redemption were a mental event
since divinity existed only within the mind. I think that his conscious belief
system served an unconscious purpose, that it was a *counter-belief system*
which was meant to protect him from, and remedy, an already-existing
unconscious belief that would lead him to terror or despair. The psychological situation that is dreaded has in fact already happened, and he gives an

account of it in his epic poetic accounts of the Fall. His defensive and remedial belief system is a remarkably insightful account of what I called *epistemic narcissism* in the last chapter. I defined an epistemic narcissist as someone who believes only in his own ideas, a counterpart in the realm of knowledge to the libidinal narcissist in the realm of love.

It is not my plan to categorise Blake as a narcissist, but, rather, to designate as epistemic narcissism the system of belief he described and advocated. Similarly, though I imagine his description of psychic catastrophe derives from personal experience, it is the poetic account, his text, that is my source and subject, not his life.

T. S. Eliot wrote in his essay *William Blake*:

> [He] was endowed with a capacity for considerable understanding of human nature, with a remarkable and original sense of language and the music of language, and a gift of hallucinated vision. Had these been controlled by a respect for impersonal reason, for common sense, for the objectivity of science, it would have been better for him. What his genius required, and what it sadly lacked, was a framework of accepted and traditional ideas which would have prevented him from indulging in a philosophy of his own.
>
> (Johnson and Grant 1979: 509)

Eliot thought the problem a simple one of lack of personal education in Blake and a deficiency of Mediterranean culture in England. He saw Blake as an English philosophical Robinson Crusoe. This rather imperious explanation is, I think, too superficial. Blake eschewed impersonal reason, common sense and objectivity for profound psychological reasons, and as such he speaks for many others who may well be highly educated, and even infused with Mediterranean culture, but nevertheless fear that their subjective existence may be annihilated by the objectivity of others. It is a fear of the chaos which would follow should subjectivity and objectivity be integrated that I think lies at the root of the system of belief that Blake elaborates. I have described this underlying fear in Chapter 4.

Blake regarded his imagination as the divine source, the creator, and he regarded *belief* as the act of creation; self-doubt he saw as destruction:

> If the Sun and Moon should Doubt
> They'd immediately Go out.
>
> (Keynes 1959: 433)

He saw belief as truth, formed by imagination and not received by perception; not seeing is believing but believing is seeing. He wrote that 'vision is the world of imagination: is Eternity. Vision is all that exists' and he

179

claimed: 'Mental things alone are real'. The eye is an organ for projection, not perception:

> This Life's dim Windows of the Soul
> Distorts the Heavens from Pole to Pole
> And leads you to Believe a Lie
> When you see with, not thro' the Eye
>
> (Keynes 1959: 753)

Belief, treated as the truth, was for him the limiting membrane of an otherwise bottomless void, the only curb on the total mental disintegration that followed the act of creation. Creation, he thought, resulted in the catastrophic separating out from within the primal unity of the self of the intellect, with its attachment to the illusion of a material universe as a finite and measurable physical world. The infantile catastrophe is told by Blake in the form of his account of Creation in his alternative *Bible of Hell*, which consists of *The Book of Urizen, The Book of Ahania* and *The Book of Los*. He has two versions of this catastrophe, just as in the Bible the *Book of Genesis* has two versions of Creation. In the first version Urizen, the personification of intellect, creates a fathomless void in the personality by wrenching himself from the side of the whole body of the eternal self. In the second account Los, imagination personified, is faced with the impenetrable, material, objective world created by Urizen. Blake describes this as a confrontation with a solid, non-fluctuant object. Los was driven wild with impatience by this black, adamantine, impenetrable rock created by Urizen. Los smashes it into fragments, thus producing a bottomless abyss, into which he then falls. So we have in the first version the subjective account of a pre-natal quiescent psychic unity ruptured by that part of mental life that is linked to the physical senses tearing itself off, leaving a chasm within the self. The second account is from an observer's viewpoint; in this account the infant imagination, in its frustration and antipathy to the impenetrability, blackness, coldness and hardness of its primal object, smashes it to pieces and then falls into the abyss thus created:

> . . . Los fell & fell
> Sunk precipitant, heavy, down, down,
> Times on times, night on night, day on day.
> Truth has bounds error none; falling, falling;
> Years on Years, ages on ages,
> Still he fell thro' the void, still a void
>
> (Keynes 1959: 258)

This second version strongly resembles that described by Melanie Klein as the destructive attack on the internal object, resulting in states of mental fragmentation. She wrote: 'The mechanism of one part of the ego annihilating other parts . . . I suggest underlies *world catastrophe*' (Klein 1946: 24). Bion, in several of his writings, emphasised this notion of Klein's that the patient attacks his or her object with such violence that not only the object is felt to disintegrate but also the mental apparatus of the person delivering the attack. This poetic account by Blake describes this and the ensuing symptomatology in an extraordinarily vivid way.

Blake continues with his description of the Fall: 'Incessant the falling Mind labour'd, Organizing itself' (Keynes 1959: 258). The resulting organisation designed to arrest the fall, by 'the falling Mind' Los, is an imaginary perceptual world with physical dimensions and bodily characteristics. This, Blake thinks, is Los's error and the basis of the *human illusion* of physical existence in a material world in which mankind is subsequently trapped.

I see this dramatic story as an insightful account of a catastrophe that resulted from a violent fragmentation of irreducible psychic fact which was represented and experienced as a hard, unyielding object in the mind. The mind then falls into the abyss of 'unknowingness' thus created. As it falls it labours to produce a belief system that it can treat as the truth, the 'bounds' it needs to arrest its fall. Earlier Blake had propounded a dictum of absolutist subjectivity so that 'Everything possible to be believed is an image of truth' (Blake 1927: 8); so the belief system the mind creates 'as an image of truth' serves as its own safety net and remedy for chaos and the void. The enemies of belief are therefore the enemies of self-existence and the creators of chaos. The sceptics, 'the Questioners', as Blake calls them, are therefore the enemies of the mind. Professional questioners such as empirical or natural philosophers are the agents of Satan – Bacon, Locke and Newton in particular: Bacon for seeking truth through reason as opposed to revelation; Locke for his emphasis on learning through experience as opposed to Blake's belief that 'Man is a garden ready planted and sown' (Johnson and Grant 1979: 443); and Newton for formulating the laws of nature in a material universe that Blake abhorred, and proof by mathematics, which he despised. 'Science is the Tree of Death', wrote Blake (Keynes 1959: 777).

In this chapter I am concerned mainly with the nature and content of Blake's beliefs rather than the quality of his verse. However, if I regard his ideas as seriously misguided, which I do, and if I consider that poetry should be judged by the test of truth, how is it that I rate his poetic verses as highly as I do? Louis Macneice, himself a considerable poet who was convinced that poetry was ultimately vindicated by its realism, addressed this question when considering the work of another great poet with strange convictions, W. B. Yeats. 'Poetry gains body from beliefs', MacNeice wrote, but 'not necessarily because they are the right beliefs'. He went on:

181

'It is not the absolute, or objective, validity of a belief that vindicates the poetry; it is a gross over-simplification to maintain that a right belief makes a poem good and a wrong belief makes a poem bad' (MacNeice 1941: 231).

My own answer to the question of how a misguided belief can be the basis of a great poem would be to make a distinction between a true representation and the representation of the truth. Blake's poetic account is a true, vivid and insightful description of an authentic psychological position and system of belief: it is a true representation. Even though I consider this psychological position to be false, defensive and based on an untenable belief system, it is one that forms the basis of some religious creeds; it is one held consciously by quite a number of individuals and unconsciously by many more. Because he was a great poet, he offers us a special opportunity to see, by the exposition of his own thinking, into the minds of others with similar belief systems and a similar need to protect themselves from like terrors.

Earlier I described his creed as exemplifying unashamedly and coherently epistemic narcissism. It is based on a claim to possess the truth by personal revelation; its reality rests on its subjective validity and on the basis of that alone, independently of its correspondence with other known truths and regardless of its disagreement with anything outside itself. In psychoanalytic terms, it is a psychic reality that claims to be true because it is internally valid and is independent of any correspondence with external reality. We could paraphrase Blake's description of the eternal self as that of *a true self* that is only true to itself.

And in Melodious Accents, I
Will sit me down and Cry, I, I.

(Keynes 1959: 600)

From outside, this self would seem to oppose any version of reality other than its own; from inside, any belief opposing that of the true self threatens to annihilate it. Accordingly, Blake, as he wrote in his prophetic poem *Jerusalem*, saw himself as:

Striving with Systems to deliver Individuals from those Systems
I must Create a System, or be enslav'd by another Man's.
I will not Reason & compare: my business is to Create.

(Keynes 1959: 629)

Blake unashamedly propounds as the route to salvation what in psychoanalysis has been called infantile megalomania. In this state, he claims, we are what we imagine we are, and our imagination is our share of the divine.

182

In our infantile innocence, he argues, we unselfconsciously believe this and when redeemed will do so again. He celebrated this state of mind in his *Songs of Innocence.* The other part of that collection, *Songs of Experience*, is an altogether different matter. In these he brilliantly captures the cruelty of human nature and the horrors of Regency London.

> In every cry of every Man,
> In every Infant's cry of fear,
> In every voice, in every ban,
> The mind-forg'd manacles I hear.
>
> How the Chimney sweeper's cry
> Every black'ning Church appals;
> And the hapless Soldier's sigh
> Runs in blood down Palace walls.

(Keynes 1959: 216)

In Blake's view experience does not teach; it corrupts, with its deprivation, pain and provocation, and compels innocent egocentricity into giving a place to envy, jealousy and covetousness. As Jean Hagstrum wrote, 'Experience is blighted Innocence. . . . It is a congregation of social, political, psychological, and unnatural horrors. . . . The one ray of light that penetrates its darkness is that of the coming judgement that will destroy it' (Johnson and Grant 1979: 529).

> What is the price of experience? do men buy it for a song
> Or wisdom for a dance in the street? No, it is bought with the price
> Of all that a man hath; his wife, his children.
> Wisdom is sold in the desolate market where none come to buy,
> And in the withered field where the farmer plows for bread in
> vain.

(Keynes 1959: 290)

For Blake the sequence is not that of the tragic vision of life with a pattern of a beginning, a rise in maturity and fulfilment, and eventually a fall into age and death; his is the apocalyptic cycle. In this, as Northop Frye stated, 'the tragedy comes in the middle with the eclipse of the innocent vision, and the story ends with the re-establishment of the vision' (Johnson and Grant 1979: 520). For Blake Creation is the Fall; we must therefore be redeemed by revelation and imagination to believe once more in the eternal and inviolate nature of the self free from the entanglements of that state of mind characteristic of the fallen world. In biological terms, conception, not birth, is the Fall; in traditional terms, it is not the loss of paradise

183

by Adam and Eve but the separate creation of Adam and Eve. This fallen world in which we live Blake called 'generation'. In this, a world of the 'human illusion' of physicality and finite time, there were specifically two obstacles to a divine reunion of the self, namely the division of the sexes and the existence of generations. These are precisely the two ingredients that psychoanalysis has found to be the essential components of the Oedipus situation, the first unalterable facts of life that confront our wishful thinking with a disagreeable necessity and inevitably contentious future. The reality of generational and sexual difference, as solid, non–fluctuant and adamantine as that created by Urizen which confronted Los, in Blake's epic, leading him to shatter it into fragments.

Before continuing with Blake's ideas and their correspondence with some psychoanalytic theories, I would like briefly to place him and his family in a historical, literary and religious context. He was born in 1757, married in 1782 and died, childless, in 1827. Thus he lived through the American and French revolutions, and the English counter-revolution that followed, with its suspension of habeas corpus and free speech. It was a time resembling the McCarthy anti-Communist period in twentieth-century America. The poet Leigh Hunt, for example, was jailed for his writing. Such was the class-consciousness of the period that a serious literary reviewer in *Blackwoods* felt able to dismiss the poetry of Keats and Leigh Hunt on the grounds that 'All the great poets of our country have been men of some rank in society . . . but Mr. Hunt cannot utter a dedication, or even a note, without betraying the *Shibboleth* of low birth and low habits' (quoted in Coote 1995: 102). London was a violent place; poverty and homelessness were rampant, and the cruel employment of children as chimney sweeps was considered respectable. It gives one a jolt when reading Jane Austen if one remembers that she was a contemporary of Blake, such were the different worlds that existed in one country intellectually and socially.

Blake came from a much lower class than the other Romantic poets. He was one of seven children born to a small shopkeeper in Soho. He was the third child; an elder brother died and he had one sister. Of his other brothers, he is described as adoring one and hating another, whom he regarded as 'the evil one'. There is no evidence of family abuse or victimisation, but nevertheless he explained to the Jews in his epic poem *Jerusalem*:

> A man's worst enemies are those
> Of his own house and family.
>
> (Keynes 1959: 652)

He felt his parents favoured his brother John, 'the evil one'. He rarely spoke of his parents and, as Peter Ackroyd comments in his biography, Blake had a sense of himself like 'Shakespeare's Coriolanus who stood "As if a man were Author of himself" ' (Ackroyd 1995: 21). Frederick Tatham, his first biographer, five years after his death, wrote that 'he despised restraints & rules, so much that his Father dare not send him to School' (quoted in *ibid*.: 23). Blake may not have been as self-conceived as he would have liked to have professed, but he was certainly self-taught. Later he asserted: 'There is no use in education, I hold it wrong. It is the great Sin. It is eating of the tree of Knowledge of Good and Evil' (*ibid*.). He was apparently beaten once by his mother because he insisted on the reality of his visions. His parents never repeated this, although his father was tempted to do so when made anxious by the same insistence. The single beating remained with him as a grievance for life.

His parents sent him to drawing school at the age of 10 and five years later he was apprenticed as an engraver. On completion of this he gained a scholarship to the fairly newly founded Royal Academy School. The President of the Royal Academy, Sir Joshua Reynolds, was later to become one of the favourite targets in Blake's private intellectual shooting gallery. One of Reynolds's crimes was to be influenced by Locke. Blake wrote:

> Reynolds Thinks that Man Learns all that he knows. I say on the Contrary that man Brings All that he has or Can have Into the World with him. Man is Born like a Garden ready Planted and Sown. This World is too poor to produce one Seed.
>
> (Keynes 1959: 471)

He wrote in the margin of Reynolds's treatise: 'The mind that could have produced this Sentence is pitiable . . . I certainly do thank God that I am not like Reynolds' (Keynes 1959: 471). Blake's marginalia in his book collection are like artillery shells in a perpetual intellectual campaign. His first biographer, Frederick Tatham, commented: 'some men muse & call it thinking, but . . . his thought was only for action, as a man plans a House, or a General consults his Map, & arranges his forces for a Battle' (Johnson and Grant 1979: 494).

It is often said that Blake's ideas are diffuse, contradictory and deliberately inconsequential. I think not. He has ideas about the necessary theoretical co-existence of contradiction, but this is part of his advocacy of a system of individualistic subjectivism, not a penchant for unsettled belief in his own thinking. A good deal has been written about Blake's influences, and certainly the ideas of such thinkers as Paracelsus, Boehme and Leibniz find a place in his work, as does Anabaptist theology. However, what seems clear to me is that he took from others only what already fitted his own thinking and violently attacked anything he read that might negate it. Others could believe what they liked as long as it did not threaten the organisation of his ideas; he was always ready to tolerate their ideas without sharing or challenging them. If they professed to have visions and were willing, in exchange, to acknowledge the validity of his, he welcomed them.

Blake was a one-man religious organisation, with his own theology and metaphysics, whose credo was 'I must Create a System, or be enslav'd by another Man's' (Keynes 1959: 629). Nevertheless it might be helpful to place him in relation to the centuries-old religious systems from which his own emerged. He comes from a definite, though deviant, Christian tradition and from a time when dissenting, radical Protestant religions proliferated, particularly among the lower classes. Both his parents were from dissenting Christian families.

Blake asserted that mental things alone are real, describing the imagination as 'the real & eternal World of which this Vegetable Universe is but a faint shadow & in which we shall live in our Eternal or Imaginative Bodies when these Vegetable Mortal Bodies are no more' (Keynes 1959: 717). In religious terms, he was Gnostic. Gnosticism, literally, means having a special and direct knowledge of spiritual mysteries. The Gnostics were a sect of early Christians who claimed to have superior knowledge of spiritual things and interpreted the sacred writings by a mystic philosophy. Their central notion was that the material universe was a creation, *not* of God, but of a second power, Demiurgos. In the first century a group called the Docetae took from Gnosticism their particular belief that Christ's human nature and form were only apparent, and hence his acts and suffering were only apparent. In the second century the followers of Marcion of Sinope rejected the God of the Old Testament as the Demiurge, God of Law (Jehovah), and worshipped only Jesus Christ, as the God of Love, whose mission was to overthrow the Demiurge. In the third century the Manichaeans, followers of Mani, believed that the universe was controlled by two antagonistic powers, light or goodness (identified with God) and darkness, chaos or evil. Christ was sent to restore the world to light and to banish darkness. Blake was a thoroughgoing Gnostic and his religious system includes these ideas elaborated in his own way.

> Error is Created. Truth is Eternal. Error, or Creation, will be burned up the Moment Men cease to behold it. I assert for My Self that I do not behold the outward Creation & that to me it is hindrance & not Action; it is as the Dirt upon my feet, No part of Me.
>
> (Keynes 1959: 617)

Blake would have agreed with the Beatles that 'All you need is love, love./All you need is love.' Much of his poetics, though greatly removed in style and symbolism from the declarations of 1968, is in the same libertarian, libidinal spirit, and informed by many of the same beliefs. In the *Visions of the Daughters of Albion* he anticipates the banishment of sorrow by free love with a triangle of pleasure replacing the triangle of jealousy: 'I cry, Love! Love! Love! happy happy Love! free as the mountain wind!' (Keynes 1959: 194).

E. P. Thompson (1993), the famous left-wing historian, rightly described Blake as an Antinomian. He saw him as a poetic genius arising from among those bible-based, anti-establishment Protestants who formed a variety of dissenting religious groups that burgeoned at the turn of the seventeenth century. All you need is love, divine love, was the Antinomian creed, and for some of them human, sexual love was the manifest form of divine love and, accordingly, the route to salvation. The Antinomians believed that the moral law is not binding on Christians who live under the law of grace. The sect originally arose in Germany in 1535 with a doctrine of free grace. John Saltmarsh, an English Antinomian, justified free grace, or 'the Flowing of Christ's Blood to Sinners' in 1645 by saying: 'The Spirit of Christ sets a believer as free from Hell, the Law, and Bondage, as if he was in Heaven', and all he has to do, says Saltmarsh, is 'to believe' and 'he is so' (*ibid.*: 15). Thompson liked to see Blake as an exemplar of the people's religion, at war with the hegemony of Church and state. This Antinomian religion, he wrote, 'displaced the authority of institutions and of received worldy wisdom with that of the individual's inner light' (*ibid.*: 5). I would add, however, that they were also apocalyptic in their religious expectations, selectively fundamentalist in their bible reading, and guided by the visionary experiences of their leaders. Such a leader was Swedenborg, who founded a sect to which Blake briefly belonged. Such apocalyptic sects have burgeoned again in our own times, particularly in the United States, where they are currently seen as a threat to established educational values and public order, which they oppose.

E. P. Thompson, as a secular libertarian and socialist, approved of the Antinomians and thought their religion 'allowed to the individual a stubborn scepticism in the face of the established culture, a fortitude in the face of its seductions or persecutions sufficient to support Christians in the face of the State or of polite learning' (Thompson 1993: 5). Blake, however, would not altogether have approved of Thompson's ideas, for, though he stood up for Tom Paine and his *Rights of Man*, he criticised both Paine's and Voltaire's secular libertarianism. He said that 'while we are in the world of Mortality we must suffer' and continued: 'You cannot have Liberty in this World without what you call Moral Virtue & you cannot have Moral Virtue without slavery of [half-deleted] that half of the Human Race who hate what you call Moral Virtue' (Keynes 1959: 615–16). Though Blake has become an icon for some on the Left, particularly those with a libertarian left tendency, his own solutions would never have been to men's problems by social restructuring of this finite world.

187

The only solution he considered was his own system of belief in the divine self and in the divinity of other selves. These divine selves were united by their possession of a shared eternal nature, while remaining individual in their subjective beliefs, which should never be correlated. They are very much as Leibniz described his monads: '[they] have in themselves a certain perfection . . . there is a self sufficiency in them which makes them the sources of their internal actions – incorporeal automata, if I may so put it' (quoted in Ayer and O'Grady 1992: 249). It seems that in Leibniz's system monads are only related to God in their own way and cannot be judged from outside it; thus however they appear to us they are altogether satisfactory to God and part of his perfect creation. In this system, in psychological terms, the individual's subjective reality cannot be subjected to objective appraisal as there is no shared objective world, only an aggregation of subjective experiences. This monadic system has found its way into some current sociological thinking and some psychoanalytic theorising on inter-subjectivity. It sounds thoroughly postmodern. Blake adopted monadism wholeheartedly and asserted that particularity is all, that there are no general truths: 'to Generalize is to be an Idiot. To Particularize is the Alone Distinction of Merit (quoted in Johnson and Grant 1979: 440). As Blake wrote in *The Everlasting Gospel*:

> The Vision of Christ that thou dost see
> Is my Vision's Greatest Enemy
> Thine has a great hook nose like thine
> Mine has a snub nose like to mine
>
> (Keynes 1959: 748)

The divine selves are to be united only by their possession of a shared eternal nature; their subjective realities should never be correlated.

> Both read the Bible day & night,
> But thou readst black where I read white.
>
> (Keynes 1959: 748)

This can be accomplished in Beulah, a place of free love and also a place where 'Contraries are equally True' (Keynes 1959: 518). A psychoanalytic reader is inevitably reminded of Freud's description of the 'system unconscious', where:

> instinctual impulses . . . exist side by side without being influenced by one another and are exempt from mutual contradiction . . . in this system [there is] no negation, no doubt, no degrees of certainty. . . .

The processes of the system Ucs. are *timeless* . . . [they] pay just as little regard to reality. They are subject to the pleasure principle.

(Freud 1915: 186–7)

Beulah is a place where both libidinal and epistemic narcissism can be fully realised while object relationships of a sort are retained, because 'I am in you and you are in me, mutual in love divine' (Keynes 1959: 622). To love is to become at one with all other lovers, and to believe is to become at one with all other believers. As he says in *The Marriage of Heaven and Hell*, 'Everything possible to be believed is an image of truth' (Blake 1927: 8) and all is particularity; there is no generality. This is in stark contrast to the world of experience, where objectivity is attempted, the reconciliation of ideas demanded and general truths promulgated. This fallen world of experience, 'generation', is a place where differences of generation and gender cause havoc and murder.

In his poetic prophecies it is Beulah that Blake sees as the way back to Eden. In the Book of Isaiah Beulah is the name of the land of blessed marriage (Isaiah 62:4). In *Pilgrim's Progress* it is described as the final destination on earth of the pilgrims who wait to cross the river of death to the Celestial City:

Beulah, whose air was very sweet and pleasant . . . here they heard continually the singing of birds, and saw every day the flowers appear in the earth, and heard the voice of the turtle in the land. In this country the sun shineth night and day; wherefore this was beyond the Valley of the Shadow of Death, and also out of reach of Giant Despair, neither could they from this place so much as see Doubting Castle . . . In this land also, the contract between the bride and the bridegroom was renewed.

(Bunyan 1684: 161)

For Blake, Beulah was a realm of mild moony lustre and soft sexual delusions, and 'a place where Contraries are equally True' (Keynes 1959: 518). It relieved humankind of those two important distinctions that condemned us to live in a fallen world: the differences of gender and of generation. Judging from his unpublished explicit erotic drawings and his textual references to 'male-females' and 'female-males', hermaphroditism prevailed in Beulah. However, in yet another description of Beulah Blake also made clear that this earthly paradise is most obviously found 'within each district/As the beloved infant in his mother's bosom round incircled' (*ibid.*). This is not, however, contradictory, as for Blake infancy is conceived as:

Infancy! fearless, lustful, happy, nestling for delight

In laps of pleasure.

(Keynes 1959: 193)

He saw adult sexuality as its renewal. As he put it:

Take thy bliss O Man!
And sweet shall be thy taste & sweet thy infant joys renew!

(Keynes 1959: 193)

It becomes clear that Blake's idea of progress from the fallen world of generation, through Beulah to Eden is an imagined regression from adult life, through sexual daydream to a voluptuous infancy, en route to the eternal state of being unborn; in Freud's terms, from the ego to the id, from the system Cs-Pcpt to the system Ucs. This notion is very close to some so-called narcissistic phantasies described in psychoanalytic writing. In these terms Blake's developmental series was primary narcissism (innocence), followed by object relations (experience) and concluding in a resumption of primary narcissism (redemption).

In Chapter 13 I commented that I find Ferenczi's psychoanalytic speculative descriptions of primary narcissism to be almost identical to Blake's poetic accounts of our origins. Ferenczi wrote of the infant:

In its primal, narcissistic self-assurance it has hitherto only known itself; it has known nothing of the existence of objects outside itself, which, of course, include even the mother, and could therefore have no feelings towards them, either friendly or hostile.

(Ferenczi 1926: 371)

In Ferenczi's account the infant's innocence of knowledge and innocence of love are rudely interrupted by the intrusion of awareness of a world outside him- or herself:

He wants to live in undisturbed harmony with his environment, but is prevented from doing so by the existence of a 'disturbing object'; this leads to a defusion of his instincts, so that the aggressive, destructive component comes to the fore.

(Ferenczi 1926: 371–2)

So it is in Blake's scheme. He begins *The Book of Los* with a lament for a lost golden age of pre-existence:

O Times remote!
When Love & Joy were adoration,

190

And none impure were deem'd:
Not Eyeless Covet,
Nor thin–lipped Envy,
Nor Bristled Wrath,
Nor Curled Wantoness.

(Keynes 1959: 256)

There are always two views of the golden age, whether as a cultural phenomenon or an individual developmental story: one that it is recollected; the other that it is invented. The first is that something really has been lost and is now a memory; the second is that it never was and is a daydream erected to buttress us against the vicissitudes of the present. So it is in psychoanalytic theory; there are those who think we have lost an infantile golden age of primary narcissism and those who think it is fictional past used as a retreat from an unwelcome present. Blake left us in no doubt where he stood on this question: he believed we came from, belonged in and should return to the golden age.

In fact he went further: Paradise was lost, he says, not after an original sin but at the moment of creation – in psychological terms, not even at the moment of birth but at the moment of conception. His poetic and religious ideas are remarkably similar to the delusional, narcissistic beliefs of some psychotic patients described by Wilfred Bion:

The patient . . . will provide instances showing that every interpretation the psycho-analyst gives is really a thought of his. He will betray his belief that papers or books written by others, including of course his psycho-analyst, were really filched from him. This belief extends to what in more usual patients appears as the Oedipal situation. In so far as he or she admits the facts of parental intercourse . . . he is simply a lump of faeces, the product of a couple. In so far as he regards himself as his creator he has evolved out of the infinite. His human qualities (limitations) are due to the parents, by their intercourse, stealing him from himself (equated with God).

(Bion 1967: 165)

I would regard this as the ultimate version of narcissism, in which Narcissus contemplates a reflection of a self he believes he has created. The penalty for this in the myth is that he has to observe the ageing self and its fading beauty; he is like a Dorian Gray locked in the attic with his portrait waiting for death. Blake has a remedy for this: the divine self is the eternal self. *The Revelation of St John* is a biblical text that underlies all his *Prophetic Books* and his belief that 'there shall be no more death, neither sorrow, nor crying, neither shall there be any more pain' (Revelation 21:4).

191

Blake complains to a mythical mother of being victimised by his conception, his development in the womb and his birth. He describes what he calls *female space* as depriving man of *infinite space*. The offending mother he calls Tirzah in one of the *Songs of Experience*:

> Thou Mother of my Mortal part
> With cruelty didst mould my Heart,
> And with false self-deceiving tears,
> Didst bind my Nostrils, Eyes & Ears.
>
> Didst close my Tongue in senseless clay,
> And me to Mortal Life betray:
> The Death of Jesus set me free;
> Then what have I to do with thee?
>
> (Keynes 1959: 220)

According to Bion, the usual state of affairs is that thoughts require thinkers, and that thinking has evolved to deal with thoughts. The counterpart in epistemic narcissism is the belief that all thoughts are created by the thinker. In Blake's scheme of things all is created by the self as visionary thinker.

If I were to find a counterpart to Blake in the psychoanalytic movement it would be George Groddeck, who, following Nietzsche, coined the term '*das Es*' (the It), familiarly translated as 'the id'. Freud borrowed this term and included it in his tripartite description of the personality, the ego, the It and the super-ego. Though Groddeck was flattered and publicly praised Freud's use of his term, privately he thought Freud undervalued the It: 'the constructive aspect of my *It* he leaves aside', he wrote to his mistress (quoted in Gay 1988: 410). For Groddeck the It is the true self, origin of thoughts and thinker in one; the puny ego is a civilised slave of reason and morality. The Self of I (we) is, or should be, he thought, lived *by* 'the It'. For Freud it is the ego which is the hero of life's tragedy, the ultimate, individual subject assailed by biology, morality and reality. In Bion's schema the ego is the thinker whose activities are necessary to deal with the thoughts generated by the It, the source of desire and stimulus. I suggested in Chapter 1 that the ego has the capacity to attach the authority of belief to some of the thoughts, perceptions and phantasies that come its way. The ego is not the origin of its own experience; it organises and affirms its psychic reality but it does not create its substance (Britton 1995b). It does seem, however, to have the capacity to produce alternatives to reality – as in daydreaming, which is neither external nor psychic reality – and if such constructions are given the status of belief, psychic fiction comes to be treated as psychic fact.

192

As was suggested in Chapter 13, Herbert Rosenfeld's (1987) concept of a destructive narcissistic organisation forever subverting the individual's relationship with his or her good parental object and with reality has its literary exemplar in Milton's *Paradise Lost*. In this work we see Satan, the personification of pride and envy, as the destructive narcissistic self at war with his creator, represented as God. This Satanic self determinedly interferes with the object-worshipful self, personified as Adam.

Milton was Blake's idol and inspiration but, as I said in Chapter 13, Milton propounded in *Paradise Lost* an account of original sin and the Fall that was absolute anathema to Blake. In an extraordinary way Blake set about putting Milton right. Having in *The Marriage of Heaven and Hell* reversed everything and having claimed that unbeknownst to himself Milton was of the Devil's party, he went further in reforming Milton. In one of his epics, entitled *Milton*, Blake summoned Milton back from heaven, where he was reputedly restless, to become the hero of the poem. As this hero, Milton defeats in combat his shadow-self, Urizen, plus the Satanic crew of Bacon, Locke and Newton. He then annihilates those aspects of femaleness that resist the fusion with him that is necessary to complete his restoration as Albion, the original, cosmic, complete man whose division had led to the Fall.

Blake, therefore, takes Milton's model of destructive narcissism and reverses it to produce a model of epistemic narcissism in which goodness and truth are contained only inside the self and are about to be stolen by the external object world. In this model of primordial paradise there are no objects, only other subjects, all of them different and all fundamentally the same. There is no God outside the self and Satan is the sky-God worshipped by all the churches, and he is author of the oppressive moral laws typified by the ten commandments. According to Milton, humankind's fall from paradise is due to disobedience; according to Blake, it is due to obedience.

Rosenfeld's concept of a destructive narcissistic organisation was taken further by Donald Meltzer, who described a phantasised narcissistic gang within the personality; in Milton's terms this would be Satan and his crew, Moloch, Beelzebub, etc.; in Meltzer's more contemporary demonology it was characterised as an internal Mafia (Meltzer 1968), an internal gang offering seduction and threat, and demanding allegiance. John Steiner integrated this with the concept of a defensive organisation, first described by Joan Riviere (1936), to produce the concept of pathological organisations. These organisations, as Steiner described them, functioned both as defensive systems against the anxieties of the paranoid–schizoid and depressive positions and as containers for the narcissistic and object-destructive elements of the personality (Steiner 1987).

I suggested in Chapter 1 that pathological organisations are sustained by counter-belief systems which organise present and future knowledge in such a way as to protect the individual from his or her own latent beliefs. These counter-belief systems are most pronounced and vehemently articulated when they are believed by the individual to be the only barrier between the individual and a catastrophe producing psychic chaos or a mental abyss. This chaos is felt to be kept at bay only by the continuous affirmation of the counter-belief system, and anything that is likely to throw doubt on that belief system has to be violently resisted. Blake was a man who believed in non-violence, but he believed violently in his own creed and in the need to oppose doubt: 'I will not Reason & Compare: my business is to Create' (Keynes 1959: 316). We can see this frantic and aggressive assertion of belief giving rise to both physical and intellectual violence in many places in today's world.

In Chapter 1 I claimed that belief is a normal ego function which confers the status of psychic reality on conscious and unconscious phantasies. As I said earlier, Klein (1946) and Bion (1963) described how in some disturbed patients the object is attacked with such violence that not only the object is felt to disintegrate but also the personality delivering the attack. This disintegration means the patient has therefore destroyed the apparatus that enables him or her to be aware of reality. I have suggested that the belief function is part of this 'apparatus' and that it might be annihilated as a drastic negative reaction to what is believed, thus leaving the individual with no means of achieving a sense of psychic reality, as I describe in Chapter 1. I am suggesting in this chapter that Blake's system was an attempt to provide a coherent framework of dogmatic ideas, asserted as religious beliefs, to remedy the loss of the capacity for natural belief: 'truth has bounds error none; falling, falling' (Keynes 1959: 258). If it is feared that truth will not be found to end falling and to give a boundary to experience, then assertive belief becomes its counterfeit. I think that Blake feared that a state of endless uncertainty and bottomless bewilderment would follow from admitting any doubt into his belief system and that this would result in a fall into a psychic abyss. Repetitive reassertion therefore becomes the only means of restoring and sustaining belief in a viable psychic world in which to live and from which to pass on to a better one.

The infantile catastrophe is told by Blake in the form of the story of the Creation of humankind and the world in two versions. In the first version Urizen creates a fathomless void by wrenching himself from the side of the whole body of eternal man (Keynes 1959: 225–6). In the second account Los – imagination personified – faced with the impenetrable, solid, adamantine object of facts and reason, smashes it to pieces and falls into the abyss thus created (*ibid.* 257–8). In the first we have the subjective account of the tearing off from a pre-natal quiescent psychic unity of that part of mental life linked to the physical senses which is the forerunner of reason

(Urizen). Urizen is very similar to Freud's Pcpt-Cs, the conceptual fore-runner of the ego which in his account differentiates it from the id. In Blake's second account of the catastrophe an observer of the infant imagination, in its frustration and antipathy to the impenetrability and hardness of the primal mental object, smashes it up and, with it, the mental apparatus.

In Blake's account Los, the imagination, rescues the mind from falling forever by creating the illusion of a perceptual body and a physical world which then houses and imprisons the mind. Los is then also imprisoned in the process of development, which leads him into the Oedipus situation. Again Blake gives two slightly different versions of the Oedipus myth involving Los, his wife Enitharmon and their son Orc. He combines with it the Prometheus myth. In one version the son is an infant and in the other he is a 14-year-old boy, but they are essentially the same story. Los, witnessing the relationship between mother and child, feels a tight band constricting his chest each night. Each morning the band of the night falls, to become the newest link in a chain growing out of him. His wife tells him it is the chain of jealousy. So Los, followed by his wife, takes the boy and nails him to the top of the iron mountain, whereupon the chain falls from Los and is used to fasten the child to the mountain. Later they 'felt all the sorrow Parents feel and hastened to the mountain to release him'. It was too late: the chain had grown roots and they could not release their son from the chain of jealousy (Keynes 1959: 307–8).

To summarise what I have been saying I will give an interpretation of Blake's work as if it were an account of a situation in analysis. While doing this I am going to take the liberty of doing to it what Blake did to Milton's *Paradise Lost*: I am going to turn it round. The sequence as Blake gives it is as follows: first, primordial narcissism; second. catastrophe and the Fall; finally, redemption and the resumption of primary narcissism. In an ongoing imaginary analysis of a patient whose clinical material consists of Blake's writings I suggest instead the following sequence: first, a pre-analytic infantile catastrophe; next, the development of an epistemic narcissistic organisation; after some analysis, a return to the scene of the catastrophe; and, finally, the exploration of the fallen world of a murderous family life.

Blake sees the fate of humankind in a world of generational and sexual difference as one of jealousy and murderousness. We can be delivered from this only by a redemptive belief fortified by vision, and by the journey through the soft sexual delusions and moony lustre of Beulah en route to an eternity in which the distinctions between subject and object, male and female, self and other, human and divine are finally abolished.

Blake wrote in order to rescue himself and his fellow sufferers from experience. I suspect his constitution was such that the vicissitudes of everyday infantile life were purgatorial. He was a man who said of himself:

> What to others a trifle appears
> Fills me full of smiles and tears
> (Johnson and Grant 1979: 461)

And in a letter to a friend he wrote:

> O why was I born with a different face?
> Why was I not born like the rest of my race?
> When I look each one starts when I speak, I offend;
> Then I'm silent & passive & lose every Friend.

> Then my verse I dishonour, My pictures despise,
> My person degrade & my temper chastise;
> And the pen is my terror, the pencil my shame;
> All my Talents I bury, and dead is my Fame.

> I am either too low or too highly priz'd;
> When Elate I am Envy'd, When Meek I'm despise'd.
> (Johnson and Grant 1979: 469)

This gives me the sense of someone who valued love above everything else but found discrete, differentiated object relations so difficult that he had to deny their necessity while trying to preserve their essence; a man whose painful awareness of the inherent conflicts in and between human beings led him to assert that the self of the shared 'objective' world is only 'a false Body: an Incrustation' (Keynes 1959: 533) over a divine, eternal subjective self that is at one with all other subjects, in an infinite state of what might now be called inter-subjectivity; all of us as distinctly different members of one body. This, he asserted, could be acheived simply by believing it. Belief was sufficient to free us from the impediments, 'the rotten rags' (*ibid.*), of memory, reason and physical perception.

——————— 15 ———————

Publication anxiety

Publishing is to the first thought as the maternity ward is to the first kiss.
(Friedrich von Schlegel, *Athenaeum Fragments*;
in Ayer and O'Grady 1992: 407)

This chapter is about the psychological problems specifically associated with the act of publication, whether spoken or written. I am not referring to difficulties in thinking and writing, or to the complex, difficult and important ethical issues involved in publishing clinical case material. Both these difficulties affect publication. Obviously, if someone cannot write they cannot publish; if they cannot satisfy themselves that it is ethical to publish what they have written they will not feel free to do so, and if it is not ethical they should not do so. We have a duty to protect the anonymity of our patients.

I have found, however, that protecting the patient from recognition and also securing the informed consent of the patient does not relieve me, as a psychoanalytic author, of a sense of guilt, and I have found this to be the case for other analysts. We may not feel that we are betraying a confidence, but we are left feeling that we are betraying an affiliation. Nor does getting permission fully exonerate the analyst in the eyes of the patient and those who identify with the patient. The knowledge that had seemed to be the private possession of the analytic dyad has been shared with others: what had seemed to be inter-subjective experience is offered as an object for their perusal; what had seemed like the mental content of a private relationship has become the raw material for other minds. The communications internal to one relationship have become the means of furthering the development of another relationship. In its most extreme form, it seems best represented by the myth of Iphigenia, whose father Agamemnon, when en route to the Trojan war, sacrificed his daughter to get a fair wind from the gods and to propitiate his associates. And yet I also know that if I followed the example of some others and completely refrained from using analytic experience for writing I would feel I was betraying something else. In allegiance to a shared subjectivity I would be betraying a commitment to an objectivity shared with professional colleagues past and present and with psychoanalysis itself. There are circumstances, as I described in Chapter 4, where objectivity is felt to be the death of subjectivity, and others where subjectivity is felt to threaten the survival of objectivity. This conflict between one allegiance and another is to be found inside an analysis when the analyst's empathic link with the patient's subjective world is felt to be threatened if he or she takes an objective view of it. The analyst's internal communication with that aspect of him- or herself which is linked with his or her analytic ancestors and associates appears to confirm a conviction of childhood that one parent sacrificed a sympathetic understanding of the patient in order to remain united with the other parent. Where this conflict is particularly severe it is often the case that there was support for this universal suspicion in the personal history of the patient. It is expressed mythically in Jocasta's readiness to sacrifice the life of her infant Oedipus to protect her husband. In this chapter I want to emphasise the ubiquity of these problems aroused by publication – the conflict between subjectivity and objectivity, and its evocation of the Oedipal situation, with its inevitable concomitants of anxiety, betrayal, guilt and shame.

In 1989 Ted Hughes, poet and husband of the late Sylvia Plath, wrote in a letter to the *Independent* newspaper: 'I hope each of us owns the facts of our life' (*Independent*, 10 April 1989). He was provoked into writing this anguished comment by the growing literature about his dead wife, whose poetry and suicide had combined to give her a special place in the literary canon, and had released a quantity of speculative and variously informed comment on their marriage and life together. In her book *The Silent Woman*, a reflection on the Plath biographical enterprise, Janet Malcolm wrote: 'But we do not own the facts of our lives at all. The real ownership passes out of our hands at birth, at the moment we are first observed' (Malcolm 1995: 8). I think this telling image of an infant observed resonates with the feelings aroused by the idea of the analyst who, having been party to the emergence of undisclosed aspects of the patient, is contemplating describing the patient as an observer to a third party.

This feeling in the analyst is somewhat offset in practice by the fact that when writing and contemplating publishing the analyst subjectively feels him- or herself to be in a completely different situation – not that of the one who exposes but that of the one who is exposed. The tables are turned; now it is the private thoughts and opinions of the author that are about to be revealed, not only to the desired object of his or her communication –

that is, the phantasised receptive audience – but also to the observers of this attempt at communication.

This description of the analyst with conflicting claims for his or her mental allegiance – the patient's view of the world, the analyst's own, emergent view of it and the view the analyst shares with his or her psychoanalytic affiliates – may sound familiar. If it does it is probably because it echoes a passage in Freud's 'The ego and the id', where he wrote:

> we see this same ego as a poor creature owing service to three masters and consequently menaced by three dangers: from the external world, from the libido of the id, and from the severity of the super ego. Three kinds of anxiety correspond to these three dangers, since anxiety is the expression of a retreat from danger. As a frontier creature the ego tries to mediate between the world and the id . . . it behaves like the physician during analytic treatment: it offers itself, with the attention it pays to the real world, as a libidinal object to the id, and aims at attaching the id's libido to itself. Its not only a helper to the id; it is also a submissive slave who courts his master's love . . . In its position midway between the id and reality, it only too often yields to the temptation to become sycophantic, opportunist and lying, like a politician who sees the truth but wants to keep his place in popular favour.
>
> (Freud 1923a: 56)

This suggests that there is an attachment to the truth and to reality in all of us, i.e. to discovering *the way things are*, which conflicts with our own wishful thinking, i.e. *the way we would like things to be*, and also conflicts with beliefs based on morality, i.e. *the way we think things ought to be*. In other words, the reality principle is always in conflict with the pleasure principle and its upmarket version the morality principle.

I would like to discuss the interplay of these forces by considering the difficulties people experience at the point of publication. The manifest problems in publication that I have found are that some people are afraid to publish, some are too ready to publish, and in some others the conflicts inherent in publication lead to deviation, distraction or distortion of their texts. I believe that *publication anxiety* is natural unless it is denied as part of a manic defence, which may lead to overreadiness to publish.

I think publication anxiety is ubiquitous and has two sources. One is fear of rejection by the primary intended audience. The other is fear of recrimination by affiliated colleagues and possible exile from them. I think that a profound *fear of rejection by the primary intended listener* in its most serious form leads to an inability to conceptualise or, in lesser states of inhibition, produces an inability to write. Even where this fear is relatively slight and there may be no inhibition in thinking or writing, there may be a significant fear of publication, whether this is by public utterance or in written form. For the sake of clarity I call this second situation *publication anxiety*, which I want to discuss further. I think it emanates from fear of criticism by third parties who are regarded as authoritative and from fear of disaffiliation from colleagues with whom the author feels the need to be affiliated. This may result in a failure to publish written work or to speak publicly. Even if this inhibition is overcome it may still produce distortion or deviation within the text in the process of publication. If it is excessive it may cause inhibition, or, if not, it may result in distortion, deviation or distraction.

If publication anxiety is denied the result is a superficial and complacent text. Overreadiness to publish which is not justified by the content of the text is familiar to editors of journals. I refer here to more than inadequacy of material, ideas or presentation, and specifically to a blind sort of overconfident belief that whatever is said or written by the author deserves and will receive widespread approval; usually this is associated with banality. In the cases I am thinking of the phenomenon itself, rather than lack of ability in the author, is a contributing cause to the poverty of the text. It can therefore afflict previously successful writers or potentially talented authors. It is a form of intellectual complacency that can arise as part of a manic defence. It results from the unconscious phantasy of being the special representative of a superior power. This imagined superior power is itself derived by the attributive projective identification of the phantasised omniscient self into an actual object, which might be a person or a school of thought. Such projective identification gives one a sense of having a special connection with this power without one having to claim omnipotence or omniscience for the self, thus preserving reality sense while retaining the belief in having access to oracular power. It may take the form of allegiance to an orthodoxy, in which case the individual author has a *priestly* function. Or it may take an iconoclastic form in which the spirit of the new is felt to emanate from some intellectually respectable version of divine revelation, in which case the author has a *prophetic* function.

In other cases complacency is derived from an incorporative identification in which the authority of an earlier author has been imbibed together with his or her ideas and absorbed into the thinking of the author, not by intellectual assimilation, but by a process which results in the disappearance of the intellectual debt to the original author and an illusion of originality. William Blake describes this phantasised incorporation of an earlier author in the *Prophetic Book*, in which he claims that Milton entered his left foot, making him the possessor of Milton's imagination. I have a colleague with a patient who entertains a similar idea that his visions of the truth are a result of wisdom entering him through his left foot. There is always an underlying precariousness in this intellectual structure, common though it is, because the derivation of the ideas is lacking and authority is achieved only by identification. Therefore any challenge leads simply to an assertion of authoritative identity: I am, therefore it is!

The particular anxieties evoked by publication will be influenced by the intellectual context in which the author's findings emerge, that is, in the state of the *central organising theory*, of the author's scientific discipline at the time of publication. I favour the use of the term '*paradigm*', coined by Kuhn (1962) for this central theory that organises and legitimises every scientific discipline or subdiscipline. I find Kuhn's account of the nature of scientific development convincing in his *The Structure of Scientific Revolutions* (*ibid.*) and I think it applies in microcosm to psychoanalysis. He describes different phases in a natural cycle of scientific development. He suggests that a science moves from the establishment of a new paradigm, through a period of its development and application to its destabilisation by the accumulation of anomalies; this is followed by its dissolution in favour of a new paradigm which will eventually emerge. The publication anxieties of the writer are inevitably influenced by the phase of this cycle that his or her science is in at the time, whether it is in a phase characterised by confirmation, confidence and coherence, or a phase characterised by discrepancy, doubt and fragmentation.

Kuhn suggests that 'normal science' begins when a paradigm is established and provides the definition by which the science is judged (Kuhn 1962: 10). 'Normal science' includes accumulating relevant facts, addressing puzzles and making discoveries (*ibid.*: 37). Discovery, however, creates problems because it reveals anomalies in the paradigm, the central theory itself. Anomalies accumulate until the new theories they generate fragment the paradigm, leaving the scientific discipline concerned in confusion and uncertainty until a new paradigm emerges which redefines 'normal science'. Kuhn observes that 'the emergence of new theories is generally preceded by a period of pronounced professional insecurity' (*ibid.*: 67–8).

Therefore the point in Kuhn's cycle that is likely to be associated with maximal publication anxiety is when anomalies have accumulated in the subject and destabilised the existing paradigm, or when the state of the science requires the integration of previously segregated theories or facts. I mention this because I think that within our own discipline the pressure to integrate the theories of the different schools of psychoanalytic thought means that we are in a period characterised by the destabilisation of previously confidently held psychoanalytic paradigms.

At this point in the cycle the scientific writer fears that his or her publication may damage the authority of the guardians of the paradigm and demoralise his or her affiliates (depressive anxiety), or the writer may fear the wrath of the guardians and exile from the affiliates (persecutory anxiety). I see this as cast in the mould of the Oedipus situation. The writer wishes to publish his or her view of his or her primary (scientific) object. The writer would like his or her version of this object to be unique because this would give the writer possession of it; he or she alone would know the truth of the object. On the other hand, the writer desires the approval of his or her ancestors and wishes to be at one with his or her scientific affiliates, his or her scientific family, who have their own view of this object. The compromise usually desired is to claim a share of the truth by making an individual contribution that adds to the total truth and also affiliates the writer with his or her fellows in their shared knowledge.

This compromise is tenable during the phase of what Kuhn calls 'normal science'. When the paradigm is no longer satisfactory authors who publish new facts fear that they may be the messenger with bad news, and workers who publish a new theory feel that they risk destroying their own subject or alienating themselves from their scientific home. At an earlier point in the cycle, when the paradigm is authoritative and appears infinitely extendible, publication is easier for those who are happy adding 'facts' to expand, exemplify and refine the paradigm. This is the phase of 'normal science'. For more restless, ambitious or determinedly original spirits the fear in this phase is that they will not find creative space for themselves.

This problem, as applied to poetry, was addressed, in terms of the Oedipal situation, by Harold Bloom in his concept of 'The Anxiety of Influence' (Bloom 1973). He described this as the fear in a poet that a dominant predecessor (such as Milton) had already taken possession of the field from which, he or she hoped, would come his or her own potential poetry. Abrams discusses Bloom's concept in his *Glossary of Literary Terms*:

> The 'belated poet's' attitudes to his precursor . . . are ambivalent . . . compounded not only of love and admiration but also of hate, envy and fear of the father poet's pre-emption of the son's imaginative space . . . [He] safeguards his own sense of autonomy and priority by reading a parent-poem defensively, in such a way as to distort it beyond his own conscious recognition. Nonetheless, he cannot avoid embodying the malformed parent-poem into his own doomed attempt to write an unprecedentedly original poem; the most that even the best belated poet can achieve is to write a poem so 'strong' that it effects an illusion of priority.
>
> (Abrams 1957: 82)

Judging from his letters, this 'anxiety of influence' was what Donald Winnicott felt in relation to Melanie Klein in 1952 in the aftermath of her production of a new paradigm, the theory of the paranoid-schizoid and depressive positions. A new generation of analysts clustered around this paradigm, rapidly applying and utilising it; they became known as the Kleinians. Winnicott suggested in a letter sent jointly to Anna Freud and Melanie Klein that 'rigid patterns . . . create iconoclasts or claustrophobics' and added: 'perhaps I am one of them' (quoted in Rodman 1987: 72). He wrote to Klein in November 1952: 'I personally think that it is very important that your work should be restated by people discovering in their own way and presenting what they discover in their own language' (quoted in *ibid.*: 34). Later (3 February 1956) he wrote to Joan Riviere, his former analyst and Klein's most authoritative ally, to complain that they would not acknowledge that he had a contribution which added to Klein's:

> you and she spoke to me and within the framework of friendliness you gave me to understand that both of you are absolutely certain that there is no positive contribution to be made from me to the interesting attempt Melanie is making all the time to state the psychology of the earliest stages. You will agree that you implied that the trouble is that I am unable to recognise that Melanie does say the very things that I am asking her to say. In other words, there is a block in me.
>
> (Winnicott; quoted in Rodman 1987: 94)

He added a sentence which makes the point I made earlier about fear of exile:

> If I contribute to psychoanalytic theory, it is not of course necessary for me to be accepted by either yourself or Melanie Klein, but I do in fact mind tremendously if I really have a positive contribution to make, however small, and if this cannot find acceptance either with you or with Melanie. (Winnicott; quoted in Rodman 1987: 96)

He did not have a 'following' at this time and had already asked (18 November 1955) Anna Freud if she could provide an audience for a paper he proposed to write. This paper was to be critical of what he called 'Mrs. Klein's temporary (I hope) insistence on what she calls innate envy, something which involves the idea of a variable genetic factor' (*ibid.*: 93). To publish this challenge he needed, apparently, a supporting power to neutralise the rejection he feared from his former authorities:

> I am writing to you because I am wondering whether you have a group that I could write this short paper for so that it could be discussed. I would be quite contented, of course, if you were to say that it would be best if I were to write it and send it to you . . . I need an audience of at least one so that I may orientate to the presentation of my idea.
>
> (Winnicott; quoted in Rodman 1987: 94)

Winnicott did not appear to see, however, that Klein might feel the need of a group of adherents to confront the hostile opposition to her ideas that she was encountering. In his letter condemning 'Kleinism' and begging her to 'destroy it' he implicitly compares her to Darwin and Kleinians to Darwinians. (As I describe below, Darwin needed a group of followers before he could bring himself to publish his theories.) Winnicott wrote to Klein:

> I have no difficulty whatever in telling anyone who asks me, from the bottom of my heart, that you are the best analyst as well as the most creative in the analytic movement. What you do not meet, however, is the opposition to Kleinism which I used to think was simply an invention of Glover's but which I now have to admit exists as something which is as much a barrier to the growth of scientific thought in the Society as Darwinism was to the growth in biology greatly stimulated by the work of Darwin himself.
>
> (Winnicott; quoted in Rodman 1987: 37)

Darwin, although sometimes made anxious by the fervour of his followers, for example Huxley, would not have seen it like that; he relied on the support of the Darwinians.

I would like to take Charles Darwin and the long-delayed publication of his theory of evolution as an illustration of the situation where, in a context of changing science and anomalous facts, an author suffers acute publication anxiety and consequent inhibition. Darwin's new paradigmatic theory of evolution arose, in Kuhn's terms, when the 'normal science' of natural history was finding too many anomalous facts for them to be contained within its general theory. His theory fascinated him; the idea of ever publishing it terrified him. It was several years before he wrote even a pencil sketch of it, and seventeen years after he had written it, when it was finally to be published as a book, he still wanted to call it 'An abstract of an essay on the origin of species and varieties through natural selection' His publisher, Murray, knew his trade well enough to produce the theory under the title *The Origin of Species*. However, under the influence of Darwin's pessimism and diffidence, he published only 500 copies. Even to the last, Darwin asked his friend and disciple Lyell: 'would you advise me to tell Murray that my book is not more unorthodox than the subject makes inevitable?' (quoted in Desmond and Moore 1992: 47).

We have in Darwin an amazingly bold thinker who was tormented by the thought of publishing his theories and convinced of catastrophe for himself and everyone else important to him if he did so. He suffered greatly from neurotic symptoms, depression and psychosomatic ill health which fluctuated wildly in keeping with his fears of publication and its consequences. The threads of the conflict are evident from his letters and journals from the moment of the germination of his ideas during the voyage of the Beagle. Darwin came from a historically freethinking family but lived in and was educated in a society that had reverted to religious orthodoxy in belief and piety in practice. He was supposed to join that body of professional naturalists who were at the same time members of the Anglican clergy. Though evolution was touted by radicals in England, it was not thought tenable by the naturalist establishment from which Darwin drew his scientific sustenance. Even if evolution was to be accepted in place of orthodox creationism, some form of recurrent acts of creation were to be thought of by such dominant figures in biology as Owen. The figures Darwin learnt from and admired were very good 'scientists' within their own definition: this meant precise work, painstaking collection, mastery of detail and abhorrence of general ideas. Darwin, secretly developing his ideas and anticipating criticism, prepared himself by becoming the greatest of imaginable collectors, fact-finder and examiner in detail. He needed all this, not to provide him with ideas, but to substantiate the ones he already had. He published these accounts of detailed work and observations, and earnt a considerable reputation as a consequence, but his general theory of evolution remained totally private until he had a potential disciple, Joseph Hooker.

From the beginning of his career in research on the voyage of the Beagle he was ambivalent about his findings and the scientific ideas which they generated in him. He was isolated from scientific colleagues and making findings which were increasingly discrepant from the orthodox views held in geology, palaeontology and biology. On the one hand, he entertained fantasies of great discoveries; on the other, he feared that a word of scientific disapproval from Henslow, his scientific paterfamilias, would finish him. When he wrote to him in 1835 he told of his incredible findings and swore that 'no previously formed conjecture warped my judgement' (quoted in Desmond and Moore 1992: 165). To his father and sisters, however, he boasted that his findings would be crucial 'to the theory of the formation of the world' (quoted in *ibid.*: 165). In 1836, while still waiting to know Henslow's response to his notes, he wrote:

> I look forward with no little anxiety to the time when Henslow, putting on a grave face, shall decide on the merits of my notes. If he shakes his head in a disapproving manner: I shall then know that I had better at once give up science, for science will have given me up.
> (Darwin; quoted in Desmond and Moore 1992: 183)

The response was enthusiastic. Darwin became increasingly successful in his scientific work and married happily, but remained sick with worry. He was steadily collecting every sort of fact 'which may throw light on the origin & variation of species' (Desmond and Moore 1992: 286). In 1839 his ideas were advancing, his conviction growing, his anxiety increasing: his findings and theories would have been music to the ears of street atheists, but not of course to Henslow (*ibid.*). In May 1842 he produced a 35-page sketch of his evolutionary theory in pencil. In late 1843 and early 1844 he confessed to Joseph Hooker that 'I am almost convinced quite contrary to the opinion I started with that species are not (it is like confessing a murder) immutable' (quoted in *ibid.*: 314). Relieved by Hooker's non-hostile, interested response, he expanded it into a full 189-page essay. Despite the growth of a circle of followers around him, this essay remained unpublished and he was only pushed into doing anything with it in 1858 by the sickening news that Wallace had produced something like his long-cherished secret theory of natural selection. Prompted by this, he allowed his friends and supporters Hooker and Lyell to make the theory public at the carefully chosen, relatively small Linnean Society. They read extracts from his essay – part of a letter Darwin sent to Gray on the subject in 1857 – and Wallace's paper to a largely uncomprehending society. Finally, in November 1859 there was the actual publication, which he called 'the appearance of my child' (quoted in *ibid.*: 476). He wrote in anxious antici-pation to Henslow: 'I fear you will not approve of your pupil', and to other respected colleagues such sentences as 'you will fulminate anathemas', 'Lord, how savage you will be . . . how you will crucify me alive' or '[to you] it will seem an abomination' (quoted in *ibid.*: 476).

He had two fears of the consequences of publication. One was that the scientific establishment which had raised him would destroy him; the other was that he would be responsible for the triumph of anarchy over authority and the consequent destruction of society. It seems clear that Darwin was powerfully prompted from within to reveal that he knew the secrets of the origin of the world which his scientific fathers did not. His ideas fascinated him but any thought of publishing them made him ill. It was not until he was bolstered by a band of junior 'siblings' that he exposed his theory and, even then, the fear of the fathers remained. Darwin, however, did not compromise in his thinking and there was no distortion in his text to facili-tate affiliation. The one misrepresentation was that he wanted it believed that he was forced, against his wishes and previous convictions, reluctantly and slowly, to his conclusions by accumulated evidence. In reality, his enor-mous research efforts were to test his theory, to provide irrefutable evidence for it and to protect himself from any imputation of being unscientifically speculative.

I would like to turn from complete inhibition of publication to consider the possible effects of the same forces in producing *distortions* within the published text. What I have in mind is the distracting or distorting effects on direct communication arising from the wish to further or preserve affiliation with the significant peer group or parental figure. To illustrate what I mean I would first like to use a portion of an important paper by Karl Abraham, 'A short study of the development of the libido, viewed in the light of the mental disorders' (Abraham 1924). I have chosen this because it is a publication of an analyst I unequivocally admire for his straightforwardness and his independent thinking, and yet he is led by anxiety when describing an important anomaly to wobble and to weaken his text.

He was writing 'Notes on the psychogenesis of melancholia' (Abraham 1924: 418–501) which was very much his own subject. He, unlike Freud, had analysed a number of manic–depressive patients and shared his findings with Freud, who doubtless used them in his own groundbreaking papers 'Mourning and melancholia' (1917c) and 'The ego and the id' (1923a). Nevertheless, at the time that Abraham was writing this paper the castration complex and the father complex were very much in the ascendant in Freud's theorising, e.g. 'A seventeenth century demonological neurosis' (Freud 1923b) and 'The infantile genital organisation: an interpolation into the theory of sexuality' (Freud 1923c). Abraham was about to say something with a very different emphasis. He thought the whole psychological process in melancholia centred around the mother, and he said:

> If we want to realise the full strength of the melancholic's hostility toward his mother, and to understand the particular character of his castration complex, we must keep in mind Starcke's theory that the withdrawal of the mother's breast is a 'primal castration'.
>
> (Abraham 1924: 463)

In this paper Abraham was about to shift the psychoanalytic ground on which subsequent understanding of depressive states of mind would be understood and he thus threatened the prevailing paradigm. I think we can detect anxiety about this, with a risk of distortion in the text, from which he appeared to recover, but he lost some directness and force in the process. I would suggest that certain phrases were used for their totemic significance to emphasise his affiliation with Freud. There is, just after the passage that implies that the introjected mother, rather than the father, forms the feared super-ego a distinctly placatory footnote in deference to Freud. Abraham began with the claim:

> In every male melancholic I have hitherto analysed I have been able to satisfy myself that the patient's castration complex was quite predominantly connected with his mother, whereas in other kinds of patients it is usually much more in evidence in relation to the father.
>
> (Abraham 1924: 460)

207

Then he qualified this:

> Nevertheless I was able to discover that its connection with the mother
> was a secondary one and the result of a tendency to invert the Oedipus
> situation. When thoroughly analysed the hostility of the melancholic
> towards his mother is seen to have roots in the Oedipus complex. In
> fact, his ambivalence really applies to both parents alike. And his father
> is also the object of a process of introjection. Many melancholic symp-
> toms, as, for instance, certain self-reproaches, show their original
> relation to both parents quite clearly.
>
> (Abraham 1924: 460–1)

He reasserted his claim:

> What I have just said does not invalidate my previous statement that in
> melancholia the whole psychological process centres *in the male* round
> the mother; it only seeks to emphasise the fact that the process has
> more than one determinant.
>
> (Abraham 1924: 461)

Abraham went on to make quite clear that the *ego ideal* is built on the
introjected original love object, the mother, quoting the patient as using the
mother's tone of voice and expressions. It is in this paragraph, in which the
concept of the super-ego as heir to the classical Oedipus complex is most
in question, that he used the deferential footnote below:

> The patient has introjected his original love-object upon which he had
> built his ego ideal; so that object has taken over the role of conscience
> for him, although, it is true, a pathologically formed one. Our material
> goes to show that the pathological self-criticism of the melancholic
> emanates from this introjected object.★

This paper was clearly addressed to the *reader*, and Freud's presence in
Abraham's mind and in the text at these points served as a distraction. It is, I
think, of some significance that the primary importance of the father was
almost reinstated in the text and the supremacy of the castration complex
implied at a moment when Abraham's thinking was clearly moving in

---

★ Freud's *The Ego and the Id* appeared shortly after I had written this part of my book. In it he
gives such a lucid account of the process that I need only refer the reader to its pages. To give a
résumé of it would be to render it less clear.

(Abraham 1924: 461)

another direction. I point this out, not to criticise Abraham or indict Freud, but to give an example of what I think may be omnipresent in our publications. Small distortions, totemic use of terms, detours into irrelevant references, links made with other work not clearly connected to the thesis are all prompted by our desire for affiliation and our fear of exile.

As a final illustration of this, where less important issues are at stake but the same dynamic is operating, I will take a short passage from the beginning of a fairly recent paper, read to the Klein Group of the British Society in 1983.

The author began by describing a situation in analysis where a patient has rid him- or herself of knowledge and feelings by projective identification. The author was about to raise the implications for analytic technique of this clinical situation and to suggest a change. He began by describing the dilemma:

> the knowledge born of previous experience in the analysis may now only have a home in the analyst. If this knowledge is of the existence of a person capable of love and desirous of communication now apparently only existing in the analyst's mind his own loneliness or frustration may prompt him to demand the patient admits it, or he may be tempted to try and sell it to the patient.

We then had a distraction in the form of an ancestral reference:

> Perhaps it was situations like this which prompted Bion to enjoin us to forfeit memory and desire in order to discern the current state in the analysis.

The author then put forward his argument:

> Paradoxically, however, the situation would seem to depend at these moments on the analyst's secure containment of his own unspoken knowledge and reality. This, I think, fluctuates with our capacity to sustain our point of view without need of the patient's confirmation or acquiescence, thus leaving us free to make explicit the patient's view of things, leaving our own position implicit in our ability and readiness to do so.

The subsequent two paragraphs muddied the waters, however, because reference was made to clarifying a number of situations that might arise as a consequence of 'splitting', 'evacuation', 'fragmentation', 'annihilation' and 'omnipotent phantasy'. The flow of the idea had been completely interrupted but no one could doubt that it was a Kleinian paper after that barrage. In the process the author also managed to mention contributions by Rosenfeld, Joseph and Segal in the space of ten lines. As a consequence the resumption of the argument of the paper was much less clear than it would have been.

I would not be so free with my comments if I were not the author of the paper in question, which is why I chose a paper of my own for scrutiny. The idea put forward in the paper found its way into print some years later in a larger context, without the diversion of the irrelevant affiliative references to ancestral figures. However, when I was publicising this idea of mine verbally in 1983, anxious to bind myself to my ancestors and affiliates, I succeeded in distracting myself – and probably everyone else – by alluding to a number of familiar shared Kleinian concepts, one principal totemic figure and all three of my analytic supervisors in just twenty lines.

I offer this as a commonplace example of publication anxiety which results in the sort of genuflection to be found in many papers. There are more serious distortions that can occur in texts, where affirmation of shared ideas, attacks on shared enemies or declarations of shared origins can be felt necessary to satisfy a wish for affiliation. Sometimes this simply corrupts the language, sometimes it changes the meaning of the discourse.

I think anxiety about affiliation may be prevalent in psychoanalysis now, when greater movement between theoretical groupings and schools of thought is taking place. There seems to be a feeling of uncertainty as to whether psychoanalytic theory will disintegrate or reintegrate. Under these circumstances one would expect increased publication anxiety and conflict, with consequent disguise or distortion within the text. In the terms I used in Chapter 6 we are probably in a Ps(n+1) position, which demands patience and requires faith – not a reasserted, coherent belief system acting like a rallying point for the faithful, but faith in the onward development of psychoanalytic ideas.

References

Abraham, K. (1924) 'A short study of the development of the libido, viewed in the light of the mental disorders', *Selected papers of Karl Abraham*, trans. Douglas Bryan and Alix Strachey, London: Hogarth Press (1973).

Abrams, M. H. (1957) *A Glossary of Literary Terms*, 4th edn, New York: Holt, Rinehart & Winston (1981).

—— (1971) *Natural Supernaturalism*, New York: W. W. Norton & Co.

Ackroyd P. (1995) *Blake*, London: Sinclair-Stevenson.

Ayer, A. J. and O'Grady, J. (1992) *A Dictionary of Philosophical Quotations*, London: Blackwell.

Bachelard, G. (1964) *The Poetics of Space*, trans. M. Jolas, Boston, MA: Beacon Press (1969).

Balint, M. (1952) 'Early developmental stages of the ego', *Primary Love and Psycho-Analytic Technique*, London: Hogarth Press (1973).

—— (1968) *The Basic Fault*, London: Tavistock Publications.

Barag, G. (1947) 'The question of Jewish monotheism', *Imago* IV: 8–25.

Basch, M. (1983) 'The perception of reality and the disavowal of meaning', *Annual of Psychoanalysis* XI: 125–53.

Beckett, S. (1979) *The Unnameable*, in *The Beckett Trilogy*, London: Pan Books.

Bick, E. (1968) 'The experience of the skin in early object relations', in E. B. Spillius (ed.) *Melanie Klein Today*, vol. 1, London: Routledge (1988).

Bion, W. R. (1956) 'Development of schizophrenic thought', *International Journal of Psycho-Analysis* 37: 344–6.

—— (1957) 'On arrogance', *Second Thoughts*, New York: Jason Aronson (1967).

—— (1959) 'Attacks on linking', *Second Thoughts*, New York: Jason Aronson (1967).

—— (1962a) 'A theory of thinking', *Second Thoughts*, New York: Jason Aronson (1967).

—— (1962b) *Learning from Experience*, Maresfield Reprints, London: Karnac Books (1984).

—— (1963) *Elements of Psycho-Analysis*, Maresfield Reprints, London: Karnac Books (1984).

—— (1966) 'Catastrophic change', unpublished paper.

—— (1967) 'Commentary', *Second Thoughts*, New York: Jason Aronson.

—— (1970) *Attention and Interpretation*, London: Tavistock Publications.

—— (1992) *Cogitations*, London: Karnac Books.

Blake, W. (1927) *The Marriage of Heaven and Hell*, ed. Max Plowman, London and Toronto: J. M. Dent & Sons; reproduced in facsimile from the original copy of 1825–7 in Fitzwilliam Museum, Cambridge.

Bloom, H. (1973) *The Anxiety of Influence*, Oxford: Oxford University Press.

Britton, R. (1983) 'Some technical difficulties in speaking to the patient', unpublished paper read to the British Psycho-Analytical Society.

—— (1985) 'The Oedipus complex and the depressive position' *Sigmund Freud House Bulletin* 9(1): 9–12 (Vienna).

—— (1986) 'The effects of serious parental psychological disturbance as seen in analysis', unpublished paper read to the British Psycho-Analytical Society.

—— (1989) 'The missing link: parental sexuality in the Oedipus complex' in J. Steiner (ed.) *The Oedipus Complex Today*, London: Karnac Books.

—— (1991) 'The Oedipus situation and the depressive position' in R. Anderson (ed.) *Clinical Lectures on Klein and Bion*, London: Routledge.

—— (1993) 'Fundamentalismus und Idolbildung', in J. Gutwinski-Jeggle and J. M. Rotmann (eds) *Die klugen Sinne pflegend*, Tübingen: Edition Diskord.

—— (1995a) 'Reality and unreality in phantasy and fiction', in E. S. Person, P. Fonagy and S. A. Figueira (eds) *On Freud's 'Creative Writers and Day-dreaming'*, New Haven, CT: Yale University Press.

—— (1995b) 'Psychic reality and unconscious belief', *International Journal of Psycho-Analysis* 76(1): 19–24.

—— (1997a) 'Subjectivity, objectivity and the fear of chaos', Melanie Klein Memorial Lecture, at Psychoanalytic Center of California, 11 January (unpublished).

—— (1997b) 'Psychic reality and unconscious belief: a reply to Harold B. Gerard', *International Journal of Psycho-Analaysis* 78: 335–40.

Britton, R. and Steiner, J. (1994) 'Interpretation: selected fact or overvalued idea?', *The International Journal of Psycho-Analysis* 75(5/6): 1069–78.

Brontë, E. (1992) *Emily Jane Brontë: The Complete Poems*, ed. J. Gazari, London: Penguin Books.

Browning, R. (1845) 'The lost leader', *Thirty Poems by Robert Browning*, ed. W. S. Mackie, London: Macmillan (1965).

Bunyan, J. (1684) *Pilgrim's Progress*, London and New York: George Routledge & Sons (1864).

Chasseguet-Smirgel, J. (1974) 'Perversion, idealisation and sublimation', *International Journal of Psycho-Analysis* 55: 349–57.

—— (1981) 'Loss of reality in perversions – with special reference to fetishism', *Journal of the American Psychoanalytic Association* 29: 511–34.

Cohn, N. (1993) *Cosmos, Chaos and the World to Come*, New Haven, CT, and London: Yale University Press.

Coleridge, S. T. (1818) 'Milton', in S. Elledge (ed.) *John Milton: Paradise Lost*, 2nd edn, New York: W. W. Norton (1975).

—— (1985) *The Rime of the Ancient Mariner, Samuel Taylor Coleridge*, ed. H. L. Jackson, Oxford: Oxford University Press.

Coote, S. (1995) *John Keats: A Life*, London: Hodder & Stoughton.

Desmond, A. and Moore, J. (1992) *Darwin*, London: Penguin Books.

Deutsch, H. (1942) 'Some forms of emotional disturbance and their relationship to schizophrenia', *Psychoanalytic Quarterly* 11: 301–21.

Elledge, S. (1975) *John Milton: Paradise Lost*, 2nd edn, New York: W. W. Norton.

Feldman, M. (1995) 'Grievance: the underlying Oedipal configuration', unpublished paper read at the West Lodge Conference, March.

Ferenczi, S. (1926) 'The problems of acceptance of unpleasant ideas in advances in knowledge of the sense of reality', *Further Contributions*, London: Karnac Books (1980).

Fonagy, P. and Morgan, S. (1991) 'Two forms of psychic change in psychoanalysis', unpublished paper read at the Institute of Psychiatry, London, March.

Flew, A. (1979) *A Dictionary of Philosophy*, London: Macmillan.

Freud, S. (1893–5) *Studies on Hysteria* (by Josef Breuer and Sigmund Freud) *The Standard Edition of the Complete Works of Sigmund Freud*, vol. II, London: Hogarth Press (1950–74).

—— (1895) 'Project for a scientific psychology (1950) [1895]', *The Standard Edition of the Complete Works of Sigmund Freud*, vol. I, London: Hogarth Press (1950–74).

—— (1896) 'Letter 46, May 30 1896. Extracts from the Fleiss papers', *The Standard Edition of the Complete Works of Sigmund Freud*, vol. I, London: Hogarth Press (1950–74).

—— (1897a) 'Draft N, Letter 64, 31 May 1897. Extracts from the Fleiss papers', *The Standard Edition of the Complete Works of Sigmund Freud*, vol. I, London: Hogarth Press (1950–74).

—— (1897b) 'Letter 71, 15 Oct. 1897. Extracts from the Fleiss papers', *The Standard Edition of the Complete Works of Sigmund Freud*, vol. I, London: Hogarth Press (1950–74).

—— (1899) 'Screen memories', *The Standard Edition of the Complete Works of Sigmund Freud*, vol. III, London: Hogarth Press (1950–74).

—— (1900a) *The Interpretation of Dreams*, *The Standard Edition of the Complete Works of Sigmund Freud*, vol. IV, London: Hogarth Press (1950–74).

—— (1900b) *The Interpretation of Dreams*, *The Standard Edition of the Complete Works of Sigmund Freud*, vol. V, London: Hogarth Press (1950–74).

—— (1904) *The Psychopathology of Everyday Life*, *The Standard Edition of the Complete Works of Sigmund Freud*, vol. VI, London: Hogarth Press (1950–74).

—— (1907) 'Delusions and dreams in Jensen's Gradiva', *The Standard Edition of the Complete Works of Sigmund Freud*, vol. IX, London: Hogarth Press (1950–74).

—— (1908a) 'Creative writers and day-dreaming', *The Standard Edition of the Complete Works of Sigmund Freud*, vol. IX, London: Hogarth Press (1950–74).

—— (1908b) 'Hysterical phantasies and their relation to bisexuality', *The Standard Edition of the Complete Works of Sigmund Freud*, vol. IX, London: Hogarth Press (1950–74).

—— (1910a) 'Leonardo da Vinci and a memory of his childhood', *The Standard Edition of the Complete Works of Sigmund Freud*, vol. XI, London: Hogarth Press (1950–74).

—— (1910b) 'A special type of choice of object made by men', *The Standard Edition of the Complete Works of Sigmund Freud*, vol. XI, London: Hogarth Press (1950–74).

—— (1911a) 'Psycho-analytic notes on an autobiographical account of a case of paranoia', *The Standard Edition of the Complete Works of Sigmund Freud*, vol. XII, London: Hogarth Press (1950–74).

—— (1911b) 'Formulations on the two principles of mental functioning', *The Standard Edition of the Complete Works of Sigmund Freud*, vol. XII, London: Hogarth Press (1950–74).

—— (1912) 'Recommendations to physicians practising psycho-analysis', *The Standard Edition of the Complete Works of Sigmund Freud*, vol. XII, London: Hogarth Press (1950–74).

—— (1913a) 'The theme of the three caskets', *The Standard Edition of the Complete Works of Sigmund Freud*, vol. XII, London: Hogarth Press (1950–74).

—— (1913b) *Totem and Taboo*, *The Standard Edition of the Complete Works of Sigmund Freud*, vol. XIII, London: Hogarth Press (1950–74).

—— (1913c) 'On beginning the treatment', *The Standard Edition of the Complete Works of Sigmund Freud*, vol. XII, London: Hogarth Press (1950–74).

—— (1914) 'On narcissism', *The Standard Edition of the Complete Works of Sigmund Freud*, vol. XIV, London: Hogarth Press (1950–74).

—— (1915a) 'Observations on transference-love', *The Standard Edition of the Complete Works of Sigmund Freud*, vol. XII, London: Hogarth Press (1950–74).

—— (1915b) 'The unconscious' *The Standard Edition of the Complete Works of Sigmund Freud*, vol. XIV, London: Hogarth Press (1950–74).

—— (1916a) 'On transience', *The Standard Edition of the Complete Works of Sigmund Freud*, vol. XIV, London: Hogarth Press (1950–74).

—— (1916b) 'Introductory lectures on psycho-analysis: lecture XXII', *The Standard Edition of the Complete Works of Sigmund Freud*, vol. XVI, London: Hogarth Press (1950–74).

—— (1917a) 'A metapsychological supplement to the theory of dreams', *The Standard Edition of the Complete Works of Sigmund Freud*, vol. XIV, London: Hogarth Press (1950–74).

—— (1917b) 'Mourning and melancholia', *The Standard Edition of the Complete Works of Sigmund Freud*, vol. XIV, London: Hogarth Press (1950–74).

—— (1917c) 'Introductory lectures on psycho-Analysis: lecture XXIII', *The Standard Edition of the Complete Works of Sigmund Freud*, vol. XVI, London: Hogarth Press (1950–74).

—— (1918) 'From the history of an infantile neurosis', *The Standard Edition of the Complete Works of Sigmund Freud*, vol. XVII, London: Hogarth Press (1950–74).

—— (1919) 'The uncanny', *The Standard Edition of the Complete Works of Sigmund Freud*, vol. XVII, London: Hogarth Press (1950–74).

—— (1923a) 'The ego and the id', *The Standard Edition of the Complete Works of Sigmund Freud*, vol. XIX, London: Hogarth Press (1950–74).

—— (1923b) 'A seventeenth century demonological neurosis', *The Standard Edition of the Complete Works of Sigmund Freud*, vol. XIX, London: Hogarth Press (1950–74).

—— (1923c) 'The infantile genital organisation: an interpolation into the theory of sexuality', *The Standard Edition of the Complete Works of Sigmund Freud*, vol. XIX, London: Hogarth Press (1950–74).

—— (1924a) 'The dissolution of the Oedipus complex', *The Standard Edition of the Complete Works of Sigmund Freud*, vol. XIX, London: Hogarth Press (1950–74).

—— (1924b) 'The loss of reality in neurosis and psychosis', *The Standard Edition of the Complete Works of Sigmund Freud*, vol. XIX, London: Hogarth Press (1950–74).

—— (1925) 'Negation', *The Standard Edition of the Complete Works of Sigmund Freud*, vol. XIX, London: Hogarth Press (1950–74).

—— (1927a) 'The future of an illusion', *The Standard Edition of the Complete Works of Sigmund Freud*, vol. XXI, London: Hogarth Press (1950–74).

—— (1927b) 'Fetishism', *The Standard Edition of the Complete Works of Sigmund Freud*, vol. XXI, London: Hogarth Press (1950–74).

—— (1927c) 'Humour', *The Standard Edition of the Complete Works of Sigmund Freud*, vol. XXI, London: Hogarth Press (1950–74).

—— (1928) 'Civilisation and its discontents', *The Standard Edition of the Complete Works of Sigmund Freud*, vol. XXI, London: Hogarth Press (1950–74).

—— (1933a) 'New introductory lectures: lecture XXXI', *The Standard Edition of the Complete Works of Sigmund Freud*, vol. XXII, London: Hogarth Press (1950–74).

—— (1933b) 'New introductory lectures: lecture XXXV', *The Standard Edition of the Complete Works of Sigmund Freud*, vol. XXII, London: Hogarth Press (1950–74).

—— (1935) 'Postscript' to 'An autobiographical study', *The Standard Edition of the Complete Works of Sigmund Freud*, vol. XX, London: Hogarth Press (1950–74).

—— (1937) 'Constructions in analysis', *The Standard Edition of the Complete Works of Sigmund Freud*, vol. XXIII, London: Hogarth Press (1950–74).

—— (1938) 'An outline of psychoanalysis', *The Standard Edition of the Complete Works of Sigmund Freud*, vol. XXIII, London: Hogarth Press (1950–74).

—— (1939) 'Moses and monotheism', *The Standard Edition of the Complete Works of Sigmund Freud*, vol. XXIII, London: Hogarth Press (1950–74).

—— (1941) 'Aug. 22 [1938]. Findings, ideas, problems', *The Standard Edition of the Complete Works of Sigmund Freud*, vol. XXIII, London: Hogarth Press (1950–74).

Gardner, M. (1960) *Alice in Wonderland* and *Alice Through the Looking Glass*, in *The Annotated Alice of Lewis Carroll*, London: Penguin Books.

Gay, P. (1988) *Freud: A Life for Our Time*, London and Melbourne: J. M. Dent.

Gekle, H. (1986) *Wünsch und Wirklichkeit*, Tübingen: Suhrkamp Verlag.

Gill, S. (1989) *William Wordsworth: A Life*, Oxford: Oxford University Press.

Goethe, J. W. von (1774) *The Sorrows of Young Werther*, quoted in *The International Thesauraus of Quotations*, compiled R. T. Tripp, London: Penguin Books (1973): 51.

Heimann, P. (1942) 'Sublimation and its relation to processes of internalisation', *International Journal of Psycho-Analysis* 23.

Heimann, P. and Isaacs, S. (1952) 'Regression', in M. Klein, P. Heimann, S. Isaacs and J. Riviere (eds) *Developments in Psycho-Analysis*, London: Hogarth Press (1970).

Hindle, M. (1994) *Mary Shelley: Frankenstein*, Penguin Critical Studies, London: Penguin Books.

Hoffer, W. (1981) 'Infant observations and concepts relating to infancy', in M. Brierley (ed.) *Early Development and Education of the Child*, London: Hogarth Press (1986).

Holmes, R. (1989) *Coleridge: Early Visions*, London: Hodder & Stoughton.

I.F. Notes (1843) Manuscript of the Fenwick Notes transcribed by E. Quillinan and Dora Quillinan (neé Wordsworth): 123: this manuscript is in the library of the Wordsworth Trust and this extract is reproduced by kind permission of the Trustees.

Isaacs, S. (1952) 'The nature and function of phantasy', in M. Klein, P. Heimann, S. Isaacs and J. Riviere (eds) *Developments in Psycho-Analysis*, London: Hogarth Press (1970).

Jaques, E. (1968) 'Death and the mid-life crisis', *International Journal of Psycho-Analysis* 46: 502–14.

James, H. (1981) *The Portrait of a Lady*, Oxford: Oxford University Press.

Johnson, M. L. and Grant, J. E. (eds) (1979) *Blake's Poetry and Designs*, New York: W. W. Norton & Co.

Jones, E. (1957) *Sigmund Freud: Life and Work*, vol. I–III, London: Hogarth Press.

Joseph, B. (1989a) 'The patient who is difficult to reach', in M. Feldman and E. B. Spillius (eds) *Psychic Equilibrium and Psychic Change*, London: Routledge.

—— (1989b) 'Different types of anxiety and their handling in the analytic situation', in M. Feldman and E. B. Spillius (eds) *Psychic Equilibrium and Psychic Change*, London: Routledge.

—— (1989c) 'Defence mechanisms and phantasy in the psychological process', in M. Feldman and E. B. Spillius (eds) *Psychic Equilibrium and Psychic Change*, London: Routledge.

—— (1989d) 'Transference: the total situation', in M. Feldman and E. B. Spillius (eds) *Psychic Equilibrium and Psychic Change*, London: Routledge.

Jung, C. G. (1959) 'The archetypes and the collective unconscious', *The Collected Works of C. J. Jung*, vol. 9, London: Routledge, Kegan & Paul.

Keynes, G. (ed.) (1959) *Blake: Complete Writings*, Oxford: Oxford University Press.

King, P. and Steiner, R. (1991) *The Freud–Klein Controversies 1941–45*, London: Routledge.

Klein, M. (1924) 'An obsessional neurosis in a six-year-old girl', *The Writings of Melanie Klein*, vol. 2, eds R. Money-Kyrle, B. Joseph, E. O'Shaughnessy and H. Segal, London: Hogarth Press (1975).

—— (1926) 'The Psychological Principles of Early Analysis', *The Writings of Melanie Klein*, vol. I, eds R. Money-Kyrle, B. Joseph, E. O'Shaughnessy and H. Segal, London: Hogarth Press (1975).

—— (1928) 'Early stages of the Oedipus conflict', *The Writings of Melanie Klein*, vol. 1, eds R. Money-Kyrle, B. Joseph, E. O'Shaughnessy and H. Segal, London: Hogarth Press (1975).

—— (1929) 'Personification in the play of children', *The Writings of Melanie Klein*, vol. I, eds R. Money-Kyrle, B. Joseph, E. O'Shaughnessy and H. Segal, London: Hogarth Press (1975).

—— (1930) 'The importance of symbol-formation in the development of the ego', *The Writings of Melanie Klein*, vol. I, eds R. Money-Kyrle, B. Joseph, E. O'Shaughnessy and H. Segal, London: Hogarth Press (1975).

—— (1935) 'A contribution to the psychogenesis of manic–depressive states', *The Writings of Melanie Klein*, vol. I, eds R. Money-Kyrle, B. Joseph, E. O'Shaughnessy and H. Segal, London: Hogarth Press (1975).

216

—— (1940) 'Mourning and its relation to manic-depressive states', *The Writings of Melanie Klein*, vol. I, eds R. Money-Kyrle, B. Joseph, E. O'Shaughnessy and H. Segal, London: Hogarth Press (1975).

—— (1945) 'The Oedipus complex in the light of early anxieties', *The Writings of Melanie Klein*, vol. I, eds R. Money-Kyrle, B. Joseph, E. O'Shaughnessy and H. Segal, London: Hogarth Press (1975).

—— (1946) 'Notes on some schizoid mechanisms', *The Writings of Melanie Klein* vol. III, eds R. Money-Kyrle, B. Joseph, E. O'Shaughnessy and H. Segal, London: Hogarth Press (1975).

—— (1948) 'The theory of anxiety and guilt', *The Writings of Melanie Klein*, vol. III, eds R. Money-Kyrle, B. Joseph, E. O'Shaughnessy and H. Segal, London: Hogarth Press (1975).

—— (1952a) 'Origins of transference', *The Writings of Melanie Klein*, vol. III, eds R. Money-Kyrle, B. Joseph, E. O'Shaughnessy and H. Segal, London: Hogarth Press (1975).

—— (1952b) 'Some theoretical conclusions regarding the emotional life of the infant', *The Writings of Melanie Klein*, vol. III, eds R. Money-Kyrle, B. Joseph, E. O'Shaughnessy and H. Segal, London: Hogarth Press (1975).

—— (1952c) 'On observing the behaviour of young infants', *The Writings of Melanie Klein*, vol. III, eds R. Money-Kyrle, B. Joseph, E. O'Shaughnessy and H. Segal, London: Hogarth Press (1975).

—— (1955) 'On identification', *The Writings of Melanie Klein*, vol. III, eds R. Money-Kyrle, B. Joseph, E. O'Shaughnessy and H. Segal, London: Hogarth Press (1975).

—— (1957) 'Envy and gratitude', *The Writings of Melanie Klein*, vol. III, eds R. Money-Kyrle, B. Joseph, E. O'Shaughnessy and H. Segal, London: Hogarth Press (1975).

—— (1958) 'On the development of mental functioning', *The Writings of Melanie Klein*, vol. III, eds R. Money-Kyrle, B. Joseph, E. O'Shaughnessy and H. Segal, London: Hogarth Press (1975).

—— (1959) 'Our adult world and its roots in infancy', *The Writings of Melanie Klein*, vol. III, ed. R. Money-Kyrle, B. Joseph, E. O'Shaughnessy and H. Segal, London: Hogarth Press (1975).

Kris, E. (1935) 'The psychology of caricature'; reprinted in *Psychoanalytic Exploration in Art*, New York: International Universities Press (1952).

Kuhn, T. S. (1962) *The Structure of Scientific Revolutions*, 2nd edn, Chicago: University of Chicago Press (1970).

Lacan, J. (1979) *The Four Fundamental Concepts of Psycho-Analysis*, ed. J.-A. Miller, trans. Alan Sheridan, London: Penguin Books.

Laplanche, J. and Pontalis, J. B. (1973) *The Language of Psycho-Analysis*, London: Hogarth Press.

MacNeice, L. (1941) *The Poetry of W. B. Yeats*, Oxford: Oxford University Press.

Malcolm, J. (1995) *The Silent Woman*, London: Macmillan.

Matte-Blanco, H. (1988) *Thinking, Feeling, and Being*, London: Routledge.

Meltzer, D. (1968) 'Terror, persecution and dread', *International Journal of Psycho-Analysis* 49: 396–401.

Mill, J. S. (1924) *Autobiography*, ed. J. J. Goss, New York: Columbia.

—— (1950) *Mill on Bentham and Coleridge*, ed. F. R. Leavis, Cambridge: Cambridge University Press.

Milton, J. (1975) *John Milton: Paradise Lost'*, ed. S. Elledge, 2nd edn, New York: W. W. Norton & Co.

O'Shaughnessy, E. (1981) 'A clinical study of a defensive organisation', *International Journal of Psycho-Analysis* 2: 359–69.

Rank, O. (1915) 'Das Schauspiel im Hamlet' *Imago* 4.

Riesenberg Malcolm, R. (1992) 'As-if: the experience of not learning', in R. Anderson (ed.) *Clinical Lectures on Klein and Bion*, London: Routledge.

Rey, H. (1979) 'Schizoid phenomena in the borderline', in J. LeBoit and A. Capponi (eds) *Advances in the Psychotherapy of the Borderline Patient*, New York: Jason Aronson.

Rilke, R. M. (1910) *The Notebooks of Malte Laurids Brigge*, trans. S. Mitchell, New York: Random House (1983).

—— (1969) *Letters of Rainer Maria Rilke 1910–1926*, trans. J. B. Greene and M. D. Herter Norton, New York: W. W. Norton & Co.

—— (1981) *An Unofficial Rilke*, ed. and trans. M. Hamburger, London: Anvil Poetry.

—— (1987) *The Selected Poetry of Rainer Maria Rilke*, ed. and trans. S. Mitchell, London: Pan Books.

Riviere, J. (1936) 'A contribution to the analysis of the negative therapeutic reaction', *International Journal of Psycho-Analysis* 17: 304.

Rodman, F. R. (ed.) (1987) *The Spontaneous Gesture: Selected Letters of D. W. Winnicott*, Cambridge, MA, and London: Harvard University Press.

Rosenfeld, H. A. (1964) 'An investigation into the need of neurotic and psychotic patients to act out during analysis', *Psychotic States: A Psycho-Analytical Approach*, New York: International Universities Press (1965).

—— (1965) *Psychotic States: A Psycho-Analytical Approach*, New York: International Universities Press.

—— (1971) 'A clinical approach to the psychoanalytic theory of the life and death instincts: an investigation into the aggressive aspects of narcissism', *International Journal of Psycho-Analysis* 52: 169–78.

—— (1987) *Impasse and Interpretation*, London: Routledge.

Rundle Clark, R. T. (1959) *Myth and Symbol in Ancient Egypt*, London: Thames & Hudson.

Sandler, J. (1976a) 'Dreams, unconscious phantasies and identity of perception', *International Review of Psycho-Analysis* 3: 33–42.

—— (1976b) 'Counter-transference and role-responsiveness', *International Review of Psycho-Analysis* 3: 43–7.

Sartre, J.-P. (1943) *Being and Nothingness*, trans. H. E. Barnes, London: Editions Gallimard (1958).

Searle, J. R. (1995) 'The mystery of consciousness: part II', *The New York Review of Books* XLII(18) (16 November): 4–61.

Segal, H. (1952) 'A psycho-analytical approach to aesthetics', *International Journal of Psycho-Analysis* 33: 196–207.

—— (1957) 'Notes on symbol formation', in E. B. Spillius (ed.) *Melanie Klein Today*, vol. 1, London: Routledge (1988).

—— (1964) *Introduction to the Work of Melanie Klein*, London: Hogarth Press (1973).

218

—— (1980) *Melanie Klein*, New York: Viking Press.

—— (1994) 'Phantasy and reality', *International Journal of Psycho-Analysis* 75(2): 395–401.

Shakespeare, W. (1969) *Midsummer Nights Dream, The Complete Pelican Shakespeare: Comedies and Romances*, London: Penguin Books.

Shawcross, J. (ed.) (1968) *Biographia Literaria by S. T. Coleridge*, vols I and II, Oxford: Oxford University Press.

Shelley, M. (1826) *The Last Man*, ed. M. D. Paley, Oxford: Oxford University Press (1994).

—— (1831) *Frankenstein (or, The Modern Prometheus)*, eds M. J. Weiss and C. F. Reasoner, Laurel-Leaf Library, New York: Dell (1965).

Shengold, L. (1989) *Soul Murder: The Effects of Childhood Abuse and Deprivation*, New Haven, CT: Yale University Press.

Sohn, L. (1985) 'Narcissistic organisation, projective identification and the formation of the identificate', *International Journal of Psycho-Analysis* 66: 201–13.

Spark, M. and Stanford, D. (1966) *Emily Brontë: Her Life and Work*, London: Peter Owen.

Spillius, E. B. (ed.) (1988) *Melanie Klein Today*, vol. 1, London: Routledge.

Steiner, J. (1979) 'The border between the paranoid-schizoid and the depressive positions in the borderline patient', *British Journal of Medical Psychology* 52: 385–91.

—— (1985) 'Turning a blind eye: the cover up for Oedipus', *International Review of Psycho-Analysis* 12: 161–72.

—— (1987) 'The interplay between pathological organisations and the paranoid-schizoid and depressive positions', *International Journal of Psychoanalysis* 68: 69–80.

—— (1993) *Psychic Retreats*, London: Routledge.

Tripp, R. T. (1973) *The International Thesaurus of Quotations*, London: Penguin Books.

Thompson, E. P. (1993) *Witness Against the Beast*, Cambridge: Cambridge University Press.

Vaihinger, G. (1912) *Die Philosophie des Als Ob*, Berlin.

Voltaire (1759) *Candide; or The Optimist*, in *Voltaire: Candide and Other Tales*, trans. T. Smollett, revised J. C. Thornton, London: J. M. Dent (1937; reprinted 1982).

Wallis Budge, E. A. (1912) *Legends of the Egyptian Gods: Hieroglyphic Texts and Translations*, New York: Dover Publications (1994).

Warnock, M. (1976) *Imagination*, London: Faber & Faber.

Watling, E. F. (1947) *Sophocles: The Theban Plays*, trans. E. F. Watling, London: Penguin Books.

Wilcher, R. (ed.) (1986) *Andrew Marvell: Selected Poetry and Prose*, London: Methuen.

Winnicott, D. W. (1935) 'The manic defence', *Through Paediatrics to Psycho-Analysis*, London: Hogarth Press (1987).

—— (1945) 'Primitive emotional development', *Through Paediatrics to Psycho-Analysis*, London: Hogarth Press (1987).

—— (1949) 'Mind and its relation to the psyche-soma', *Through Paediatrics to Psycho-Analysis*, London: Hogarth Press (1987),

—— (1951) 'Transitional objects and transitional phenomena', *Through Paediatrics to Psycho-Analysis*, London: Hogarth Press (1987).

—— (1954) 'Metapsychological and clinical aspects of regression within the psycho-analytical set-up', *Through Paediatrics to Psycho-Analysis*, London: Hogarth Press (1987).

—— (1960a) 'The theory of the parent–infant relationship', *The Maturational Processes and the Facilitating Environment*, London: Hogarth Press (1965).

—— (1960b) 'Ego distortion in terms of true and false self', *Maturational Processes and the Facilitating Environment*, London: Hogarth Press (1965).

—— (1962) 'A personal view of the Kleinian contribution', *Maturational Processes and the Facilitating Environment*, London: Hogarth Press (1965).

—— (1967) 'The location of cultural experience', *Playing and Reality*, London: Penguin Books (1974).

—— (1971) 'Dream, phantasying and living', *Playing and Reality*, London: Penguin Books (1974).

Wordsworth, W. (1850) 'Preface to the lyrical ballads and appendix (1850)', *William Wordsworth: Selected Prose*, ed. J. O. Hayden, London: Penguin Books (1988).

—— (1979) *The Prelude 1799, 1805, 1850: William Wordsworth*, ed. J. Wordsworth, M. H. Abrams and S. Gill, New York: W. W. Norton & Co.

—— (1984) *William Wordsworth*, ed. S. Gill, The Oxford Authors, Oxford: Oxford University Press.

—— (1985) *William Wordsworth: The Pedlar, Tintern Abbey, the Two Part Prelude*, ed. J. Wordsworth, Cambridge: Cambridge University Press.

—— (1994) *William Wordsworth*, ed. S. Gill and Duncan Wu, Oxford Poetry Library, Oxford: Oxford University Press.

Wu, D. (1993) *Wordsworth's Reading 1770–1799*, Cambridge: Cambridge University Press.

Index

Abraham, K. 207–9
Abrams, M.H. 202
Ackroyd, P. 184–5
adhesive identification 50
a elements 22
affiliation anxiety 207–10
Anrita 55
Antinomians 187
anxiety 6–7, 61; affiliation 207–10;
    existential 7, 146–65; of influence
    202–3; publication 197–210
Apophis 55
a process 22
archetypes, theory of 122
'as-if' syndrome 9, 15–16, 59–68, 172–3
associationism, theory of 134
asymmetry 67
the authentic 166
authoritative identity 200–1
auto-erotism 112
Ayer, A.J. 14, 41, 45, 49, 57, 188, 197

Bachelard, G. 120, 121
Bacon, F. 181
Balint, M. 70, 71, 80, 101, 171
Basch, M. 59
Beckett, S. 107, 158
β elements 22
belief function 194; disorders of 14–18
belief(s) 1–2, 8–18, 181–2, 194; archaic
    89–90; counter- 16–17, 178, 194;
    failure to relinquish 17–18; illusional
    16–17; reality testing of 9, 13, 14;

religious *see* religious beliefs;
    relinquished 9, 12, 13, 14, 17, 18, 90;
    scientific 7, 201–6; surmounted 89–90,
    93; suspension of 15–16, 59–68;
    unconscious 8–9, 11; wish-fulfilling
    16–17
Bergson, H. 41
Bick, E. 20, 50
Bion, W.R. 13, 34, 100, 181, 191, 192;
    theory of containment 3, 6, 19–28
    passim, 53, 56, 58, 69, 74, 106, 148;
    notion of innate pre-conceptions 33,
    122, 159; notion of nameless dread 7,
    43, 54, 55–6, 58; on philosophy 2; on
    regression 71, 74, 81; on reversible
    perspective 60–1; on thinking 23, 33,
    97–8, 192
Blake, W. 34, 40, 127, 166, 167–8, 169–70,
    171, 172, 178–96, 200; *The Book of Los*
    180, 181, 190–1, 194; *The Book of
    Urizen* 180, 194–5; *The Everlasting
    Gospel* 188; *The Good and Evil Angels*
    167–8; *Jerusalem* 182, 184; *The Marriage
    of Heaven and Hell* 167–8, 189, 193;
    Revelation of St John 191; *Songs of
    Experience* 183, 192; *Visions of the
    Daughters of Albion* 187
Bloom, H. 202
body and soul 26–7
borderline syndrome 46, 56, 172
British Psycho-Analytical Society 110
Britton, R. 4, 26, 41, 42, 44, 53, 90, 95, 97,
    109, 192

reality principle 67, 112, 199
Rée, P. 152
regression 70–81
rejection, fear of 199–200, 203–4
religious beliefs 15–16, 60, 119, *see also*
    Blake, W.; Milton, J.; theology
Revelation of St John (Blake) 191
reverse perspective 60–1
Reynolds, Sir Joshua 185
Riesenberg Malcolm, R. 61
Rilke, R.M.: *Duino Elegies* 5, 56, 93,
    146–65; *The Notebooks of Malte Laurids
    Brigge* 148–9, 152, 153–4; *Sonnets to
    Orpheus* 146, 147, 148, 160, 162, 163;
    Turning Point 156
Rime of the Ancient Mariner (Coleridge)
    142–3
Rita 55
Riviere, J. 3–4, 71, 193, 203
Rodman, F.R. 61, 119, 203, 204
Rosenfeld, H.A. 4, 5, 46, 53, 57, 70, 71,
    75, 79, 119, 149, 168, 193
The Ruined Cottage (Wordsworth) 143
Rundle Clark, R.T. 19

Salomé L.A. 151, 152, 153, 163
Saltmarsh, J. 187
Sandler, J. 6, 126
Sartre, J.-P. 45, 48–9, 57
Schelling, F.W.J. von 139
Schlegel, F. von 197
Schreber case 15
scientific belief 7, 201–6
screen memory 20, 133
Searle, J.R. 43
Segal, H. 18, 32, 34, 70, 95, 110–11,
    137–8, 147, 164
selected fact, use in interpretations
    97–108
self, true and false 118–19, 151, 166, 168,
    169, 171, 172–3, 182
self-psychology 166
Shakespeare, W. 113, 120
Shawcross, J. 15, 121
Shelley, M. 114–15, 146
Shengold, L. 102
skin erotism 50
Sohn, L. 5, 60
Songs of Experience (Blake) 183, 192

Sonnets to Orpheus (Rilke) 146, 147, 148,
    160, 162, 163
Sophocles 29, 36
soul and body 26–7
Spark, M. 115, 116
Spillius, E.B. 6
Stanford, D. 115–16
Steiner, J. 4, 7, 37, 59, 69, 75, 95, 97, 119,
    151, 193
Steiner, R. 110
Strachey, J. 3, 15, 59
subjectivity 1, 13, 41–58, 68, 198; hyper-
    46, 50
sublimation, theory of 109
Swedenborg, E. 187
symbolic capacity 32, 44
le symbolique 44
symbolism 109, 137–8
symmetry 67–8; negative or inverse 61,
    66–7

Tatham, F. 185
theology 2, 119
thick-skinned syndrome 46, 50, 51–4
thin-skinned syndrome 46, 47–51, 53, 56,
    57, 79, 172
thinking 23, 33, 97–8, 192
third position: establishment of 92–3; lack
    of 42
Thompson, E.P. 187
Tintern Abbey (Wordsworth) 129–30, 142
transference 66; negative 50; positive 50;
    total 83, 94, *see also* counter-
    transference
transference illusion 17, 37–8
transference love 37, 125
transitional space 16, 61, 121
triangular psychic space 13, 41–2, 92, 121
Tripp, R.T. 109
truth 34–5, 54–5; source of 166
Turning Point (Rilke) 156

unconscious 10, 11, 188–9
unconscious belief 8–9, 11, 14
unheimlich experience 89–90, 93

Vaihinger, G. 15, 16, 60
Vallon, A. 129, 143
Visions of the Daughters of Albion (Blake)
    187